Copyrights Reserved © 2023 Serena Mastin

All rights reserved. All original additions, including illustrations and chapter summaries, are copyright © 2023 by Serena Mastin and may not be reproduced, distributed, or transmitted in any form or by any means, including photocopying, recording, or other electronic or mechanical methods, without the prior written permission of the publisher, except as permitted by U.S. copyright law. All the content used in this book belongs solely to the author. This work depicts actual events in the life of the author as truthfully as recollection permits and/or can be verified by research. Occasionally, dialogue consistent with the character or nature of the person speaking has been supplemented. All persons within are actual individuals; there are no composite characters. The names of some individuals have been changed to respect their privacy.

Acknowledgments

It would be impossible for me to acknowledge all those who have been instrumental in my writing journey. With a grateful heart, I recognize the following individuals for their contribution to the production of this book, Marshall Krupp, Cathryn Mora, Ken Faught, RJ Johnson, Paul Sage, Steven Ochoa, Ashley Barrett, and Marley Penagos for providing unending inspiration and support.

Dedications

This book is dedicated to my mother, Dorene, for her strength in overcoming insurmountable obstacles with a relentless drive to fight for her children and her unconditional love. My sister Faye for her support, protective nature, and nurturing during the darkest times in both our lives, and my stepdad Ken for showing my mother what true love is and for accepting my sister and me as your own. For my children, Adian, Nevaeh, and Ashton, may you never be exposed to the darkness I have faced but find beauty in following the light.

Table of Contents

Chapter 1: Why Me	9
Chapter 2: Unlovable	19
Chapter 3: You Asked For It	35
Chapter 4: No One Understands Me	51
Chapter 5: Downward Spiral	61
Chapter 6: Breaking-Point	73
Chapter 7: The One That Got Away	83
Chapter 8: Without Purpose	95
Chapter 9: Heavyweight	107
Chapter 10: Broken	119
Chapter 11: Escape	135
Chapter 12: Love Is Blind	147
Chapter 13: Uphill Battle	159
Chapter 14: Baggage Reclaim	173
Chapter 15: I'm Not Enough	187
Chapter 16: Spiral of Lies	201
Chapter 17: Rebuilding	217
Chapter 18: Exposed	231
Chapter 19: Unraveling	245
Chapter 20: Shattered	259
Chapter 21: Denial	277
Chapter 22: Surrender	295
Chapter 23: Unhinged	311
Chapter 24: Enough	331

Prologue

We are most vulnerable during our first few years of life. The people and circumstances we are born into dramatically affect our personalities, which means that for many of us, any damage afflicted during those years marks us for life. Unfortunately, the pain and trauma we endure at a young age remain dormant within us, waiting to be discovered and healed. Often emerging in our young adult years as we uncover our identity.

As children, we experience life based on our environment and cannot choose or control our surroundings. I experienced this first-hand as I was exposed to severe trauma, sexual abuse, and adverse childhood experiences. The abuse was so explicit that I repressed memories of specific events to cope with reality and to adapt to the environment. It wasn't until later in life that these memories resurfaced, allowing me to articulate what happened clearly.

Living with the repercussions of these events, even the seemingly insignificant moments, permanently changed my emotional and mental state and significantly impacted the course of my life. Yet, despite intense counseling, seeking personal growth, and professional guidance, I found myself repeating the same cycles.

Until I had enough.

I initially wrote this book to continue my healing process, never intending to expose the most intimate moments of my life. Although, at times, it was an agonizing process, resurrecting painful memories and physically reliving each experience, it was also one of the most powerful methods of healing. The more I released the raw, vulnerable, and explicit stories, the more I realized that I could no longer hide my truth.

In exposing my story, I hope to inspire and awaken the spirit, empower others, and seek the courage deep within to stop hiding and bring those stories into the light.

I refuse to remain in the shadows, allowing the darkness to consume me. Instead, I choose to step into the light.

Brace yourself as the story you're about to read may be unsettling to sensitive readers.

Chapter 1: Why Me

As a little girl, I had long, greasy blonde hair and wore dirty, ripped clothing. My face was often covered in dirt from playing in the streets of the rundown mobile home park where I lived with my father, mother, and older sister, Faye. One of my earliest memories was after hours of riding my bicycle up and down the street; I felt the cold wind on my skin as the sun began to set. My bare feet peddled faster as I raced to the end of the street, swiveling side-to-side with each stroke as the training wheels stabilized my speed. Finally, I jumped off the ragged seat, leaning my bike against the steps of the rundown porch near the front door, as I made my way into the living room of our single-wide mobile home. The living room was dark, with the sun barely peeking through the blinds; the room felt frigid; dimly lit candles surrounded the house, and a soft breeze from the door shutting behind me swept through the room. As I stepped barefoot on the carpet with my dirt-stained feet, I reached above the giant television set on the tips of my toes to find a video of The Frog and the Toad. I pressed the videotape into the VCR and sat a few inches away from the television screen, eager to watch my favorite movie.

As the film began to play, the screen started to flicker. The scene of the children's movie disappeared in a snowy pixelated pattern; I remember the sound of the static screen ringing in my ears as I scooted closer, and it suddenly stopped. Then, it was silent, and the movie scene changed; I saw a woman with dark hair sitting naked in a shallow bathtub; the picture seemed so natural as if someone had taken it on a home video camera. I felt a sense of curiosity and continued to watch intently as I noticed a tear running down her cheek; her expression was emotionless as she reached for a razor on the side of the tub and began to slide the razor blade against her wrists slowly. I quickly lost my curiosity and was frozen with fear. I watched the blood run down her arms as she slowly laid her head against the rim of the tub and allowed her arms to lay beneath the water; the blood continued to contaminate the clear water as she closed her eyes and seemed lifeless in a pool of her own blood.

I sat in silence for a moment as I processed my emotions and quickly started to feel the weight of what I witnessed; I jumped from the floor and started screaming, "Mommy, mommy" as I rushed down the dark hallway towards my mother's room, she was napping and woke up in a panic, asking me why I was so upset. I couldn't articulate what I had seen at age four, so I pleaded with her and wrapped my little fingers around her hands, pulling her toward the living room, but the screen was black when we stood in front of the television. My mother slowly kneeled and kissed me on my head.

She said, "Everything is okay,"

Then she walked away as I stood in the dark living room, shaking with fear, unable to communicate the tragedy I had encountered.

It was as if I inherited tragedies as a legacy. In the late '70s, my mom was a single mother and had been in several toxic relationships after losing her father to cancer at the age of sixteen. Her father's death impacted her deeply as a teenager, which led her to one unhealthy relationship after another, eventually leading to my father, Vince, the most devious of them all.

My mother raised my older sister Faye alone, and Vince promised her he would take care of them. Shortly after, they got married and started sharing their lives together. After I was born in 1980, the deception, manipulation, and brainwashing began. My father immersed himself in a satanic community. He became a cult leader engaged in drug abuse, explicit sexual encounters, human sacrifice, and bestiality as part of his religious practice. My mother was brainwashed by my father's manipulation and satanic rituals, making it impossible for her to realize the magnitude of the deception, let alone protect us. Many nights, I would hear my mother scream, see them fighting, throwing dishes, and witness Vince holding a gun against my mother's head, threatening to kill her if she didn't comply. We lived under constant surveillance; he had strategically placed tape recorders and cameras throughout the house. He monitored every conversation and even had cult members follow us when we left the house.

I had a childhood so disturbing that even the wildest reaches of your imagination would shake at a glimpse of what I experienced every single day in the madhouse I called home.

For Satanic cults, the primary purpose of sex is developing a connection between physical pleasure and a form of painful stimulation. I remember getting ready for bed one night. As I approached my bedroom, it was dark, I could barely make out my surroundings, yet I could hear a person moaning and gasping for air. The sounds coming from my room were terrifying for me as a young child, yet I continued to tiptoe towards the bedroom door in my onesie pajamas with my wet stringy hair dripping down my back.

As I quietly peeked through the door, the moans grew louder, and I thought someone was in pain. Suddenly I realized that two people were thrusting back and forth on the top bunk of my bed. Not fully understanding what was transpiring, I continued to lean forward with my eyes squinting, trying to make out a visual until I realized the two individuals were having sex. I quickly pulled away; my heart was pounding as I leaned against the door and made my way down the hallway. The house was dark and filled with candles. I was terrified to walk past the kitchen, as I frequently saw the silhouette of a man watching me from outside the kitchen window. So, I closed my eyes and pretended I was invisible as I paced quickly past the kitchen into the living room, curled up in a blanket on the couch until I fell asleep.

Vince actively molested my ten-year-old sister Faye and convinced her that he would sexually abuse me if she resisted. Little did she know that when my sister and mother were away, he would threaten to kill my mom if I didn't allow him to abuse me sexually. The trauma was so intense that I repressed many memories, except one that, to this day, is clearly embedded in my mind.

One afternoon, when my mother and sister were at the grocery store, Vince insisted I shower. I could feel chills run down my back as I slowly removed my clothes. He stood naked as he towered over me in the shower; I was shaking in terror as the water poured down my head, my eyes filled with tears as I solemnly glared at his thin pale body.

His devilish hands lavished my body with soap as he pressed his hands around the base of my neck, tightly gripping my hair, and forced himself into my mouth. I felt a piece of me shatter inside as I disconnected from my body. I tried to erase these memories by removing myself emotionally and imagining that I was somewhere else, but my body felt weak, leaving me in a dismal psychological state. Finally, as I started to reenter reality, I found myself wrapped in a damp towel hiding in the closet.

I heard the front door slam and could distinguish the sound of my mother's voice; my body shivered as I was frozen in fear behind the hanging clothes that shielded me from the pain. My mother slid the wooden closet door open and reached her arms around my tiny body. I couldn't articulate what had just happened because I knew my father would hurt my mother if I told her what he had done, so I clenched my lips and held back the tears as she wrapped her comforting arms around me. I laid my head in her arms and felt a sense of relief as she carried me into my room.

These sexual experiences with my father often continued when my mother was away. It wasn't until years later that I realized he had taken my virginity at the young age of five. I endured so much trauma that I separated my emotions from feeling physical pain. As a result, I was numb and disassociated from reality. It was as though my brain selectively erased terrifying moments yet left shattered fragments of memories hidden like a dark shadow in my mind. I coped with the pain by creating an imaginary world and pretending that everything was okay to shield myself from the horror of what was happening to me. It was my only method of survival.

Like a tree without the sun, it bends to seek light to survive, yet when left in darkness; the roots become frail. Similarly, the traumatic experiences of explicit sexual abuse hindered my childhood development. As a result, I lived in darkness, which ultimately led me to find safety in hiding.

One evening after dinner, a fight broke out between my father and mother. My mother frantically grabbed my sister and me, rushing us toward our bedroom. She knelt and whispered softly with a terrified look in her eyes.

She said, "Stay in your room. Do not come out no matter what you hear."

She closed the bedroom door, and within seconds an outpour of yelling and screaming began. My sister and I pressed our ears against the thin walls, where we could hear banging and crashing; the noises intensified as the trailer started to rattle. We listened intently and suddenly heard our mother belt out a blood-curdling scream; without hesitation, we bolted towards the dining room. We halted just in time as a dish flew past us and shattered against the wall. The dining room was filled with broken dishes, and chairs knocked to the floor. Before we could fully grasp what was happening around us, I saw my father holding a gun against my mother's head. With a surge of adrenaline, Faye lunged at my father, using all her strength to pull him down. I ran furiously up and over her, jumping onto my father's back, hitting, and screaming.

I yelled, "Don't hurt, mommy!"

Viciously pulling the thin hair off his balding head as he wrestled us to the ground. Then, with a manipulative tone, he glared at my mother.

Vince said, "See what you've done."

The last memory I have of my father was an unusually eerie night; I stood behind him in our tiny kitchen with my bare feet sticking to the linoleum floor. I pressed the tips of my toes as high as possible, curiously perching my head around his body to see what he was preparing. But instead, I saw him churning a wooden spoon in a large cast iron pot with a glossy black glaze over the gas flame while he chanted words I couldn't grasp. I remember being enchanted by the vapor pouring over the sides. Later I learned that he was brewing a spell to sacrifice my sister and me to the cult over a black cauldron; he intended to offer us as a sexual sacrifice to the cult.

The following day was filled with chaos, I woke up suddenly to my sheepdog, Gypsy, barking uncontrollably, and my mom was rushing around the house in a panic. The sun was so bright that the entire room seemed white as my eyes adapted to the light. I was confused and disoriented as my mother abruptly pulled me out of bed.

She said, "We must leave now, grab your things, let's go!"

I didn't understand why we had to leave so quickly and cried for my dog Gypsy as my mother rushed me out the door. Moments later, we were running through the streets of the mobile home park, making our way to a local grocery store where my mother used a payphone. I heard her frantically dialing and pleading with the caller to come and pick us up immediately as if we were running from something. She hung up the phone quickly and gripped my hand firmly. I felt a rush of adrenaline as she led my sister and me to the center island in the middle of a busy intersection.

I was still trying to fully comprehend why we were in such a hurry and leaving everything behind when a car quickly pulled up next to the center island and stopped without warning. I realized it was my grandparents, and they were motioning us to get in the car, "hurry," they said. Excitedly, I jumped in the car yet immediately felt an immense tension filling the vehicle.

My grandparents seemed panicked, and the tires screeched as we drove away. I could feel my mother's heart pounding and her breathing heavy as I scooted closer to her.

She whispered, "Everything will be okay."

My mother saved us that morning from a monster that I called my father, who used and abused us for his demented desires and the horror of being offered as a sexual sacrifice to the cult. As a child, I adapted to my environment. No matter how traumatic the situation may have been, I thought it was normal to serve as a sacrifice for those whose purpose was to protect you. I didn't understand the complexity of our situation or even realize the magnitude of damage that would follow me later in life. But it became evident as I started to piece everything together.

A few days after we escaped, I heard whispers and chatter between my mother and grandparents on a seemingly calm spring morning as they sat around the dining table near the large window that overlooked the front porch near the entry door. My little feet pressed into the carpet as I quietly crept across the long hallway near the dining room; the floorboards rubbed against each other, making it impossible for me to sneak around my grandparent's house with a cacophony of squeaks and creaks.

I heard a sudden knock at the door and curiously peeked my head around the doorway, trying to make out the silhouette of the person talking. The sun seeped into the living room as the door began to open, the bright light felt warm, and I leaned closer to hear the conversation. I saw my mother speaking to a man I had never seen before. She seemed unsettled, so I wrapped my arms around her, clenching her leg tightly, and nestled beside her as I could feel her energy suddenly change.

I had an extraordinary bond with my mother; it was almost as if I could hear her thoughts, feel her body language shift, and be highly sensitive to every emotion she experienced. At this moment, I felt a deep sadness running through her body, and before I could fully grasp the thoughts running through her mind, the strange man at the door knelt to reach for me.

As he pried me away from my mother, I thrust my body back and forth with every ounce of my strength, kicking and screaming; I felt my fingertips pulling towards her. If I could reach them just a little further, I could touch her one last time. But instead, the man struggled as I pushed and hit him in a hysterical rage, screaming and yelling for him not to take me away.

He placed me in the back of an old station wagon and tried to calm me down as he secured me against the seat with a worn fabric seat belt. I was determined to fight, kick, bite, and lunge my body around to slide out of his grip. The car door locked, and my screams were silenced as the shock set in. I pressed my face against the dirty car window, desperately seeking my mother's touch, tears running down my cheeks. I wept as the man slowly drove my sister and me away.

My sister was all I had left; I felt numb; my body and mind had created a shield to protect me from sensing the weight of what had just transpired. The man continued driving for what seemed like hours and pulled the old station wagon into a covered parking lot beneath a large building. He escorted us from the vehicle to an elevator leading to a social worker's office.

I later realized that my mother's nightmare was just beginning as she lost her parental rights due to her inability to protect my sister and me from the abuse we endured. As a result, we were ripped from her arms and admitted into the witness protection and foster system. The man guided us through the office and sat me on a tall chair before a cluttered desk covered in files and papers. I could barely see the woman behind the desk as she leaned over, slightly lowering her gaze in my direction.

She asked, "Do you know where you are?"

I nodded my head from side to side in confusion, with my eyes swollen with tears.

She replied, "I am a social worker for an agency that protects children. I'm here to help find you and your sister a safe home."

The legacy of child sexual abuse – and how I survived, continued to haunt me with each traumatizing event throughout my life. I am a survivor of the terror, isolation, destruction, and evil that surrounded me. So much of the power of an abuser lies in silencing the victim, and I will no longer be silenced. This is a small glimpse of how my journey began.

Chapter 2: Unlovable

The following days were a series of sleepless nights, pain, guilt, silence, tears, but most of all, fear. Sexual abuse severed me, slicing me to my core, and the aftermath continued to plague me for years to come.

What most people who have suffered sexual abuse won't tell you is that the apologies and attempts at empowerment after aren't always helpful. The damage is done, and for many of us, we can't believe that the abuse is over. Even after the abuser is gone, the pain still remains, and we will become our own abusers in their place. Those destructive messages you allow to fill your mind continue haunting you.

The confusion, dissociation, desensitization, and emotional trauma followed me as I was thoughtlessly tossed from one foster home to the next. Every night, I yearned for my mother. I grew weary that my only glimpse of her would be from the witness stand as the counselors, social workers, and court-appointed advocates vigorously interviewed me.

A counselor led me to a small room for one of my first sessions, where my mother accompanied me. The room was dimly lit, with an oversized armchair on one side and a small sofa on the other. The counselor had a calm demeanor; his eyeglasses were rather large, covering up more than half of his oval face. He slowly sat back in the oversized chair and, with a gentle tone, began to ask me questions. Without saying a word, I crawled to the floor and curled into a fetal position behind the sofa. The counselor curiously observed my behavior, then addressed my mother.

He asked, "What is she doing?"

My mother replied, "She's hiding."

As a small child, I didn't have the language to explain what had happened to me, so I blocked the horrific memories from my mind. The pain was too much, even without words. So, as psychologists, social workers, and doctors all asked intimidating questions I couldn't understand. The intense pressure engulfed me in their attempt to investigate the grave details of my life. To me, it was merely more adults demanding answers that I couldn't articulate.

Over the next five years, my sister Faye and I relocated to over a dozen foster homes after being removed from the only place we knew as home. My mother was required to follow a stringent case plan to earn her rights back as a parent, and my father was incarcerated for the sexual abuse he inflicted on my sister and me.

Many of the foster homes were foreign and disturbing. In addition, my sister and I were separated on multiple occasions, so even the comfort of having my big sister there to protect me was ripped away.

The witness protection program was elusive about our whereabouts. At times, we would relocate in the middle of the night to strange new places with unrecognizable foster parents who housed several foster children in each room, making each transition daunting and intimidating. In this state of constant confusion, a few distressing situations were permanently ingrained in my mind.

It was late one evening as I sat in the back seat of an unmarked car; I could barely reach the window and sat solemnly gazing at the moon as it glistened behind the passing trees. Finally, the vehicle stopped in front of a small single-story house on the main street with a large oak tree covering the front windows. As the driver escorted me into the house, I was approached by a man and a woman with porcelain skin, hooded eyelids draped over their dark brown eyes, and straight jet-black hair. They kindly invited me into their home.

    The front door led to the living room, where I sat quietly on a small sofa; my feet could hardly reach the floor. After the driver disappeared, the woman motioned for me to follow her. It seemed like they were from a different planet, as she spoke in a language I didn't recognize. Although I couldn't understand what she was saying, I aimlessly followed her as she guided me down a narrow hallway. The rooms were cramped and had two sets of bunk beds in each room; children were sleeping in most of the beds as she led me to an empty bunk. I crawled into the bottom bunk and buried myself beneath the sheets.

    The following morning was filled with unique sounds: children chattering, feet stomping, dresser drawers banging against the wood stands, and dishes shuffling in the kitchen. Hesitant to move, I pretended to sleep and pulled the blankets over my head. The woman approached me, motioned me out of bed, and led me into a small bathroom. She quickly removed my clothes and pointed to the bath; I noticed that the bathtub was empty, so I apprehensively stepped in and sat on the cold porcelain tub floor; she ran the water long enough to fill a small cup and dumped it over my head, my damp hair covered my face and dripped down my tiny body. I was shivering in the tub, so I tried to reach towards the knob to run the warm water, and she immediately steered my hand away. She began to wash my hair and body as I sat in the empty tub, then filled the small cup up once more to rinse off the remaining suds. I was puzzled as to why the tub wasn't full of warm water so I could play in the bath, but she quickly wrapped me in a towel and dressed me before I could complain.

    Once I was clothed, she grabbed my hand and walked me toward the kitchen. The once chatter-filled house was empty and quiet as I realized all the children had left for school. I stood in the kitchen trying to discern the language she spoke to the man sitting at the table, but I still couldn't detect what they were saying. She placed me in a booster seat, pushed me closer to the table, and impatiently nudged me to eat, but I didn't recognize the food, so I pressed the small plate away and refused.

The man looked at me with confusion and assertively handed me a fork, but I continued to turn away. My mind was racing, and I tried to communicate that I wasn't hungry, so I jumped off the booster seat in an attempt to find my way back to my bunk. The man gestured to me to sit on a small stool in the kitchen; he set a large bowl in front of me, handed me a raw potato, then guided my hand with a metal tool to illustrate how to peel the potato. I thought it was an unusual situation but continued to follow directions peeling the potato until it was bare.

Once I finished, he cut the potato into long slices, and the woman dropped them in a hot pan. I could hear the oil crackling and began to smell a delicious scent, an aroma so powerful it made my mouth water. The man picked me up, set me back in the booster seat, and set a hot plate of French fries before me. I was filled with joy as I devoured the French fries. Every day thereafter, I was delighted to sit on the small stool peeling potatoes and eating French fries for almost every meal.

Although this environment felt strange, I began to find comfort in this foreign place. One mid-afternoon, the woman took me on a memorable trip. I overheard her tell the man that we were going to a place called Chinatown. It sounded to me that we were going on an adventure to a faraway place in another land.

The streets were filled with outdoor vendors, and people were rushing around in a frenzy. It was exciting to see the commotion; I clutched her hand tightly as she hurried through the shops. She stopped at what I thought was a pet store and bought a beautiful white duck. My eyes lit up with curiosity as I imagined the duck was my new fluffy friend. When we returned to the house that day, she let the duck out of the cage and into the backyard.

The backyard was overflowing with colorful plants and fruit trees, the air was crisp, and the smell of mint and basil filled the garden. I eagerly chased the duck as it waddled around the yard and played outside for hours. That evening, the house was unusually crowded with people. Several older women with jet-black hair and warm porcelain-toned skin moved quickly around the kitchen, preparing something special for what seemed like a celebration. I curiously peeked around the corner, observing all the commotion as I noticed a few white feathers lightly coating the tile floor. I thought that silly duck must have waddled through the house.

As I further inspected the kitchen floor, the woman shouted, "Shoo! Shoo!" and signaled me to get out of the way; I slowly lifted my head to acknowledge her and realized that my pet duck was lying on the kitchen counter lifeless. I shuttered and felt a whirlwind of emotions run through my body; I stood in horror as I realized they were preparing to cook my only friend. I ran back into my room and hid under the covers as I cried myself to sleep.

Shortly after, the mysterious driver appeared again. By now, I understood he was taking me to another unknown location each time the driver arrived. This particular time, he surprised me with a bright yellow toy bus to keep me occupied; I could see his eyes glancing back at me through the rearview mirror as we drove through the residential streets. He pulled next to a charming two-story house and held my hand as we approached two large wooden double doors.

An older woman with thin white hair opened one of the wooden doors and invited me in. The entryway had high vaulted ceilings and a long staircase wrapped around the room's right side with landings, elegant posts, and wooden handrails leading to a second-story loft overlooking the entryway. I was awestruck and slowly stepped forward as she closed the door behind me, and I heard the familiar sound of the old station wagon engine starting as the man drove away.

She asked me to remove my shoes and guided me to an accordion door latched with a small hook beneath the stairs. As she slid the accordion door to one side, I saw an unlit corridor with one room and a bathroom. The woman sternly instructed me to stay in the passageway until mealtime and forbid me from wandering around the house. The room was sparse, with an empty shelf and a twin-sized mattress on the floor. I heard the accordion door abruptly slide shut and the sound of the hook latching. The old woman was gone, and I was alone, locked in this dreary space.

As I settled into my new home, I sat with my legs crisscrossed on the stained carpet floor, playing with my naked Barbie dolls, using my imagination to keep myself entertained. Finally, a few hours passed, and I heard the woman approaching as she unhooked the latch; she told me to sit at the dinner table with an ascetic tone. As I entered the kitchen, I noticed two other children sitting at the table with their heads knelt, silently staring at the floor. I energetically slid into a chair next to a young boy who appeared to be my age.

I said, "Hello!"

He looked over and shrugged his shoulders while waiting for his plate of food. The old woman set a dish full of soggy vegetables before me, and I immediately pushed it away. The woman glared at me with her beady eyes.

She said, "If you don't eat it, you'll go straight to bed."

All I could think was that my mother never made me eat vegetables, and when I refused to eat at the foreign house, they made French fries. So, I sat in silence as I watched the other children make sour faces as they swallowed the soggy vegetables on their plates before I could muster up the courage to take a bite.

The old woman shouted, "Go to your room; if you don't like what I've made, you can go without!"

In a fit of anger, I stomped my way back to the room as she aggressively latched the door behind me.

After several days, I quickly realized the old woman never wavered from the routine. We were only allowed to come out of our rooms during mealtime and for one hour to play. I rarely saw the other children because she rotated our schedules for playtime each day. So, I swayed back and forth lopsided on a broken swing set in the dirt backyard or watched a blurry cartoon on the snowy television set in the empty loft. Then, once I heard the timer bell ring, she escorted me back to isolation in the locked hallway.

One night as I was getting ready for bed, my ears perked up as I didn't hear the familiar sound of her latching the hook on the accordion door. I hoped she had forgotten and slowly crawled onto the thin mattress on the floor. I pretended to sleep and pulled the covers over my head, curiously waiting for her to go upstairs. I laid awake quietly, listening for her footsteps against the stairs. I heard her footsteps grow faint, followed by the sound of the upstairs bedroom door sliding shut. The house was silent; I struggled to keep my eyes open as I lay motionless under the blankets; I waited a few more hours to be entirely certain that she was asleep.

I was still wearing my ripped, faded blue jeans covered in dirt from the yard with my favorite blue sequin unicorn sweater. I was fully capable of taking care of myself at six years old, and I was determined to escape in search of my mother. I couldn't imagine spending one more day in this prison. My heart was pounding as I meticulously planned my escape.

I slowly crept out of bed and reached for a wrinkled plastic bag with my two naked Barbie dolls nestled inside. I tiptoed down the dark hallway with my bare feet so I wouldn't make a sound, then slid my tiny fingers through the side of the accordion door to investigate if the latch was unhinged. Yes! She forgot to latch the hook. With a surge of excitement, I continued to carefully slide around the doorway without making a sound.

I felt my body anxiously shaking as I stood in the moonlit entryway beneath her bedroom. Then, with determination, I moved swiftly towards the enormous wooden doors and slowly turned the bolted lock. The old door creaked open just enough to squeeze my body between the gap; I listened intently to make sure everyone was sound asleep and gently closed the door behind me.

The night was cold and dark. My heart continued to race as the brisk wind grazed my face. I rushed down the sidewalk, following the path of the dimly lit streetlights, until I saw bright headlights from an oncoming car; I froze in terror, standing in the center of a driveway only a few houses away from where I started. I heard the clinking chains behind me as the garage door began to open, and the car turned towards me. I stood like a deer in headlights contemplating my next move but couldn't move my feet.

    Finally, the car stopped, and I heard the gear shift into park with the bright headlights beaming straight at me; my eyes couldn't adjust fast enough to visualize the driver, yet I could hear the driver's door squeak open. A beautiful woman with long dark hair tenderly approached me and, with a gentle voice, asked, "where are your mommy and daddy?" I took a deep breath and softly replied, "I'm trying to find my mommy." She seemed like an angel sent to save me as she tenderly clutched my hand and guided me inside her home.

    Walking through the entry door, I saw a mountain of stuffed animals in the living room. I ran as fast as possible and plunged into the soft pile of teddy bears, dolls, and fluffy pillows. I rolled around, snuggling the plush animals as I sunk into the couch. The angelic woman knelt beside me and asked if I knew my phone number; without a second thought, I spouted out the only number I knew. She thoughtfully pressed each number as the pool of dolls enchanted me.

    I distinctly heard the rings when a man answered. Her expression seemed concerned as she hung up the phone and quickly dialed another number, this time she only pressed three buttons and turned her head away as she whispered into the phone. I was gleaming with excitement, so I didn't bother to concern myself with what she said and eagerly bounced up and down on the couch. I was finally going to see my mommy.

    Moments later, my excitement quickly faded, and my stomach began to turn as I heard sirens approaching. There was a loud knock at the door; I took a deep breath, and the door slowly opened. The bright flashes of red and blue lights immediately grabbed my attention as a tall police officer in a dark blue suit knelt and opened his palm, motioning me to place my hand in his; he seemed like a gentle giant and asked me why I ran away.

The only words I could utter were, "Am I in trouble?"

He shook his head and said, "We need to take you back to the house you came from."

My feet slowly stepped backward as I pushed him away with both hands.

I demanded, "I want to see my mommy and sister!"

Tears filled my eyes as he wrapped his arms around me, lifting me off the ground with his strong arms and carrying me back to the foster home.

I shouted, "I don't want to go back. She made me eat my vegetables."

He smirked and continued walking towards the old woman's house. I was too young to clearly articulate my thoughts or explain that she routinely isolated the children and locked us away, and I was too exhausted and defeated even to try.

In this monumental moment, I realized that I was alone.

*****

After that night, I was tossed from one foster home to the next. The driver would often appear at night, and I would wake up the following day in an unfamiliar place. I moved so many times that I lost count. Between foster homes, distant relatives, and Juvenile Hall, I was exposed to a variety of unusual characters.

Before I lost all hope, my sister and I were reunited and placed with our aunt and uncle. My mother was living with our grandparents after the court revoked her parental rights as she attended mandatory classes and enrolled in a nursing program, relentlessly fighting to regain custody.

Finally, the judge appointed my aunt, Evelyn, and uncle Collin as our legal guardians and allowed monitored visits with my mother. They were raising two teenagers of their own in addition to my sister and me, so I can't imagine the pressure they may have felt. Let alone dealing with the repercussions of our childhood trauma.

By this time, I had difficulty identifying, expressing, and managing my emotions. As a result, I experienced intense and ongoing emotional upsets; I was diagnosed with Dissociation and Depersonalization Disorder, Attention-deficit Hyperactivity Disorder (ADHD), Dyspraxia - also known as Developmental Coordination Disorder (DCD), and Post-Traumatic Stress Disorder (PTSD). I had trouble focusing and listening; I withdrew, regressed, and lost previously acquired skills. In addition, frequent night terrors haunted me, which led to difficulty sleeping. As a result, bedwetting and sleepwalking became a regular nightly routine.

My Uncle Collin was a handsome man with a gentle face; he was playful, kind, and charming. He would often impersonate cartoon characters, keeping me giggling for hours. My aunt Evelyn was tall and thin with dark skin, thinly shaped eyes, and a mysterious beauty that would often captivate me. However, she was a strict woman with a cold disposition and didn't have the patience to tolerate my defiance.

Oddly, my aunt Evelyn displayed affection towards my older sister Faye, and I often felt dejected and shunned because I was impossible to control. As a result, I felt unwanted, unlovable, and rejected with every encounter.

She repeatedly punished me for my behavior without explanation; I stood stoic and unflinching as she spanked me. I responded with indifference. After all, it paled in comparison to the infliction I endured. I had become numb to the pain. She exhibited cruel and unusual methods of punishment in her effort to seize control over my unruly behavior.

On many occasions, without warning, I found myself standing in the corner of a dark room for hours with my nose pressed against the wall. Other times I remember being sound asleep on the top bunk bed, waking up to her pulling me by my hair onto the floor and dragging me to another room to discipline me for something I had done earlier that day.

One memory forever embedded in my mind was a bright sunny morning. Aunt Evelyn asked me to shower, so I gathered my clothes and went to the bathroom. I closed the door and started running the shower water. I was in a playful mood that morning, so I pulled my shirt over my face; the shirt's neckline was so tight that it wrapped snugly around my forehead, draping down my shoulders. My panties were dangling from my ankles as I stood in front of the bathroom mirror, making funny faces, and singing songs.

I reached under the counter to explore the interesting items stored in the cabinet and noticed a tall bottle of mouthwash. I began to imagine that I was performing a show as I pranced around the bathroom with the shirt on my head and my panties around my ankles. Unfortunately, I must have lost track of time as the shower was still running, and I heard the bathroom door violently swing open. I was startled and jumped backward, quickly turning my back towards the large bathroom mirror, hiding the mouthwash behind me.

Aunt Evelyn shouted, "What are you doing?"

Without realizing that she could see the mouthwash clenched between my fingers in the reflection of the mirror. I panicked, wiggling from side to side.

I replied, "Nothing!"

She forcefully grabbed my arm, dragged me down the hall to the living room, and stood me directly in front of the bay window facing the street. In her effort to teach me a lesson, Aunt Evelyn harnessed her power and authority by publicly humiliating me. I felt paralyzed as my nine-year-old naked body was exposed, facing the large bay window, with my shirt still draped around my head and my panties wrapped around my ankles. My older cousin had his friends over that day, and they passed by repeatedly with expressions of embarrassment and shame on their faces.

These moments tarnished my self-esteem and continued to fuel my rebellion, making me even more impossible to control.

Over the years, her patience ran thin as I continued to act out and test her boundaries. I exhibited repeated and persistent patterns of anger, defiance, and backtalk. I had trouble managing my emotions and was hostile or aggressive towards grownups and other children. I frequently stole money from my aunt's coin jar, ditched school to buy candy at a local liquor store, and initiated fights with other students at my elementary school. I sought attention in destructive ways yearning for some form of love and acceptance. The more infuriated she became with my uncontrollable behavior, the more consequences became unbearable.

I remember standing in front of a small mirror in the hallway as she hovered behind me, forcing me to stare at my reflection as the tears rolled down my cheeks.

Aunt Evelyn grumbled, "Look at yourself!"

Then she would tap my head with a wooden spoon if I looked away. The tapping became more intense as it continued to rub against the same spot over and over again. Finally, I flinched and closed my eyes for a brief moment, and just as I lifted my head; I started screaming uncontrollably. The wooden spoon had punctured my skin, and a thick strand of blood began to seep through my white-blonde hair, dripping down my forehead. Aunt Evelyn panicked, rushing me to the bathroom, leaning my head over the side of the tub, and hysterically running the water through my hair. I was shocked and frozen as I watched the blood-stained water swirl down the drain.

These negative experiences made me feel hollow inside, and my mind powerfully protected me from feeling anything at all. However, the one feeling that never dissipated was the desire to see my mother. I yearned for her and prayed every night that I would live with her again. I counted the days until our weekend visits and cherished every moment we spent together until my aunt realized that the visitation time with my mother was the one thing she could take from me that would force me to comply.

On many Saturday mornings, I would wake up excitedly, shuffling around my room to find my favorite outfit and effortlessly skipping through the house, gleaming joyfully. Only to find out that my aunt had canceled my visit with my mother due to my prior behavior. Forcibly separating me from my mother was the cruelest form of punishment. It induced anguish, despair, guilt, shame, and resentment. I desperately longed for the moments I spent with my mother because she was the only person who truly loved me.

As the years went on, my uncle Collin was in a treacherous battle with cancer and spent many days in hospitals surrounded by people desperately praying over him. He was eventually placed in hospice care, where he took his last breath. I can't imagine the darkness my aunt faced as she pushed through the grieving process. Yet, I was terrified that the loss of my uncle would make her anger and intolerance grow stronger until the day arrived when my mother's parental rights were reinstated.

I had been dreaming of this moment for years. I was ten years old at the time and was filled with a deep sense of comfort, knowing I was finally going home.

Or so I thought.

Chapter 3: You Asked For It

Be careful what you ask for because you might get it. I prayed vigorously for this moment, yet I underestimated the gravity of my experiences and how they would drive me to isolation—leading me to push those I loved most away.

My sister, Faye, and I packed all our belongings and moved into my grandparent's home, where my mother had lived for several years while we were in foster care.

My grandparents lived on the corner of a busy street next to an elementary school. The house's exterior was painted a pale yellow framed by layers of red brick leading up to two casement windows with a large brick fireplace towering over the rooftop. Plush grass and succulent plants filled the front yard, surrounded by black wrought iron fencing and a red brick walkway that led to the large front porch.

I felt the cool breeze against my skin as the gate squeaked open, and I quickly ran down the red bricks toward the door where my grandmother stood. My grandmother had coarse white hair with tight curls that thinly wisped around her head. Her skin was pearl white with layers of wrinkles, small scowling eyes, and thick glasses. She was an unaffectionate woman and always seemed anxious or impatient in my presence.

The screen door slammed shut as I carelessly passed her to explore my new home. The living room was dreary, with a lingering musty smell, filled with trinkets and doilies, ancient lamps, and pictures with wood paneling covering the wall surrounding the fireplace mantel.

A burgundy reclining chair divided the living room from the old wooden dining table where she would sit for hours playing crossword puzzles, gazing out the front window while plucking white hairs from her chin.

The kitchen was tucked behind the dining room, with bright sage-colored walls, wood paneling, and thick floral wallpaper. A long gloomy hallway led to a den and three bedrooms. I skipped through the hallway, basking in my freedom as I found my way to my new room. I gleamed with joy as my mother and I were finally reunited.

As the days passed, I realized my mother was not around as often as I had hoped. Instead, she worked tirelessly every night and slept most of the day. My grandmother cared for me while my mother worked, and I grew more anxious as I scavenged around the house. She constantly shouted, "Stop that!" "Calm down" and "Don't touch that" at my every move. The floorboards creaked as I tried to sneak through the house in an effort not to agitate her, and I would feel her cold, wrinkled hands grip me firmly from behind as if I was an intruder. I felt a deep sense of sadness as the fantasy of living with my mother slowly faded and the reality set in. This was not the happy ending I thought it would be.

On one particular day, I sat silently on the living room floor, twirling my fingers through the carpet strands while staring at the blank television screen, completely dissociated from the world around me. Then, I heard the sound of the wrought iron gate squeaking open and immediately snapped back into reality. It was a comforting sound; I knew that meant my Momma was home from work. However, my resentment for my grandmother grew deeper as I would listen to her complain about my behavior each day as my mother walked through the door.

I was nauseated by my sister Faye because she had such a strong bond with my grandmother; she was always such a perfect angel and could do no wrong. Yet my grandmother would scornfully glare at me as if I was the spawn of Satan. Moreover, my biological father led a satanic cult, tormenting my family, so I didn't particularly appreciate being associated with him, let alone perceived as such.

One afternoon I was mischievously lurking around the house, finding trouble in every corner. I pretended I was a spy as I quietly tiptoed into my grandparent's bedroom on a mission to steal a piece of candy from their bedside table. The room was dark, with the sunlight barely peeking through the blinds; I carefully slid the small drawer open just enough to squeeze my fingers through the opening. Chills ran down my spine as I could feel the wrapper of the decadent chocolate suddenly slip through my fingers as my grandmother forcefully snatched my hand away from the drawer.

I jumped and shouted, "I hate you!"

I ran around her frail body, trampling my way to my room. I knew I was in trouble, but she couldn't catch me if I ran fast enough. I hid behind my bedroom door, sinking into the closet as the door swung open.

I yelled, "I didn't do anything."

I then buried myself behind the clothes hanging off the closet rod. She reached behind the sliding door and clutched her hands around my neck. I froze in terror, taking a deep gasp for air as she pulled me out of the closet; she glared into my eyes with disgust and grumbled under her breath as she walked away.

She said, "I wish you were never born."

That evening, I sat with my arms crossed and my nose scrunched, glaring at my grandmother, disgruntled at the dinner table. My mother, sister, and grandparents shared stories about their day; they laughed as they passed the plates around the table. I was outraged. *How could she?* I thought to myself as she pretended as if nothing had happened. Then, without a word, I pushed my chair back, jumped off the seat, and stomped to my room. My mother followed me and peeked around the doorway.

She asked, "What's wrong?"

I couldn't find the courage to tell her what my grandmother had said.

I replied, "Nothing, I'm just tired,"

I sat silently on my bed as they finished dinner without me that night.

There are perhaps no more painful thoughts than that of *Nobody wants me. They don't care about me. Why am I even here?* These self-attacks continued to fuel my insecurities as the days went on. I struggled to articulate my emotions, and a dark depression weighed over me as I felt unlovable and unwanted.

Each night I sat in the bathroom gazing at my mother as she brushed her hair, preparing to leave for work. I didn't want her to go and followed her every move, refusing to leave her side. This particular night before leaving for work, she handed me a tape recorder with a tiny cassette tape.

Momma said sweetly, "I made this just for you."

I clenched it tightly in my hands and asked curiously, "What is it?"

She said softly, "Listen to it before you go to bed as a reminder that I'm always with you."

She gathered her things, tightly tucked me under the covers, gave me a gentle kiss then rushed out the door. I bounced out of bed and fervently watched her through my bedroom window as she drove away, staring at the taillights of her car until they disappeared into the night.

I climbed back into bed, eagerly placing the cassette tape into the recorder, and pressed play. I laid my head against my soft pillow listening intently as the music began to play. I heard my mother's angelic voice singing, *"I've got a mansion, just over the hilltop, in that bright land where we'll never grow old, and someday yonder, we will never more wander. But walk the streets that are pure as gold."*

I felt a deep sense of calm and warmth cover my body as I played it repeatedly until I fell asleep. My heart had never felt so at peace, and I continued to play that same song every night after she left for work.

As the months and years went on, my mother became actively involved in the church; it became a safe haven for each of us as we found a community that accepted us. We attended every Sunday, and many times throughout the week, I began to connect with others my age and actively engaged in youth group activities.

My mother started attending a singles group hosted by the church; she seemed slightly apprehensive and started acting a little funny. Something was very different about her demeanor, but I couldn't put my finger on it. After church, I looked forward to going out to a nice restaurant for brunch. We sat around a long table as families from the morning service gathered together, laughing and sharing stories.

On one occasion, I noticed a man named Ken gazing at my mother with a peculiar gleam in his eyes. His cheerful face, rosy cheeks, and silly jokes lit the entire room in laughter. He had a jolly belly that shook every time he chuckled, dark hair with gray streaks, and a playful personality.

My mother skeptically looked in his direction, making it known that she was not the least bit interested in his flirtatious banter, but he was persistent in attracting her attention. With lovestruck eyes, he admired her as she gracefully declined his efforts. Yet, it seemed like only a few days had passed when his endearing charm wore down my mother's apprehensive exterior. After that, they became inseparable, spending every waking hour sitting on the front porch of my grandmother's house laughing and giggling as if they were teenagers.

My mother would visit him at a local gas station he managed each night. When we arrived, he leaned over the counter with a comforting smile and in a kind-spirited voice.

He said, "Choose anything you'd like."

I shuffled through the endless shelves of snacks and treats with excitement, scavenging for the largest candy bar I could find. As I was shuffling through the towering shelves, I caught a glimpse of him handing my mother a tiny thimble and sneaking a soft kiss. I felt my heart drop into my stomach and rushed towards the counter with disgust.

I shouted, "Ewww, gross!"

They giggled in embarrassment while I rolled my eyes, then continued to indulge in my candy bar. As we drove away that night, my mom explained.

She said, "The thimble symbolized his love for me, and he asked me to marry him."

My bright blue eyes felt like they were glued wide open as I sat in shock, feverishly asking a million questions.

I said, "But you've only known him for a few weeks?", "Is he going to be my new dad?" "Wait! When are you getting married?", "Does this mean we have a new family?"

My mother replied, "We're getting married in two weeks."

Confusion and enthusiasm filled my thoughts as the unanswered questions raced through my mind. I was elated by this seemingly strange situation. We are finally going to be a real family. The following two weeks were a whirlwind, and they included Faye and me in every aspect of planning the big day—dress shopping, hairdressers, makeup, cake tasting, gift registry, and flowers. I felt like this was my big day too! Yet, as crazy as it may have seemed, I had an odd sense of peace knowing that God placed this man in our lives so we could let go of the past and create the next chapter.

My new dad had an enormous family, initially making me slightly overwhelmed because I had become quite comfortable only having my mother, grandparents, and Faye. His family hosted several events at my new papa and grandma, Vovo's house, where a massive group of family members would gather around a large table in the living room.

Their rowdy banter and boisterous laughter would fill the space while the kids would run recklessly through the house. Each family member had their own unique personality; I felt lovingly accepted by some and alienated by others. As a result, I often felt a deep sense of loneliness, even amid the crowd. I couldn't seem to connect with his family or adapt to the new environment, so I continued to shield myself from judgment by pretending to be a normal child. At times, the intense commotion felt so paralyzing that I would retreat into the guest room, disconnected and isolated from all the festivities.

One unsettling night after the family began to disperse, one of my stepdad's sisters invited me to spend the night at her home. I was twelve years old at the time, and she had a son just a few years older, so I was hopeful for the opportunity to spend quality time with them. She was high-spirited, funny, and affectionate, always making me feel loved and welcome, so I jumped at the opportunity. I quickly gathered my things and jumped in the back seat of her car.

My cousin was quiet and polite and even offered to sleep on the sofa that night so that I could take his room. As we approached the apartment, my cousin was greeted by a friend, Damon, who I had noticed attended our church. Damon and my cousin went into his room for what seemed like forever. Finally, I realized it was getting late, so I put on my nightgown and started gathering blankets and pillows, tucking them into the couch. Then, I gently knocked on my cousin's room door.

I said, "I don't want to bother you, so I'll sleep on the couch tonight instead."

I heard muffled voices as I walked away.

They replied, "Ok, goodnight."

I snuggled between the couch cushions with a mountain of blankets and fell asleep. The blankets must have fallen to the floor as I tossed and turned. I could feel a cool breeze against my legs as I suddenly felt the touch of someone's hand against my calf; I pretended to sleep patiently, waiting for their next move; with utter stillness, they deliberately began to press my nightgown up towards my thighs. I turned to my side restlessly, pretending to sleep as I repositioned myself, and I could feel the person jump back away from my body as they slowly walked away.

I trembled with fear and prayed. *Please, God, don't let them hurt me.* I curled up in a ball nestled between the cushions and slowly drifted back to sleep. Again, I awoke to someone lifting my nightgown over my thighs, but I felt a cold chill as I lay entirely still this time. My heart began to beat rapidly as I realized that the nightgown was draped over my stomach, exposing my panties. I could hear heavy breathing and felt them carefully position their arms on each side of my body. I could smell the musky sweat of a teenage boy but was too frightened to open my eyes. I could feel his body shaking as he held himself up with his arms placed strategically on each side of the couch; he began to thrust back and forth against my exposed midriff in a pushup position.

I moved slightly, pretending to turn in my sleep; he instantly jumped off me and ran towards the kitchen. I knew this was my one opportunity to see his face, so I sluggishly sat up on the couch, pretending to yawn as I stretched my arms and stumbled toward the kitchen. I wiped my eyes to portray that I was waking up and squinted slightly to get a better view. I could make out Damon's silhouette standing off to the side of the dimly lit kitchen. I reached for a glass of water as he quickly moved past me, returning to my cousin's room. My knees felt so weak that I could hardly move my legs. In horror, I stood in the kitchen trembling as I leaned over the counter, placing my hands over my mouth, trying to hold back the tears. Finally, I mustered the courage to lay down on the couch and tightly tucked the blankets around me.

A few hours passed, and I fell into a deep sleep until the same cold hands pressed against my nightgown. I shuddered at the idea of his relentless pursuit, and I found him in the same position once more; I thought, *why isn't God protecting me?* He continued in a thrusting motion hovering over my body; I could feel the bulge in his pants press against my pelvis and his warm breath run over me. I was certain it was Damon this time and was confused by my body's inability to move or push him away. I laid stiff for a few moments as he continued to thrust against my body, and with a burst of adrenaline, I turned my head toward him, glared into his dark eyes, and began hitting and punching him with all my might. He fell backward off the side of the couch and swiftly jumped to his feet; I continued to plunge towards him pushing his chest as he towered over me.

I screamed, "Get off me!", "Don't touch me!"

My aunt and cousin entered the living room, puzzled by my behavior, trying to gain control of my swinging arms. My aunt held me back from attacking him and, in a confused tone.

She asked, "Serena, what are you doing?"

Before I could catch my breath to explain what had happened.

Damon uttered, "She had a bad dream, and when I checked on her, she started hitting me. She's crazy!"

I shouted, "Liar! He's lying!"

My aunt separated us and set me firmly on the sofa; she rushed to the phone, feverishly dialing, and told my mother to come to pick me up. I was filled with rage as I sat with my arms tightly wrapped around my knees, shaking back and forth until my mother finally arrived.

I said, "Momma, I'm not lying; he was trying to hurt me. Why didn't they believe me?"

I continued to explain each moment in detail. She gently held my hand.

Momma said, "I don't know, sweetie. People believe what they want to believe."

My heart sank deep into my chest as I buried myself deeper into the passenger seat, and I stared blankly out the window and quietly wept the entire drive home.

We attended church services every Sunday, and in passing, I caught a glimpse of Damon and his family from the corner of my eye. My stomach churned with nausea as I clenched my jaw and dropped my head, counting every step I took to divert my attention from any chance of eye contact.

Just when I thought I was in a safe place, the sexual trauma continued to emerge. That night was a turning point in my life. I entered my teenage years struggling with impulsiveness, rule-breaking, sensation-seeking, and hypersexuality. My self-worth was based on pleasing others, attention-seeking behaviors, and performing, leading to more guilt and shame.

I became increasingly interested in boys seeking approval and affection in unhealthy ways, further withdrawing from my mother. I couldn't understand why I was drawn to these dangerous situations and continued to repeat patterns of behavior that would eventually lead me to more pain.

I attended the youth group every week, trying to submerge myself in a safe environment. We would play games and sing worship songs, and when service ended, the girls would playfully chase the boys around the courtyard.

I was giggling and whispering with my girlfriends about a new boy who had started attending our youth group. He had light blond hair, clear blue eyes, and adorable dimples that would melt the heart of any teenage girl. He flirtatiously glanced over at me; I smiled and looked away. He attended all the youth activities, so I eagerly participated in every event with high hopes that I could see him again. Finally, he approached me, confidently introducing himself.

"Hi, I'm Calvin," he said.

Butterflies fluttered through my stomach while I blushingly looked up at him.

I replied, "I'm Serena!"

He asked if I wanted to hang out with him, my eyes lit up and without hesitation.

I said, "Yes!"

I knew the other girls would be jealous, but I couldn't resist. So, the following week, his parents dropped him off at my house. We sat on the sofa in the living room while my parents were busy doing work around the house. I was mesmerized by his sparkling blue eyes and enchanted by every story he shared. I felt lucky that he chose to spend the afternoon with me.

My parents knew he was a good Christian boy admired by many families at our church, so they weren't apprehensive about leaving us alone for a short time.

Momma said, "We have some errands; we'll be back shortly."

As they drove away, Calvin leaned in and softly kissed my lips; my heart fluttered as I was quickly immersed in the moment. He began to rub my chest; I pulled away and skillfully placed his hands around my waist. The mood awkwardly shifted, and I could feel my throat tighten as he unbuttoned his pants, exposing himself, then firmly clutched his hand around the back of my neck, forcing my face into his lap. I realized that he didn't care about me; he wasn't the "good" Christian boy everyone thought he was. Instead, his only desire was to use me for his pleasure. I detached myself from the situation, allowing my mind to disconnect as he forced himself deeper down my throat. I gagged and tried to lift my head, but his grip was too tight. I closed my eyes and reluctantly continued to satisfy his needs. After he left that day, I began to withdraw and isolate myself.

Emotional avoidance temporarily suppresses difficult emotions, yet avoiding these feelings took me down a more destructive path. My depression and anxiety led to a tornado of emotions, turning to self-harm to find a sense of relief. For example, I would lock myself in the bathroom for hours, cutting my ankles to feel something, and then wearing clothes to cover my scars, such as long sleeves or long pants, even in the hot summer weather.

When cutting no longer soothed the pain, I turned to compulsive overeating or binge eating large amounts of food, then proceeded to make myself vomit to eliminate it from my body. I often engaged in this cycle in private until my parents started to recognize my patterns.

The first time I attempted to make myself vomit was the most excruciating. I locked the bathroom door and ran the sink water to dull the noise; I started with one finger down my throat but couldn't initiate my gag reflex, so I continued to push more fingers down my throat, pressing firmly against my back tongue, still nothing.

Finally, I reached for a toothbrush and forced it down my throat, but only saliva filled my mouth. I spit the saliva into the toilet until I started to gag violently, more saliva filled my mouth, and my stomach began to press in and out as I pushed harder. I could feel my eyes swell as I unknowingly started to break the blood vessels around my eyes, and suddenly the contents in my stomach emerged.

The vomit plunged into the toilet water and splashed abruptly on my face. A small moment of satisfaction ran through my body as it became more effortless after the initial release. I smelled the putrid vomit on my hands and face, so I gargled with mouthwash and scrubbed my face until I removed the vile stench.

These episodes became a consistent part of my daily routine. First, emotional eating, overeating, then binging and purging in response to any negative emotions I experienced. I used it as a way to suppress or soothe my feelings, whether it was stress, anger, fear, sadness, loneliness, or pure boredom. I found comfort and reprieve in having complete control of my body. I became entangled in this newfound freedom.

Yet, before I could recognize what was actually happening, my daily routine revolved around the scrutinization and mental torture of overthinking any food intake—controlled entirely by the wrath of restricting, binging, purging, and vomiting up to ten times each day.

One evening at a local Mexican restaurant, I indulged in several baskets of chips and salsa, a large plate of enchiladas, and additional items at the table. Finally, I excused myself to use the bathroom, and when I returned to the table, as I scooted myself across the booth, I could see the disappointment on my parent's faces and in a disheartened tone.

Momma asked, "Did you waste the money we just spent on dinner?"

I scoffed and said, "I don't know what you're talking about."

I knew they were fully aware of my secret, so I got better at hiding it from that moment on.

Chapter 4: No One Understands Me

The more my depression progressed, the more my appearance declined. Black fishnet stockings covered my arms and legs, long black dresses, combat boots, and a spiked dog collar tightly clasped around my neck with thick winged eyeliner and pale powdered skin. My platinum blonde hair covered my face as I walked through the high school halls. The other students would mock me and taunt me yelling "Freak!" across the high school campus and whispering, "She's so weird," as they walked past me.

I couldn't focus in class, and the teachers often asked me to sit outside because I was a distraction to the other students; my grades declined, and I began to gravitate towards a group of outcasts huddled in the dark corners on campus.

One sunny afternoon my friend and I went to a local pizza place near the mobile home park where I lived with my mom and Ken. As we walked in to find a booth, we noticed two boys wearing black trench coats sitting in the back of the restaurant. We glanced at each other and giggled as we deliberately found a table just a few feet away from the mysterious boys. I was intrigued and flirtatiously locked eyes with one of the boys, then quickly looked away, pulling my hair back towards my face.

Within moments, they leaned over our booth and invited themselves to join us. One of the boys confidently introduced themselves as they slid beside us at the table.

He said, "I'm Angel, and this is Daniel,"

Daniel bashfully scooted towards me; he had greasy black hair that fell effortlessly over his dark, deep-set eyes, his skin was pallid yet flawless, and when he blushed, his cheeks would light up with rose-colored undertones.

I tried to initiate a conversation with my bubbly personality, but he seemed distant and awkward, yet intently leaned closer, seemingly engaged in my chatter. Daniel spent most of the afternoon distracted, doodling on a napkin, and as the boys left, he folded the napkin and placed it in my hand. My friend curiously pleaded with me to open the napkin as they walked away. I skeptically unfolded each side and blurted out with excitement.

I said, "He gave me his phone number!"

She squealed enthusiastically and eagerly asked, "Well, are you going to call him?"

I pretended to hesitate for a moment until we both burst into laughter, then in an apprehensive tone.

I said, "We'll see."

We rushed home before dark, and after her parents picked her up, I eagerly ran to the phone to dial his number. I nervously waited for an answer as each ring sent a tingle of goosebumps up my arms.

He answered, "Hello?"

I replied, "Daniel?"

He giggled and said, "I didn't think you would call."

I was smitten and couldn't contain my chatter. However, the more anxious I became, the more I would ramble on until Daniel graciously interrupted.

He asked, "When can I see you again?"

My stomach swarmed with butterflies, and I quickly replied, "Let's meet tomorrow at the pizza place."

I couldn't sleep that night replaying the conversation in my mind. It felt like the day slowly crept by as I patiently waited for the hour to arrive where we could meet again. As I walked toward the restaurant, I noticed Daniel crossing the street from the corner of my eye. As he approached, I realized he was exiting the apartments across from my mobile home park. He hugged me tightly and said, "Why don't you come to my house? My mom isn't home."

I was slightly nervous, but I decided to test the waters to see if he was like all the others. We spent the afternoon talking for hours, he continued to be shy, not making any sudden moves, and as I left that evening before sunset, he kindly walked me home. It was like a breath of fresh air; I was surprised that he didn't try to force me to do anything but was gentle and warm. As we approached the front porch of my mobile home, he turned to walk away. I reached for his hand and pulled him in close, giving him an innocent kiss on the cheek.

We were inseparable from that moment on, spending every waking hour together. One night, my parents began questioning our relationship; they had an undeniable suspicion that he was trouble and demanded that I stop seeing him. He enchanted me, and I couldn't bear the thought of being apart. They didn't understand; he was all I had, the only person who truly loved me. My parents and I fought for hours as I passionately defended my love for him, but they wouldn't waiver. Finally, I couldn't take it anymore, and I slammed my bedroom door and began to sob with rage.

I mumbled to myself, "How could they?" "They don't even know him." I love him."

As I wiped my tears, I felt a surge of adrenaline run through my veins. I furiously fumbled through my room, gripping my backpack and filling it with random clothes. Just then, my mother opened the bedroom door with a confused expression.

She said, "What are you doing?"

I looked her dead in the face, pushing my way through the doorway; I bolted towards the front door.

I said, "I'm leaving!"

Ken ran towards me, shouting, "Get back here!"

I grabbed my skateboard, leaning against the porch, and threw it to the ground, placing my foot on the front of the board, balancing my stance, and pushing my back foot to gain momentum as I raced away. I could still hear my dad yelling as I sped down the street.

He screamed, "Look what you're doing to your mother!"

As my adrenaline continued to fuel my unruly behavior, I saw a familiar neighbor standing on his porch and begged him to let me in. In his late twenties, he was an unusual man; he was glamorous and wore fashionable clothes, ornate jewelry, and makeup. He was known as the neighborhood drama queen because he would argue with his roommates so loud that the entire mobile home park could hear them ranting. He hurried me through the front door and whispered in my ear.

He said, "Don't worry, baby girl, you're safe here."

I flipped my skateboard up and placed it tightly under my arm as I quietly rushed toward the back bedroom of his mobile home.

He said, "You can hide here."

I followed his direction as he pointed to the closet. I nestled my body between the draping fabric and held my knees close to my chest as he quietly closed the closet door. I knew my parents wouldn't find me there and would likely go directly to Daniel's apartment to talk to his mom. So, I hid quietly in the closet until the sun began to set, then snuck out the backdoor and lurked behind every shrub until I covertly made it to Daniel's house.

I threw pebbles at his bedroom window; he peeked through the blinds and rushed to sneak me into his room while his mother was busy in the kitchen. That night I snuggled under his arm, tucked my head tenderly on his chest, and fell asleep ignorant of the consequences the following days would bring.

I woke up abruptly to his mom yelling, as she stood in his doorway.

She screamed, "What the Hell is she doing here?!"

I immediately jumped off his bed, frantically gathered my things, and rushed out the door. I stood alone in the dark apartment complex, contemplating my next move, when I realized I had nowhere to go. I walked through the moonlit streets solemnly until I finally gave up and went home.

The porch steps creaked as I walked towards the front door; with my heart pounding and anxious thoughts racing, I slowly turned the doorknob and tiptoed into the house. My parents were still awake, infuriated with my unruly behavior, but neither spoke a word. The silence continued the following day as I despairingly sat at the kitchen table. Finally, my mother approached me.

She said, "I give up."

I pleaded with her to forgive me, yet I could see the pain in her tired eyes; she had fought so hard to get me back, and this was who I'd become. I was dejected and couldn't defend my actions. I knew my rebellious temperament was leading me down a dark path.

I continued to struggle in school, and it seemed like the world was crumbling around me. The boys at school repeatedly ridiculed and slut shamed me because of my clothes. My friend Corey overheard a group of boys whispering about me behind my back as I carelessly walked away. The rumors spread like wildfire, and just as the bell rang for lunch, I saw Corey confronting one of the boys who started the gossip from a distance. Corey was a gentle giant with long dark hair and a calm demeanor, so this was entirely out of character. I panicked, pushing my way through the crowd of students. Before I could get close enough, the boy grabbed Corey by his long hair and pulled him to the ground. He raised his clenched fist, and just as he swung to hit Corey, I lunged toward him and jumped on his back, recklessly swinging, and hitting the boy's skull. He flung me from side to side, trying to wrestle me from behind, but I clenched my legs tightly around his waist and continued punching in every direction.

The students pressed in the surrounding chaos, chanting, "Fight, fight, fight!"

Before I knew it, I was being roughly pulled off him by campus security. I quickly found myself sitting in the principal's office with my hands clenched tightly as I waited for my mother to arrive. The drive home was silent, and when I tried to explain, my mother's face was stone cold with the most devastating look of disappointment.

Within a few weeks, my parents were looking to relocate. My outbursts and uncontrollable behavior drove a wedge between us, and I couldn't help but think we all needed a fresh start.

We drove for hours on a winding road leading to a three-story A-frame cabin tucked away on a desolate street. Cedarwood planks ascended through the trees, exuding tranquil energy, warmth, and refuge. Wooden decks wrapped around every floor, fronted by a soaring wall of windows that overlooked breathtaking forest views as far as the eye could see. The second story was an open-concept living space with 16-foot ceilings, a small kitchen, a living area, a primary bedroom, and a bathroom. A narrow stairwell led to a mezzanine overlooking the main living room. I crawled up the stairs through a small opening.

Jokingly I said, "This is my room!"

But before I knew it, we packed our things in boxes and moved into this mysterious mountain hideaway, and my parents enrolled me in Rim of the World High School, located at the top of the mountain overlooking a vast valley.

The sound of my alarm would repeatedly chime until I knew I couldn't press the snooze button any longer, so I sat up in my bed and made my way to the shower to get ready for school. Unfortunately, the pipes were so old that the furnace would take forever to heat the water, and I was running out of time to get ready for school, so I mustered up the courage to quickly stand under the ice-cold water. I pulled my long black velvet dress over my shivering body, laced my tall black boots, and swaddled my arms inside a heavy trench coat as I prepared to walk through the snowy streets toward the bus stop at the top of the driveway. The large yellow school bus stopped abruptly as the driver motioned me to climb in.

I stood at the front of the bus trying to locate an empty seat while the other students dressed in jeans and flannels glared and whispered, watching my every move. Finally, I sat alone, pressing my face against the frosty window, drowning out their constant chatter. The bus made several stops and each time the students would glare and mumble as they passed the empty seat beside me. The bus drove near the edge of the mountainside, and with every nauseating turn, I solemnly stared at the endless sea of clouds that covered the valley below.

As soon as the bus stopped in front of the school, I waited for all the students to exit and walked to the public restroom. A girl stood by the empty stall smoking a cigarette and smugly moved aside so I could lock myself behind the metal door. I sat on the cold porcelain seat, looking down at the mud-stained tile, and heard the main door squeak open; with all the commotion, I didn't realize the girl had thrown her cigarette butt under my stall. I pulled my fishnet stockings up over my waist and draped my black velvet dress down my legs. I opened the stall door to find a woman from campus security hovering over me; she firmly grabbed my arm and marched me to the principal's office. They suspended me on my first day of school.

This bizarre little town started to wear me down as the months passed. I was an outcast and the center of all the small-town gossip. I was miles away from all my friends and began to feel isolated, so I continued to withdraw as my depression deepened. Finally, a few days before my sixteenth birthday, I demanded to go down the mountain to see my friends, but my mother shut down my requests. She was busy cleaning the kitchen as I smugly sat at the table, looking her straight in the eyes.

I said, "I'm going whether you like it or not."

My mother stopped what she was doing with a defeated look on her face.

She said, "If you leave, don't come back."

In a fury of anger, I pushed my chair back from the table and climbed up the narrow stairs to the loft; I paced back and forth as I deliberated my exit strategy.

I recklessly began shoving my things in a large black bag, fiercely stomping through the house. I laced my boots, grabbed my trench coat, and slammed the front door behind me. I didn't know where I was going or how to get there, but I knew that if I wanted a future for myself, I'd have to make it on my own. So, with determination and despair, I started walking down the graveled mountainside, away from my family and into the night.

Chapter 5: Downward Spiral

I stood silent at the top of the desolate street, afraid to look back, so I continued forward. Pride and determination fueled me to keep going, yet my heart was hollow.

I was a wanderer. I didn't care where the journey would take me - the desire for independence and freedom fueled me. But I chose to take this path alone. I was unaware of the course before me or if it would lead to suffering or poverty; it was all the same to me - because it was all I'd ever known.

The night grew cold as the sun faded beneath the trees. I walked several miles and stopped at a gas station near the main road to use the pay phone. I called several friends, pleading for them to pick me up, but it was too late in the evening for anyone to drive that far. I leaned against the glass outside the convenience store and slowly slid down, using my backpack to prop me up; I felt hopeless with my head in my hands. Finally, a teenage girl that I had recognized from school approached me.

She said, "Are you okay?"

I replied in desperation, "I have no place to go."

She said, "Why don't you spend the night at my place tonight?"

We stayed up talking most of the night as I shared my story. I told her I had been alone for so long that I couldn't adapt to a normal lifestyle and never felt accepted. She listened intently to every word. She was like an angel who rescued me from the cold dark night.

The following day, my friends arrived and drove me back to the city I had left behind. I slept at a different friend's house each night until I quickly wore out my welcome. I experimented with marijuana and alcohol at first but quickly immersed myself in a world of drugs. The drug dealers seemed to care for me like a lost puppy.

One of the drug dealers would sneak me in through his window at night; his parents were both hearing impaired, so I would hide in the closet when they entered the room. Unfortunately, he had several friends who snuck in and slept over, so I made his tiny closet my safe haven from them. I gathered pillows and blankets, nestling my body in a ball beside his dirty laundry, gently sliding the door shut as I heard the others arrive. I closed my eyes, covered my ears, and lay silent while he and his friends snuck other girls into his room for sex. No matter how tightly I covered my ears, the sounds of moans and groans crept in through the thin closet door.

I would wake up with my stomach growling each morning, afraid to open the closet door. I waited quietly, listening for the girls to leave, trying to hide the sounds of my grumbling stomach. Finally, I slid the closet door open just enough to peek through the crack inspecting the empty room. I saw him leaning over a glass table as he invited me to come out. He rolled up a dollar bill and snorted the white powder lines carefully distributed on the glass. He handed me a small clear bag tied in a knot with white rocks inside.

He said, "You can't stay here another night, but this will help your hunger and help you stay awake."

That morning, I crawled out the window and began walking through the residential streets with no end in sight. I found myself drawn to the powder substance. I noticed a shopping center ahead and navigated my way through the aisles to a bathroom in the corner of the store. I hid inside a dingy bathroom stall with the toilet still running, the stench of urine and feces lingering. I reached into my pocket only to find some loose change rattling around.

So, I wrestled through my backpack, finding an unused tampon. I stripped the paper packaging, so the applicator was exposed and dismantled the larger outer tube that holds the tampon. I discarded the smaller tube and cotton. I then pulled out my compact mirror, placing it strategically on the lid of the stainless-steel trash container. I used my school ID card to crush the rocks in the white bag and then precisely formed a small line of powder. Placing the end of the tampon applicator against my nostril - I took a deep breath, pressing my other nostril closed as I inhaled the white dust.

As the powder entered the narrow channels between my eyes, I felt a burning sensation piercing my head. I lifted my head back with tears dripping down my face and immediately felt an extreme burst of energy and focus. It was euphoric.

This clever concoction swallowed me whole and made me feel invincible.

In the following weeks, I navigated the streets, using public transportation to apply and interview for several positions, enrolled in the high school I previously attended, and continued falling deeper into my addiction.

As summer ended and my Junior year began. I juggled three jobs, taking the bus across cities to work for just a few hours. I desperately searched for a safe place to stay but could barely afford the bus fare. I wandered the streets hopelessly at night, trying to find refuge. My life spiraled in circles as I secretly used my addiction to cope with the pain and keep my eyes open long enough to make it through the night.

There was a park directly across from the high school I attended; large oak trees encircled the wide-open areas. The park lighting illuminated grass fields while the picnic shade structures were hardly visible from the street. I noticed a wooden bench tucked away from direct exposure, and when all my options failed, I curled up on the bench and wrapped my coat tightly around my arms and legs.

The night sky was scattered with dark clouds as the park lights radiated between the trees. The cold breeze whistled through the leaves, brushing against my skin, my teeth chattered, and my body felt numb. I gently placed my bag beneath my head and fell asleep. I tossed and turned on the rigid bench surface and woke up to the sun rising in the early morning hours. Water droplets covered my face from the morning dew; I rubbed my eyes, reacclimating them to the light, and slowly sat up on the bench, stretching my arms to dull the throbbing aches and pain.

I heard the school gates sliding against the concrete and briskly gathered my belongings. When the gates opened, I knew I only had a few minutes to sprint through the school halls to the girl's locker room. I shuffled for the soap and toothbrush at the bottom of my bag and quickly undressed, submerging myself beneath the tepid shower water. I let out a sigh of relief as I savored every moment. The first-period bell rang, and I immediately snapped back into reality. I carefully tiptoed across the wet tile to reach for the thin paper towels hanging in a dispenser near the sinks. I abrasively dried my trembling body, fumbling to pull my dress over my head, laced my boots, and thoughtlessly applied my makeup.

The powder substance echoed through my mind, *just one more time. It's the only way to get through the day.* I cunningly positioned myself behind the lockers and inhaled a small line, then rushed to my first class sniffing and wiping my nose as the chemical-like taste dripped down my throat.

After the last period bell rang, I ran through the campus to the bus stop, so I didn't miss the upcoming departure time. Once the bus arrived, I found a seat on the bench closest to the driver to avoid the musty smells of the other passengers; rancid body odor, old food, and exhaust fumes swirled through the poorly circulated air.

I reached my first destination and threw on my red hat and white apron as I shuffled through the promenade to the Popcorn Palace in the far corner of the mall. I made it just in time to clock in before my shift started. Between customers, I hid in the dingy break room, devouring a bag of stale jalapeno cheddar popcorn as my only meal of the day.

After my shift ended, I wiped the counters, swept grit, hair, and other large particles from the trampled floor, and rigorously mopped from one end to the other. I tightly wrapped several bags of trash, placing them outside the security gates and pulling down the gates to lock the store. The security guard waited for me to exit the premises to discard the trash in the large dumpsters behind the building.

Just then, my friend Ronnie sped past me in a 1969 black Chevy Camaro, leaning his head slightly out the driver's side window.

He said, "Let's go!"

I jumped in, and we were on our way to find trouble. We drove up to a local billiard hall to play pool. I was exhausted from the night before, so I headed toward the bathroom to snort a line of meth before the shenanigans began.

As I exited the restroom, I saw my friend Shanae sitting at a high-top table, arguing with her boyfriend near the entrance. Shanae was seventeen and six months pregnant; she had bristly black hair pulled back in a bun, wearing an oversized white shirt with red sweatpants. They always argued, so I glared in his direction but didn't pay much attention until her boyfriend forcefully grabbed her by the arm and pushed her from behind.

He yelled, "Get your ass outside."

I watched skeptically through the barred windows as the argument progressed in the parking lot. The loud music and the noise from the billiard hall muffled their voices, so I couldn't hear what they were saying. He towered over her; raised his fist angrily, and leaned closer, threatening her. I noticed the terror on her face as she stepped backward and flinched like a cornered animal. Just then, he violently pushed her against the chain-link fence.

I screamed, "Stop!"

Frantically running towards them, and without hesitation, I felt a sudden surge of adrenaline, clenched my fist, and lunged forward, striking him directly in the face. He looked up and chuckled, then, with blunt force, took a straight shot to my face. Blood poured from my nose as my eyes immediately welled up, sending a jolt of sparks across my entire face.

Ronnie rushed toward us before I could comprehend what had happened, lifting me feverishly off the ground.

Ronnie yelled, "Get in the car!"

I fled towards the Camaro, slid in the back seat, and slammed the door. Then, I quickly rolled down the window.

I screamed, "Shanae! Get in!"

But she refused and demanded to stay with her boyfriend. Confusion struck me while the pain flooded my face and began to pulsate from the direct impact of his fist. Then, as the chaos faded in the background, I laid my neck against the seat and used my shirt to absorb the blood, applying pressure to my nose. I could see Ronnie glaring at me through the rearview mirror as my eyes peered through a wild tangle of hair slightly covered by my blood-stained shirt.

With an annoyed tone, Ronnie said, "Now, where will you stay tonight? You can't come to my house."

He knew that I frequently spent the night with Shanae, so I reluctantly asked him to pull over so I could use the payphone.

I tried several numbers, but the phone rang with no answer, leaving voicemails on every answering machine until I finally ran out of quarters. Then, I suddenly remembered a close friend from school, Jared. His mother once told me that her door was always open if I ever needed a place to stay. I knew it was a long shot, but I had memorized the streets and asked Ronnie to take me there. He pulled up to the house, and just as I shut the passenger door, he screeched his wheels and sped off.

I stood momentarily at the base of the driveway, contemplating how to explain the swelling, and bruising around my eyes. Finally, I took a deep breath and, with my head down, walked towards the dimly lit entryway. I pressed the doorbell and stepped back with my hands shaking, awaiting an answer. I gazed at the oversized arched windows and noticed the lights flicker throughout the house. The door slowly creaked open, and his mother stood in the doorway with a concerned look. She was tall with long thick, auburn hair, deep-set blue eyes framed by smile lines, and her skin had a warm undertone. As I looked up, his mother stepped back and gasped.

She said, "What happened to your face, sweetie?"

I was humiliated and replied, "It's been a long night."

Jared must have heard the commotion and poked around the corner behind her.

He said, "What are you doing here?"

I replied, "I had no place to go."

His mother gently leaned forward, wrapped her arms around me, and invited me inside.

The following day, I awoke to the comforting smell of pancakes and bacon as his mother prepared breakfast. She brought me an ice pack to hold over my face because the swelling was so bad I could hardly open my eyes. The ice began to melt, so I went to the bathroom to find a towel. I glanced at my reflection in the mirror, with my eyes swollen so tightly I could barely make out the purple, black, and dark blue rings above and below my eyelids. I was humiliated and embarrassed, gently trying to cover the dark spots with my makeup powder. I stood in the bathroom for a few moments, calculating my next move. I couldn't stand to be a burden, so gracefully, I excused myself from breakfast.

I said, "Thank you so much for everything, but I should go."

I collected my things and thanked them repeatedly as I said goodbye. Then, I walked down the street just a few blocks over to the public bus station and waited for the next bus to arrive. Using my low-income bus pass, I traveled a few cities away to visit my best friend, Christi, for a few days of reprieve. Christi had short, spiked platinum blonde hair, pale skin, freckles, piercings covering her face, and an edgy punk rock style that demanded the attention of anyone she passed. She was also one of the most intelligent and kind-hearted people I have ever met. I admired her young wisdom as she always spoke the truth most authentically, and I needed her more than anyone at this moment.

Christi and her older brother John - who often reminded me of Sid Vicious from the Sex Pistols, lived in an unfinished room with their sister and her family in a modest part of town.

When I arrived on her doorstep, Christi rushed in for a bear hug, practically lifting me off the ground. I basked in the brief moment and began sharing the details from the previous night. I always found a sense of comfort in Christi as she listened intently without judgment while nursing me back to health until my wounds healed.

I stayed with Christi for several days until a crossfire broke loose between her family, and the feuds began to unravel. So, Christi, John, his friend Rocky, and I rebelliously left her sister's house to find our next adventure. We walked for hours tormenting each other, making jokes, loitering in shopping centers, and dodging police cars as they passed.

Then, as the night progressed and the breeze set in, we stumbled upon an abandoned house in a run-down neighborhood. The yard was overgrown with weeds and shrubs; the city boarded up the creepy windows with wood pallets, and the exterior paint peeled from the walls. We snuck around the back of the house and found a broken window to climb through. The inside of the condemned house seemed to be demolished, covered with debris and trash. Giant holes exposed the pipes from the rotting walls, the carpet ripped from the surface, dismantled furniture camouflaged the floors, and the smell of a decomposing animal lingered in every room.

If the walls could talk, I imagined the horror stories they would tell. While scavenging through the vacant house, we found an old dirty mattress leaning against the corner of an empty room. John and Rocky tipped the mattress over, filling the room with dust and dirt as it violently hit the floor. The four of us snuggled together in the center of the mattress and shared stories for hours until we couldn't keep our eyes open and fell asleep.

By the following evening, John and Christi went home, and Rocky reassured me that I could stay with him. Rocky was short and stocky with deep brown eyes, rough skin, and a mohawk that towered eight inches in the air. He lived in a small house with a large family, and when we arrived, his mom was hustling around the kitchen preparing a mountain of food while yelling at the kids running in and out of the back door through the kitchen.

His mother scowled at me as I entered the kitchen and started speaking to Rocky in Spanish, so I couldn't understand what she was saying, but her expression made me uneasy. Rocky scoffed at his mom and told me to wait in his room. I sat on the matted carpet floor, waiting patiently for him to return. I could hear him stomping down the hall; he abruptly entered the room, slamming the door behind him.

He said, "You can't stay here."

I folded my head in my hands, exhausted and defeated.

He said, "Don't worry, I have a plan."

Skeptical of his tone, I said, "It's late, and the public transportation stops running soon."

He said, "Follow me."

I begrudgingly followed him behind his house down a long driveway that led to a detached garage. The decrepit structure was filled to the brim with old tools, boxes, rusted bikes, and spider webs spanning the wooden beams. He gave me the combination of the padlock on the door.

He said, "You can pretend to leave, then when it gets dark, you can sneak in and sleep here tonight."

I sighed and nodded, terrified of what would happen if I got caught. I left shortly after and waited down a back alley near Rocky's street until the stars lit up the sky. I nervously watched his house until the lights faded and slowly crept down the long driveway to unlock the shed. He left me a blanket and pillow on the cement floor, so I curled up under a workstation and closed my eyes.

After hours of tossing and turning on the cold cement, I finally began to fall asleep. I abruptly awoke to the screech of the shed door opening and saw Rocky's father hovering over me, yelling in Spanish. I jumped up like a thief in the night and ran as fast as I could before his father could call the police. I sprinted and weaved through the dark alley for what seemed like forever until my lungs began wheezing, and my knees collapsed as I fell to the ground. I looked in both directions to make sure no one was in sight, then reached for the bag of powder to get me through the night.

Wandering through streets in the middle of the night, I hid behind dumpsters and vacant buildings as police sirens circulated the area. I heard whistles and hollers from every direction. I could see the reflection of headlights as a car slowly lurked behind me. I picked up my speed, briskly walking towards a gas station, when the car stopped a few feet ahead of me, waiting for me to pass. The driver tried to get my attention, but I continued with my eyes fixed on the convenience store just a few blocks away.

Navigating the streets is an endless pit of shame, guilt, and despair, yet I was determined to prove all who doubted me wrong.

Chapter 6: Breaking-Point

It was a Friday afternoon, and rumors of a party were circulating through campus. A small and pale, anorexic-looking girl with excessive acne scars and greasy platinum blonde hair sitting beside me in class leaned toward me, a mischievous grin plastered on her face.

"Let's go to the party together; you could stay the night at my place." She whispered.

Maya had a bad reputation; she was known for sleeping around, backstabbing, lying, and gossiping. Despite her manipulative behavior, I had worn out my welcome with many of my close friends and needed a place to crash.

I lived solely for my survival, splitting my time between three jobs and the endless mounds of homework required to pass all my classes. So, the idea of a party, a taste of the normal High School rites of passage that my peers took for granted, was too tantalizing to pass up. Despite my gut reminding me that Maya could be bad news, I emphatically said, "Yes!"

That evening we flooded her bedroom with music and danced around the bathroom, applying our makeup, and tossing clothes in every direction, trying to find the perfect outfit. I laughed and smiled, and danced around, delighted to forget my reality and get to play the part of a normal teenage girl for just a moment.

Her parents dropped us off at a fast-food restaurant near the party, and as they drove away, I curiously asked Maya why they didn't take us there.

"I lied. I told them I was staying the night at your house and that your parents were meeting us here." She told me.

My heart fell into the pit of my stomach as she knew damn well I didn't have a place to go. Annoyed and irritated, I began walking away. Just then, some boys from our school pulled up and asked if we wanted to "pregame" before the party. Maya flirtatiously batted her eyes, leaning over the passenger window.

Maya said, "Let's do it!"

I rolled my eyes and reluctantly climbed into the back seat. One of the boys pulled out a small plastic bag from his wallet filled with thin strips of translucent paper and told us that we should take one if we wanted to have a good time. Unaware of the power of this small piece of dissolvable paper, I placed it under my tongue, and it melted instantly.

I could hear the loud music playing from down the street as we approached the party. The music was so intense that I could feel the ground vibrate under my feet as I stepped out of the car.

Teenagers swarmed the house, dancing, drinking, smoking, and forming small groups in every corner. As I walked through the crowd, I assumed those boys must have been lying because I didn't feel any different. So, I distanced myself from the mass of people and stood alone in the corner, trying to organize my thoughts.

Suddenly, time, movement, color, and sound started to shift and change. The loud music became muffled, and the chaos around me seemed to move in slow motion. The shadows on the walls began to flow in sequence, and people's faces morphed into putty.

I began to panic; sweat dripped down my neck; I pushed through the crowd trying to find Maya. Then, finally, I spotted her sitting on someone's lap.

I said, "I'm leaving."

She bounced up and said, "We just got here?"

I ignored her and tried to concentrate on finding my way out. Waves of confusion and clarity flowed in and out like a current during low tide. I closed my eyes and took a deep breath; just then, I recognized Jared standing across the room. I desperately rushed toward him.

"Is there any way I can stay at your place tonight?" I begged. He looked at me strangely and started laughing.

"Are you tripping?" Jared asked.

I tried to control my body language to appear alert or semi-normal, but everything swayed back and forth. Finally, Jared interjected before I could compose a response.

"Not tonight, but I bet you can stay with my friend Jake. His dad isn't home." He told me.

With relief, I thanked Jared repeatedly as I scanned the room, trying to decipher where his friend Jake was standing.

Jared laughed and replied, "Oh, he's not here. Remember, he lives around the corner from my house."

Embarrassed, I giggled while attempting to hide my utter confusion and casually walked away.

I managed to find one of the boys who drove us there and pleaded that he drop me off. As I stumbled toward the car, Maya followed closely behind me and jumped in the back seat. I tried to play it cool, acting like my brain wasn't a puddle of mush. Despite my state of mind, I managed to navigate the driver to Jake's house.

Maya and I stood at his doorstep as the car drove away, and Jake peeked through the window, motioning us to come in. Jake was nineteen, and we were sixteen, so he naturally treated us like immature young girls. He was tall and muscular with a shaved head and blue eyes, wearing blue shorts without a shirt.

As I walked into the house, a dark storm of clouds came rushing in, and I couldn't explain the altered reality I was experiencing. I tugged on Maya to go to the bathroom with me; we stood in awe, staring at our reflection in the mirror. I watched closely as my face began to morph into a roaring lion. Then, terrified, I quickly looked away and opened the bathroom door. Jake was blocking the doorway, hovering over me as I tried to squeeze by. He tightly gripped my arms and forcefully pushed me toward a dark empty room. Maya followed closely, and he locked the door behind us. The drug may have altered my senses of space, distance, and time but the moment I heard the door latch, I had extreme clarity.

Jake demanded that we remove our clothes; I laughed nervously, testing his response, hoping he was joking. However, his eyes pierced through my soul as he didn't waver. Maya stood beside me as we gradually undressed, standing completely naked and trembling before him. Jake pushed Maya aside and told her to sit in the corner of the room.

He forced me to lay naked on the coarse carpet, with my voice shaking.

I whispered, "No, no, please don't."

He placed one hand over my mouth and started undoing his pants with the other. Maya reached forward, trying to pull him off me, but he propelled her tiny body across the room. I turned slightly to visualize Maya, but she was cowering in a ball in the corner, watching me with a shameless expression. Aware of what was about to happen, my body froze, and the entire room went silent, with only the sound of the humming ceiling fan.

My whole body went cold. I couldn't move. I felt trapped inside myself. With my eyes glossed over, watching the ceiling fan's blades circulate, trying to drown out the sounds of his grunts, listening to the fan hum, I imagined I was in a different place. His forceful movements penetrated my stomach with every thrust. It felt like my insides ripped open as he violently defiled my body. I was humiliated and felt powerless, lying under his massive body, but even more repulsed that Maya watched the entire time with a disturbing glare as if she wished he would have chosen her. After he finished, he stood over me, lingering until I acknowledged his dominance. Then, in a patronizing tone.

He said, "You wanted it."

Laughing under his breath, he casually exited the room as if nothing had happened. Tossed away like a piece of trash lying naked on the floor, emotionless. I curled into a fetal position pulling my knees to my chest, wrapping my arms tightly around my body, shivering as I cried in silence, acting as if nothing happened.

I peeked my eyes open to observe Maya's demeanor and mirrored her behavior, concealing my pain, minimizing the experience, and blaming myself.

The aftermath of this violation is not only ingrained in my mind but also tangled up in everyday life in the form of unconverted, invasive memories. It affected my psychological state and reached out with force to the people around me, including my family and social environment. Eventually, my ability to focus in class and at work plummeted.

I was relentlessly determined to press on as my body and mind deteriorated. The weeks passed, and the cycle continued until I finally found a room to rent with a family I knew from the church we previously attended.

The room was empty but had a cozy window seat with a shelf-style bench and cushion. I could envision myself nestled in a blanket for hours, waiting for the sun to set.

I bought a lightly used fold-out floor sleeper at a local thrift store. It rolled into a chair while I studied and rolled out into a bed on the floor with a detachable back cushion that I used as a pillow each night. Although the room was sparse, I was safe from roaming the streets and began to feel a sense of belonging.

A few days later, the school counselor called me into the office. Anxiously I waited outside his door, wondering what I could've done this time. Finally, he invited me in and handed me a large box of canned food donated during a recent food drive. I clumsily carried the oversized box home that day, excited to see what was inside. I peeled back the taped edges and scavenged through the contents - macaroni and cheese, pasta noodles, sauces, soups, and even a few old cans of sardines. It was the highlight of my day, the family was away at work, and often when they were home, they kept to themselves while I isolated myself in the room, so I took advantage of the empty house and eagerly started cooking in the kitchen. I enjoyed a hot bowl of spaghetti before catching the bus to work.

I lived for little moments like these; as small as they may seem, they fueled me and gave me the strength to keep going.

However, my body and mind deteriorated more each day as I became further entangled in my addiction. The cost of meth was far cheaper than the cost of food, suppressing my appetite for hours, so I began to use it daily, seeking different methods to consume my drug of choice. It started by grinding up shards of crystal and snorting up to eight lines a day, then quickly evolved to smoking the crystals in a small glass pipe. The feelings of empowerment, high energy, excitement, and racing thoughts powered me through the day. But my body became weak as the days blended into weeks and months.

My light blonde hair covered my pale blotchy face as the chemicals seeped through my skin, creating a rash of open sores, bumps, and scars. I appeared sick, with skin barely hanging from my bones, frail as I struggled to stand upright with protruding ribs over my hollow stomach. I communicated with senseless and irrational babble with intense moodiness and irrational outbursts. This seemingly harmless 'survival' initiative was slowly killing me.

Then, like a volcano on the verge of eruption, it all ended abruptly. After several days without sleep or proper nutrition, I fainted during my shift at work. My manager rushed me to the break room, shaking me hysterically until I regained consciousness. The dark secrets I carefully kept hidden rose to the surface. I was exposed. Then in a child-like tone.

I begged, "Please call my momma."

My mother and Ken drove several hours to pick me up and pack my things. After all the damage I had done to dismantle our family, they still welcomed me with open arms. Listening without judgment as I shared the experiences I endured. I couldn't fathom their unrelenting love for me after all the pain I caused them and everyone I encountered.

My mother tucked me in and gently kissed my head as tears rolled down my face. I slept for weeks, only awake long enough to bathe, and eat. My mother nurtured me through my recovery while I experienced debilitating pain, night sweats, involuntary shaking, and withdrawals as my body expelled the toxic chemicals. She never made me feel unloved or unwanted. She never judged me; she accepted me in my darkest moments, at times sacrificing her own needs but never with resentment, only with grace and unconditional love.

My stepdad Ken was so patient and kind, loving me despite my choices. He supported my mother through all the challenges and pain she endured while I was away. He is the only real dad I have ever known. He isn't perfect, but he is present, consistent, active, caring, supportive, fair, and comforting, and he taught me what a father should be. He always put us first, and even when everything seemed to be falling apart, he was the glue that kept us together.

My mother enrolled me in home school so I could finish my last few credits, and after a few daunting months of healing and studying, I finally graduated high school just after my seventeenth birthday.

I sat on the steps beneath the front door while my mother and I discussed the future. I stared at the large pine trees as the sun peeked through the shade; a cool breeze swept over the tops of the trees as they swayed back and forth. We were enjoying the pine-scented air and embracing this peaceful moment together.

She asked, "What do you want to do with your life?"

I sat silently for a moment and then with a sigh of uncertainty.

I replied, "What do you think I should do?"

She said, "You are bright, beautiful, and strong, but most of all, you are resilient. You can do anything you put your mind to."

After all that I had done to tear our family apart, the heartache my mother endured, the endless nights not knowing where I was, I didn't deserve her grace, yet she gave it so freely without hesitation, and most of all, she still believed in me.

Chapter 7: The One That Got Away

As we sat on the steps of my parent's cabin, I pondered my future, unclear where to begin or where my journey would take me. My mother encouraged me to pursue a career in real estate. She knew that I needed a path where I could have the freedom to evolve and find myself, so I took the next steps to obtain my real estate license.

As much as I wanted to stay tucked away in their cabin in the woods, I knew I was wild and free, so I packed my things and moved down the mountain once more—this time with the loving support of my parents, cheering me on.

I rented a room and started applying for internships at local real estate offices to establish a foundation. At the same time, I juggled two other jobs and continued to use public transportation as I navigated through life.

I sat at the bus stop on the corner of a busy intersection, waiting for the next bus to arrive. A nearby friend saw me sitting and slid onto the bench beside me. We hadn't seen each other in months, so we laughed and giggled as we shared stories catching up on our lives. Just then, an old red pickup truck drove past and honked, then made a U-turn pulling into the parking lot behind the bus stop. My friend jumped up and started talking to the driver, so I turned to glance at the person in the truck.

Everything started to flow in slow motion as I locked eyes with the driver. It was as if the world had stopped, and I was floating toward him. He had long brown hair that he casually swept to the side as he spoke; the sun danced over his features, bringing out his strong jawline, chiseled facial structure, and high cheekbones that lit up when he smiled. As I walked toward him, all the noises from the busy intersection seemed to fade away. He was the most beautiful man I had ever seen, and with just a simple introduction, I was captivated by his kind, gentle demeanor.

As the bus arrived, I snapped back into reality and ran off without even knowing his name. I found an empty seat on the bus, gazing out the smudged window in his direction as the bus drove away. My heart fluttered, and my stomach filled with butterflies as I watched the cars pass, daydreaming of this mysterious man.

When I returned home, I called my friend to inquire about the man in the red pickup truck.

He said, "His name is James!"

I suggested he give him my phone number; my friend scoffed and unenthusiastically agreed.

A few days later, I received the call that would change my life; James invited me to dinner. I tried not to reveal my excitement, but without hesitation, I accepted. I was elated, trying on every outfit I could find, practically floating through the house as I prepared for him to arrive. I meticulously straightened every layer of my bright blonde A-Line haircut, perfectly applied my black wing-tipped eyeliner, and bronzed my olive skin. I was healthy and glowing as I slipped into a little black dress with platform heels.

I sat eagerly on the edge of the sofa in the living room, awaiting his arrival, twirling my blonde hair through my fingers, tapping my legs anxiously, and counting the minutes until I heard the sound of his truck parking outside my door. I glanced in the mirror, nervously applied my nude lip gloss, took a deep breath, then, calm and collected, answered the door. As James stood before me, my heart melted into putty.

He was even more gorgeous than I remembered. He towered over me in the entryway as I blushingly glanced up at him. He was taller than I expected, his button-down shirt draped over his broad shoulders and muscular arms; the shaded stubble on his face framed his jawline, his hazel brown eyes pierced my soul, and the smell of his aftershave tickled my nose, sending a wave of goosebumps down my body.

With a modest smile, James said, "You look beautiful."

We talked for hours over dinner as if time had no meaning. I was awestruck by his gentle spirit and strong demeanor. Once we realized how much time had passed as the night progressed, he drove me home. James was the perfect gentleman; stepping out of the driver's side to open my door, he politely held my hand, walking me to the front door. He gazed into my eyes with a timid yet confident expression, softly placing my hair behind my ears; he leaned in for an innocent kiss. I cupped his face in my hands and drew him closer, not wanting the night to end.

A flood of emotions filled my body as he drove away. His beautiful soul enchanted me; he was passionate, vulnerable, and creative. He intrigued me with his self-taught musical abilities, from singing to playing guitar, keyboard, and drums. He was only a few years older than me, starting his career designing digital graphics and recording music for video games, yet everything about him utterly amazed me. His hazel eyes pierced through my soul as if his gaze had broken down the walls I built around my heart. As he intently drew me in, I felt like his presence peeled away the layers of my past, and he could see the little girl inside me yearning to be loved.

He swept me off my feet, and within a few months, I met his family, and they accepted me as their own. I introduced James to my parents, and

I could see in my mother's eyes that she adored him as I knew she would. He was perfect!

I fell deeper in love with him as each day passed, spending every waking moment together, and within a few months, we moved in together. James swept me off my feet; he would sing and record music, writing songs dedicated to me; we painted together, made pottery, explored new places, went on road trips, and created memories everywhere we went. He encouraged me to follow my dreams and even challenged me to dream bigger.

We would lay in bed naked for hours, intertwined in each other's arms, as he caressed my body and embraced all my insecurities and imperfections. We made love for hours and would wake up in the middle of the night, thirsting for more. I couldn't get enough of him and yearned for our souls to be one.

James taught me more about myself than I ever imagined. He was an old soul with so much wisdom to share, walking me through my emotions and guiding me as I navigated through the early years of my adult life.

James worked tirelessly to provide for us while I was still trying to discover myself. I jumped from one job to the next, failed my real estate exam three times, and my negative emotions slowly crept in. I felt like he was coasting through his career, and I was unstable, seeking approval, and desperate to prove my independence. Secretly embarrassed, I masked my emotions, disguising them in the form of extreme adoration instead of accepting the truth. I was discouraged because James gave so much, yet I had nothing to give in return.

I wanted to contribute, so I accepted a position as a receptionist for a stainless-steel manufacturer. The company was in an industrial area surrounded by old run-down commercial buildings, which made me uneasy, but the job gave me a slight sense of independence. So, despite my overbearing supervisor constantly looking over my shoulder, I still found joy in making people smile by answering the phone.

My mom and dad were so proud of me for starting my first real job that they wanted to do something special. They had always sacrificed beyond their means to ensure I had everything I needed, even when I didn't deserve it. But this time, they outdid themselves. As I walked up the stairs to celebrate over dinner, my mom and dad giggled excitedly, dangling a set of car keys. I squinted my eyes skeptically, observing their playful mannerisms when they simultaneously blurted out.

"We're buying a new car and giving you ours!"

It was a used 1994 baby blue Dodge Spirit, a box-shaped four-door midsize sedan with a musky worn fabric interior, a front split-bench seat to accommodate up to six passengers, cigarette residue between every crevasse, and scuffed hubcaps from my mom parking a little too close to the curb. This wasn't quite what I had in mind for my very first car, but I was genuinely grateful. I wrapped my arms around each, squeezing so tightly, and showered them with appreciation.

Later that week, during one of my shifts, I received a call from a woman seemingly impressed by how I answered the phone. I embraced those little moments and politely transferred the call. I continued to answer calls while organizing the stack of files on my desk, and the woman called again.

She asked, "Do you like your job?"

I curiously replied, "Why do you ask?"

She said, "I'm a recruiter, and I have a receptionist position that I'm looking to fill, and you would be the perfect fit. So, if you're interested, I will schedule an interview today during your lunch hour."

I looked around the lobby suspiciously to ensure no one could hear our conversation, then apprehensively replied.

I said, "I don't want to lose my job."

She said kindly, "You have nothing to lose; it'll be between you and me."

She gave me the address and asked me to arrive at noon. Nervously, I played the scenario over and over again in my mind. *Should I take the risk? What if the interview lasts too long and I lose my job? What if my boss finds out?*

I felt undervalued in my current position, and I can always devise a clever excuse if I'm late returning from lunch. So, I decided, *What the hell, she's right! I have nothing to lose.*

I anxiously watched the large glass clock positioned in the center of the wall directly in front of my desk. The small arrow pointed at the number eleven, and the long hand ticketed slowly around the face of the clock until it finally was fifteen minutes before noon. I quickly clocked out for lunch and raced to the address the recruiter provided.

The address was only a few blocks away, so I arrived with two minutes to spare. As I rushed towards the entry, I noticed two large wooden medieval doors surrounded by glass windows—a large cement monument with front-lit bold red and black letters brightly illuminated from the structure displaying the name of a national retailer specializing in rocker fashions and accessories; I frequently shopped in their stores, so

I was very familiar with their brand. I quickly ran up the steps opening the giant wooden doors.

As I walked into the lobby, I was in awe of the rock-n-roll aesthetic. Concrete floors spanned through the entrance with an oversized red velvet couch on the right, two high-back chairs to the left, and a massive rust-distressed gothic chandelier suspended from the open ceilings; framed gold records covered the walls. A sizable Persian-style rug led to an enormous fifteen-foot handcrafted wooden built-in that resembled an authentic castle with eight television screens playing music videos—an antique autopsy table with a wrought iron frame and glass top centered below the wooden altar.

As I approached the desk, I was speechless and amazed by this magical place.

The receptionist said, "Serena? We're expecting you; someone will be with you shortly."

The receptionist led me on a tour of the conference rooms, each with its own unique style. One room was called the operating room, with a large stainless-steel table and framed X-rays displayed on the walls; Moroccan furniture and decor filled another room. Then she asked me to sit in the Gothic room centered by a round black wooden table with high-back medieval chairs upholstered in red velvet, crimson-colored walls with antique iron fixtures, and a massive two-tier candle chandelier.

Restlessly I waited, fidgeting and tapping my legs. Finally, a woman with long wavy dark hair dressed in a rock t-shirt, cargo pants, and laced black boots entered the room and conducted the interview surprisingly pleasantly and thoughtfully. Her demeanor was so welcoming that it calmed my anxious fidgeting as I answered each question with confidence and optimism.

The woman stepped away for a moment; I heard my flip phone vibrating repeatedly and realized I had lost track of time. I rehearsed what I would tell my boss as I nervously waited for the woman to return.

She opened the conference room door with a smile and introduced me to a woman named Elizabeth. Elizabeth was an accomplished businesswoman who served as the CEO. She gracefully sat beside me, sharing the story of how the now Fortune 500 company began its journey from the founder's garage, ignited by a passion for combining music and fashion.

Elizabeth continued to say they were impressed by my interview and wanted me to start immediately, offering me an hourly wage higher than I had ever made before. I accepted without hesitation as they began the new hire process.

Several hours had passed, and I glanced at the clock, realizing it was already four o'clock. Once the interview was over, they asked me to start the next day, and with excitement, I practically skipped through the parking lot.

I sat in my car, emphatically thumbing through the numerous missed calls from my boss. I listened to the screaming voicemails until I mustered the courage to return her call. She answered with agitation, and I confidently told her I was giving my notice. She yelled obscenities, so I politely wished her well and hung up.

I was filled with excitement as I rushed home to tell James the news. He wrapped his arms around me and told me how proud he was that I had taken this leap of faith. We celebrated together that evening as I anxiously prepared for my first day.

The corporate office, referred to as "headquarters," was an enchanting environment, from the eclectic decor to the incredibly talented buyers and employees; the entire office was an open space concept, with each desk connected to the other. The executives didn't have closed offices; their desks strategically faced each department encouraging collaboration and engagement. It was my dream job, and I continued growing and thriving daily.

As the year progressed, I grew in my career, focusing less on my personal growth and becoming more codependent on James. I could see my constant neediness and desire for attention slowly wearing him down. The intensity of my love and infatuation for him consumed me, obsessing about his whereabouts, giving him little or no space to be free. I expressed my frustration subtly, suppressing and avoiding, isolating, or shutting down when I didn't get my way. Then, finally, James pulled me aside one evening.

He said, "We need to talk."

The conversation that every person dreads. He was kind and thoughtful, as he genuinely cared for my feelings. He expressed his concerns about my manic behavior, encouraging me to take time to focus on healing after all the trauma I endured. I sat in silence, intently listening to every word and accepting responsibility for my needy behavior. I knew in my heart James was right, but I couldn't imagine living without him and continued to beg for one last chance.

He empathetically responded, "Healthy relationships manifest themselves through healthy communication, but one of the most vital parts of a healthy relationship is loving yourself, and you're not there yet."

My heart sank into my stomach as the tears poured out, I cried uncontrollably, trying to speak, but the words were just mumbles of desperation. I felt tremendous grief, fur-lined with the fear that joy had slipped through my fingers-tips and had forever escaped me. Then, finally, the harsh reality sunk in that there would be no happily ever after for me.

With a heavy weight on my chest and tightness in my lungs, I felt like every breath I took was like swallowing razor blades. I looked up at James with my swollen tear-filled eyes.

I said, "I understand."

I placed my hand against his cheek, my fingers grazed the soft contour of his mouth, and pleaded for one last night together.

A note of misery in his voice increased the tension mounted in my chest as he graciously declined. The subtle rejection devastated me as if I was drowning in a pool of grief, gasping for air. He wrapped his strong arms around me, holding me tightly, and gently placed my head on his lap. He caressed my forehead, softly wiping the teardrops streaming down my cheeks as I cried hysterically until I fell asleep.

In the days following, I stayed with a family member that lived nearby until I could get back on my feet. But, again, the sadness and emotional suffering consumed me, bursting into tears at the slightest moment with an unrelenting agony that felt like a stabbing sensation piercing my stomach. I couldn't eat or sleep and lay awake staring blankly at the ceiling many nights.

There is a fine line between love and madness. I began to act outside of my typical nature. It felt like something inside of me took over that was so powerful it motivated my illogical actions.

It was midnight, and I impulsively sat up in my bed, my mind fixated on the memories we shared, and I couldn't take it any longer; I needed to see James. So, I hastily grabbed my jacket and drove to his apartment. I tiptoed into his back patio, gently tapping his bedroom window, desperately hoping his strength would cave. Finally, James peeked through the curtains and motioned me to enter through the sliding door. I let out a sigh of relief and felt a glimpse of hope.

The pale crescent moon radiated through the curtains illuminating a soft glow on his face as I entered the room. He tenderly touched my hand, leading my body beside him on the bed, wrapping the soft covers over me with the warmth of his body encircling me. He caressed my forehead, softly kissing my lips and pulling me closer. My grasp slid over his broad shoulders. My fingers curled gently through his hair as he drew me closer, wrapping my legs around him as we made love one last time.

That was the first time I began to accept that nothing happens without a bigger purpose– not even broken hearts, not even pain. As my mindset began to shift, I began to see my life in a different way. These pain-filled moments were lessons and signs gifting me the opportunity to step back and reflect on my journey. They were illuminating a new path for me to move forward toward healing.

James taught me so much about myself, and I admired him for the impact he made on my life; even though I knew we couldn't be together, we had an unbreakable friendship.

Chapter 8: Without Purpose

 I spent most of my time establishing my career. While I continued to grow in my position at the retail headquarters, I evolved in real estate, working as a transaction coordinator for a local real estate company on the weekends hosting open houses. During this season, I was living with my roommates Michelle and Luke. Luke was always quiet and mostly stayed in his room, and Michelle was a breath of fresh air, wild and spirited.

 One day, I was sitting on the couch waiting for my date to arrive, but the doorbell didn't ring, and I suspected he had stood me up. Then, as I started to lose hope, I received a phone call from an unknown number. I answered the phone, assuming it was my date, only to realize someone else had accidentally called the wrong number. I've always had a soft, sweet tone, so when I explained that he had the wrong number, the caller continued to spark a conversation; I giggled to myself, thinking, *who is this crazy guy?* He continued to flirt with me and ask me ridiculous questions, and when I shared that my date didn't show up, he convinced me to go on a date with him instead.

 We met that evening at a local coffee shop. I knew that if we met in a public place, I could easily sneak away if he was hideous or creepy. But, instead, I was pleasantly surprised. As he approached, I was sitting on the patio outside the coffee shop; the string lights glistened against his goofy smile when he introduced himself.

 He said, "I'm Anthony. You must be Serena?"

 I playfully responded, "You must have the wrong table."

We both laughed and spent the evening seeing who could outsmart each other with sarcasm. Anthony was tall and clean-shaven with prominent ears that added to his cuteness and dark brown hair with a short military haircut. Anthony brought out the goofy and sappy side of me. He was light-hearted and carefree, helping me see the brighter side of life and giving me a reason to laugh again.

After our first date, he called me from the military base daily, and we talked for hours. Then, when he was visiting family in the area, he would come over to my house in footie pajamas with silly cartoon-shaped slippers, jump on the bed, watch movies, and laugh endlessly together. I loved how he made me feel, and I ignored plenty of red flags, disregarding them because I enjoyed this fun-loving distraction. With his buttery words, he would melt my heart and convince me that he was coming to see me. I would get so excited running around cleaning the house, getting dressed up with my makeup perfectly applied each time. To realize that he wasn't coming.

Feelings of rejection, discarded, and abandonment began to swirl through my mind. Then, finally, I started to recognize a pattern. Anthony would say whatever I wanted to hear at the moment, but when the time came; he would make excuses for not being able to show up, especially when I needed him most. I noticed slight changes in his behavior but dismissed the signs. Instead, I was optimistic, continuing to justify his excuses and ignoring my intuition.

One night, I was severely ill. He had promised he was coming to see me and asked me repeatedly to stay up for him. I was throwing up all night with a burning fever, dozing off every few minutes and anxiously waiting for him to arrive. Anthony told me he was on his way within the hour, but then two hours passed.

Anthony said, "Don't worry, I'm on my way. I'll be there soon."

My body was weak, yet I forced myself to stay awake despite my drowsiness and nausea. Finally, after several hours had passed without hearing a word, I realized it was two o'clock in the morning. With my head leaning against the cold porcelain toilet seat, heaving, and vomiting uncontrollably, I decided that I had waited long enough—I didn't need him to take care of me; I was strong enough to take care of myself. So, I picked up the phone and told him not to come, and out of exhaustion and irritation ended our relationship that night. The most disturbing part was that he was not affected by my outburst. He didn't ask me to stay or wait for him to arrive. Instead, he was surprisingly unbothered.

After our breakup, I learned about Anthony's second girlfriend near the military base and later realized he was dating us simultaneously. Although hurt and angry, I was glad I found out sooner rather than later, so I could lose the distraction and focus on my career.

As the months passed, I was increasingly ill, vomiting at the slightest smell, and I started to feel my body changing, feeling bloated, swollen, and gaining weight even though I could barely hold anything down. It was until my roommate Michelle exchanged some playful discourse and convinced me to take a pregnancy test that I began to feel uneasy.

She curiously asked, "When was your last period?"

I scoffed and replied, "I'm always irregular, so I'm not worried, but I think it's been about three months."

Michelle cunningly replied, "There is no harm in taking a test you're well prepared for, right?"

I found it silly to consider her challenge because it had been several months since Anthony, and I separated. But she was persuasive, so I reluctantly agreed to take a home pregnancy test. I pulled down my pants and hovered over the toilet in the bathroom, positioning myself slightly above the seat. A single drop of urine barely touched the applicator, and two pink lines appeared within seconds. The test was positive—*No! This isn't happening. I can't be pregnant.* Panic set in as I threw the first test aside and anxiously unwrapped the second test.

Again, two pink lines appeared instantly within seconds of my urine hitting the applicator. My heart started racing; sweat dripped down my forehead, and with my hands shaking, I handed Michelle the applicators. She graciously set the pregnancy tests aside and hugged me; my knees buckled as I fell to the floor. Fear and disbelief poured out of my soul in the form of tears. I collapsed at her feet, trembling as she coddled my head between her arms, rocking me from side to side on the cold bathroom tile.

I couldn't believe it! I wasn't ready for a baby. I struggled to survive independently, working hard day and night, and couldn't let my progress go. I was terrified. I couldn't fathom bringing a child into the world at the age of twenty. My breathing accelerated, and as the muscles in my neck and shoulders tensed, I began to feel dizzy and nauseous. The room spun around me, seemingly the metaphor of my life spinning out of control.

Michelle lifted me off the floor and offered to take me to see my parents. As she drove, I stared blankly out the window with tears streaming down my face. My mind was racing with so many unanswered questions—I felt my plans, hopes, and dreams slowly slipping away.

As Michelle drove closer to my parents' street, I could hardly see through my swollen eyes. I slowly stepped out of the car with my body shaking in fear; despair consumed my mind with each step towards the front door. The moment I saw my mother, she stood in the doorway, inviting me in with open arms, but I was so ashamed I couldn't bear the thought of telling her. So instead, I desperately turned towards Michelle to plan my escape, but Michelle looked me in the eyes and gently nudged me forward.

With my voice trembling, I could taste the salt from the tears surrounding my lips as I quietly muttered the words.

I said, "I'm pregnant."

Without hesitation, my mom and Ken graciously embraced me and held me close.

They said, "We love you unconditionally, and we will continue to love and support you every step of the way."

I sat in disbelief as the shame and guilt pressed into my chest. I struggled to swallow in a disheveled heap as my grief poured out in a flood of emotions. My parents held me tightly, encouraging me until I finally shed my last tear. I left my parent's house that evening with a small glimpse of hope. Even though the terror of this news weighed heavily on my mind, I wasn't alone.

The following day I mustered up the courage to contact Anthony to inform him of the situation. Although deep down, I wanted to run away and hide; I knew he had a right to know—I even believed that he might want to be a part of his child's life. But unfortunately, I found his response more horrifying than the pregnancy news itself. Anthony's first response was falsely accusing me of attempting to get back with him by lying about the news of my pregnancy. He then felt compelled to tell me he was living with the other woman on the military base and raising her baby instead.

At that moment, my suspicions became validated: I realized he was with her the entire time we were together. I was his mistress when he was home visiting his family, and when Anthony would return home, he would return to her. He told me he wanted nothing to do with me and continued to deny that the baby was his; Anthony suggested I get an abortion because the pregnancy news would tarnish his reputation in the military. His tone was harsh and threatening, paranoid that he would lose his job if I told anyone. He made it very clear that this was my burden to carry and told me not to contact him again. Anthony's hurtful words left me devastated. His rejection of accepting the baby brought me to my knees. Raising a child by myself in my early twenties was something I never expected nor could imagine.

After my first doctor's visit, I struggled to believe I was almost four months pregnant. I found myself battling with conviction in deciding whether to keep the baby or consider other options, whether it would hinder my career, the future I worked so hard for—or if I could even raise a child alone.

I shared my concerns with the people I trusted. My supervisor was sensitive and comforting during this crucial time, and even though I didn't believe in abortion, the fear of raising this baby consumed me. She kindly offered to go to the abortion clinic with me so I could consider all my options.

As we arrived, I felt a dark shadow cast over me. The waiting room was still and quiet except for the hypnotic tick of an old plastic clock hanging on the wall. A smell evoking images of latex gloves and ammonia filled the sterile air. Dusty fake plants hung from the dingy white walls, and faded baby blue chairs circled the edges of the sparse room leading to the smudged glass window. The nurse behind the window pointed to a stack of papers attached to a clipboard and motioned me to sign in.

While I sat in the clinic, waiting for the nurse to call me in. I sat solemnly beside my supervisor as she placed her hand on mine. Then, with my head hanging down, the tension increased in my neck as I carefully scanned the waiting room, observing the other patients. Some sat alone, and others leaned into their partners; the room felt somber, filled with uncertainty and despair.

I saw several young women like me who didn't know whether they could raise the baby on their own. Women who faced unimaginable choices so their unborn babies wouldn't have to suffer at the hands of this cruel world. I felt their pain drifting in the air as I'm sure they could feel mine. Then, finally, the door creaked open, and the nurse called my name. My supervisor waited as I entered the cold exam room. The door shut quietly behind me, and all I could hear were whispers sweeping through the waiting room.

The paper crinkled as I sat on the edge of the examination table, intently listening to the nurse as she described the procedure; she seemed emotionless, using words I couldn't fully comprehend. Then, finally, she explained a dilation and evacuation method typically required during the second trimester, using a long, looped-shaped knife that scrapes the lining, placenta, and baby away from the uterus. I could feel my throat swell up as I sat in horror. The nurse continued to describe the side effects and risks in detail, including nausea, bleeding, and cramping. In rare cases, an infection may occur due to retained remains of the baby, or bacteria can cause fever, pain, abdominal tenderness, and scarring. I started to feel faint and mustered up the courage to mumble a few words.

I asked, "Can the baby feel anything?"

She paused momentarily as she noticed my leg fidgeting and then explained.

She said, "At this stage in your pregnancy, the baby flexes, kicks, and begins sucking their thumb, the skin starts to form, and facial expressions are possible."

I pictured this tiny human growing inside my body, so I desperately scrambled for my bag without saying a word, practically knocking her over as I rushed out of the door.

I had already made the decision. I knew I needed to own my choices and take accountability. I would never forgive myself for hurting this poor soul growing inside me. I have experienced trauma, grief, fear, shame, guilt, the duality of life and death, loneliness, community, nostalgia, and self-preservation. Yet, among all these things, I survived. And I am determined to raise this precious baby, overcoming the challenges ahead, no matter the circumstances.

I called Anthony the same day to inform him of my decision. But, instead, he cut the call short, insisted on denying that the baby was his, and told me not to use his name on the birth certificate. I knew his rejection was not a reflection of this baby but instead a reflection of him. So, I didn't contact his family to honor his request and kept my pregnancy a secret.

A few weeks later, I received an unexpected call from Anthony's older sister, Karen. Karen was tall, solidly built with generous curves, and towered over me with her bold disposition. She thrived on rumors and banter, hastily airing everyone's dirty laundry, over-dramatizing stories, and cackling with a high-pitched laugh. So, I was slightly apprehensive when Karen informed me that Anthony had abruptly slipped in the shower injuring his head. I rolled my eyes and listened as she explained that he had been admitted to the hospital.

She was obnoxiously hysterical as she claimed that he shared the important news of my pregnancy with his family.

From that point on, Karen demanded to be involved in my pregnancy. But all I wanted was to be far away from anyone remotely related to Anthony. He had already put me through enough stress, and I needed to focus on my career so I could provide for my baby.

However, Anthony's sister kept nagging me with questions regarding the baby and the pregnancy. At first, I tried to be optimistic, hoping she had good intentions or that her involvement would be positive. Until she blatantly told me that the baby in my belly was her flesh and blood, and she had a right to take this baby away from me.

She emphatically called me at work, and when I wouldn't answer her calls, she began sending me three-page-long emails about how she planned to take my baby and raise it as her own. Then, without forewarning, she would show up at my doctor's appointments pretending she was in the area and noticed my car in the parking lot. Karen was obsessed and unstoppable, no matter how many times I asked her to give me space. I was quickly overwhelmed with terror and in total fear that she would spread rumors that I was unfit to be a mother and try to steal the baby from me once it was born.

Over the next few weeks, Karen became even more unrelenting. She repeatedly reminded me that the seed growing inside me was her blood and that she would leave no stone unturned, doing everything in her power to take my baby away. Anthony might not have wanted the baby, but Karen demanded this baby would be hers.

Due to Karen's constant intimidation, her relentless pursuit to invade my privacy, dictate my every decision, and her continuous effort to initiate anxiety were beginning to impact my health. I knew I needed to stand my ground when I realized she was unwilling to back down. So, I filed a restraining order against her to eliminate unnecessary stress so I could continue my pregnancy in peace.

My action proved to be my best decision; I finally enjoyed a healthy pregnancy and glowed with excitement when I found out I was having a baby boy.

Before the final month of pregnancy, I moved into a small one-bedroom apartment. Thirty-five acres of plush grass and giant shade trees surrounded the barbeque and picnic areas of the single-story apartment complex. Each unit included a charming patio. I could feel the breeze brushing against my face as I approached the front door with my arms barely wrapped around a large box pressed against my growing belly.

I was overjoyed to finally have a sense of independence as I soaked in the smell of fresh paint and carefully walked around the pattern of vacuum lines throughout the carpet. The total living space was five hundred square feet of pure freedom. The movers perfectly placed my plush purple sofa just beneath the bay window in the living room as I unpacked the tiny baby plates and bottles in the maple-stained kitchen cabinets.

My wrought-iron canopy bed filled the limited space in the undersized primary bedroom, leaving just enough room for me to assemble the baby's new crib and position it near my bedside. I purposefully chose a crib skirt, soft fitted sheet, and baby blanket that complimented the colors of my bedding with the added touch of matching accent pillows. I was finally home.

My friends and family surrounded me with love and support. James stood by my side every step of the way, and when the time came for my delivery, he was there holding my hand. As I fawned over my precious baby boy, I chose his name, Adian Micah. The meaning behind his first name is 'little fire,' and he lit up my whole world. While the name Micah carries a deeper meaning, 'Gift from God.' from the moment they placed him in my arms, I knew he was my gift. In the first hour of wakefulness, as his skin pressed against mine, I was mesmerized by his innocence, deeply connected to this tiny human as I welcomed him to the world.

Chapter 9: Heavyweight

Navigating motherhood was like driving through a blizzard with broken windshield wipers in the middle of a desolate mountain. But the moment I looked into the bright blue eyes of my flawless baby boy, my heart melted, and every struggle seemed to float away in the wind.

Especially when we made each other laugh by rubbing noses or when I nuzzled his neck—that secret chubby spot in the back that stayed warm long after a nap. His tiny toes and mounds of rolls rumbled when he giggled.

Motherhood was magical until reality set in; the long sleepless nights made it impossible to see straight without going cross-eyed. I could barely walk after labor, let alone change diapers, breastfeed, or figure out what to do with that tiny thing between his legs.

As my maternity leave ended, the stark truth of leaving him with a caregiver weighed heavy on my heart. But I had no choice; I was alone and needed to prove that I could do this on my own.

The night before, Adian was fussy all night; after tossing and turning for hours, he finally fell asleep around three o'clock, slightly drooling breastmilk on my chest. However, the obnoxious beeps from my alarm abruptly woke us up just a few hours later.

I jumped out of bed, buckled Adian's little body in his infant seat, and placed him next to the shower as I quickly soaped and rinsed my body. His coos and whimpers were cute at first but immediately turned into wails and screams if I didn't poke my head out from the shower curtain every few seconds to remind him that I was still there.

While I scrambled to get dressed for work, I curled Adian under one arm, bouncing him on my hip while applying makeup with my other hand. I suddenly realized I was going to be late, and I had forgotten to pack his baby bag the night before. I playfully began tossing diapers and toys in the air to keep him giggling while heating his bottle and packing his things. Then just as I was finally ready to run out the door, a devastating smell filled the air, and I knew I couldn't leave without changing his diaper.

I rushed back in, laid him gently on the changing table, and began to clean up his morning massacre. I placed the new diaper under his cute little bottom and leaned in to sneak a kiss. Suddenly, he let out a little toot and squirted yellow poop all over my shirt with just enough force to spray poop on my face. I gasped, and he giggled as I frantically scampered to the bathroom to scrub my face and find a clean shirt.

Despite the challenges of motherhood, I had a bigger problem to face. I listened to everyone who had said, "You're eating for two," and I didn't realize the pregnancy's impact on my body. I couldn't remember the last time I looked in a full-length mirror. I believed that breastfeeding would make all the fat melt away. Yet, I was twenty-one years old, 5'1, and over two hundred pounds.

It wasn't until the corporate marketing department asked if I would model for their new plus-size division, that I realized I was no longer a size six but had grown to a size eighteen.

Once the "plus-size" model photos were released, I was devastated. It was not as shallow as my dress size but a much deeper pain. I struggled with an eating disorder for several years, and when I wasn't binging and purging, I was starving or punishing myself for allowing this to happen. I felt so ashamed that I was embarrassed to eat in public, looking over my shoulder and scanning the restaurant before each bite. It was like a smaller version of myself was trapped inside a larger body.

It was the assumption that people described me by my size rather than who I was. My personality, strength, intelligence, humor, and resilience could no longer hide my insecurities. I heard the dreadful statement time and time again, "Well, at least you have a pretty face."

The whole world could see me, I was exposed, and no matter how long I tried to wear my maternity clothes, I could no longer hide.

The brick-like weight pulled me down with every step—physically and mentally. I felt humiliated and desperate for a magic pill, fad diet, or skinny potion. The countless 'skinny' clothes hanging in my closet that I kept just in case I could wear them again taunted me, and without fail, I couldn't pull anything over my hips. I continued circulating the only three outfits I could fit into, wearing oversized shirts, jackets, and leggings, hoping people wouldn't notice that they were slowly ripping at the seams. I could barely afford my rent, let alone healthy food, and I refused to spend any money on 'fat clothes' because one day I wouldn't need to wear them, and besides, I didn't deserve new clothes anyway.

The drooping rolls that hung over my waist, the sagging skin around my thighs rubbing together as I walked, and the new stretch marks that magically appeared before every shower inflated the emotional torture and horrifying thoughts already haunting my mind; *No one will ever love me this way; I'm disgusting; how could anyone want me? How could I have let this happen?*

The deep-seated panic and anxiety consumed me, even over minor tasks. Cold spider-like fingers raced up and down my spine as I pushed my new baby boy in his stroller, praying that no one was staring, hoping that no one noticed that I lost my breath by leisurely playing with him at the park. Spirals of self-doubt ran through my mind as I struggled to make even the simplest decisions at the grocery store. Anywhere there are people, people who could see how big I've become would stare, whisper, and point.

The only sense of comfort I found was hiding in the car during my lunch hour, or the final slow deep exhale as I walked through the front door each night. I dreamt about the possibilities of how life would feel if I were a 'normal' weight again, but I didn't even know where to begin.

Growing up, family members and foster parents always told me to eat everything on my plate without complaining. I believed that eating healthy was having a salad with ranch dressing and extra cheese, vegetables only came from a can, and God forbid if I ever wasted food. So as agonizing as it was to see those photos, it sparked a fire inside me.

I couldn't find an easy solution, so a friend studying for his fitness training certification made me his test project. His goal was to see if his nutrition plan and exercise routine would actually work, and I was willing to try anything to feel 'normal' again.

He said, "The first step is to change your mindset and relationship with food."

Looking in from the outside, if anyone ever knew that I literally wanted to throw up, binge until it hurt, force-feed myself until even the taste of ice cream made me sick, or naturally feel tortured by any food in front of me, they would never understand. It was my way of exerting control when life felt turbulent and chaotic. Controlling my body gives me a sense of power, and I had been living this cycle for so long that vomiting after every meal was effortless and a relief. My compulsion around selecting foods, restricting, or purging neutralized the obsessive intrusive thoughts of guilt, shame, inadequacy, and failure. So now, someone would change everything with a simple nutrition plan? I doubted it.

I'd always been an overachiever, aiming to prove everyone wrong, yet I was terrified of being faced with reframing my relentless drive and harsh self-criticism with unreachable standards. My stomach twisted in knots; I felt imprisoned by my body, not good enough—not capable, competent, worthy, and lovable, but I knew he was right. I needed to change my mind set before I could change my body.

He handed me a notepad and asked me to track my daily meals for the next seven days. Count my calories, fat, protein, and sugar intake. This idea sounded insane, and I couldn't even fathom how to add this to my list of millions of things I was already juggling throughout the day. Thoughts raced through my mind; *I needed to throw up to feel a physical release and calm; how would I let go of the one thing I could control? How in the world am I going to eat six meals a day and not make myself vomit?*

I couldn't even afford a gym membership, let alone a fitness trainer. So, I didn't have a choice; this was my only opportunity to transform emotionally and physically, with a trembling voice.

I said, "I'll do whatever it takes."

The following week, he copiously reviewed my notes and handed me a list of foods I could eat. The list was much shorter than I expected, but that was the least of my worries. He then asked me to take a 'before' picture. My knees felt like they would buckle; I wanted to hide behind something as my hands clutched around my stomach with a downward gaze, and my hair covered my face as I stared at the ground. A feeling of nakedness, being on display, and the thought of someone with a perfect body observing my flaws repulsed me as I slowly pulled my oversized T-shirt over my head and stood against a white wall, shaking with only a sports bra and thin leggings. Just as the camera shuttered, I quickly grabbed my shirt to cover myself. I was an enemy of my own body.

He outlined a workout routine I could follow at home, in the park, or at a local school. Reviewing the exercises was like reading a different language, burpees, planks, and squat jacks. He patiently demonstrated each one and then asked me to perform the workout. I could feel the sweat dripping down my forehead; my heart felt like it would burst through my chest, and a wave of nausea flooded my body.

He smiled and said, "Good! Now do this same routine every day until we meet again."

Every day? Is he crazy?

He added, "Oh, one more thing! I want you to run around the high school track four times too!"

I felt mortified at the idea of running, but I was even more appalled at the thought of ever taking a 'before' picture again.

After returning home the next day, I rushed to pick Adian up from the caregiver and then sped to the high school track before sunset. I positioned his stroller in front of the track, handed him a sippy cup, and began to jog. I couldn't make it more than thirty seconds, not even halfway around the path before my chest started burning, and my lungs began wheezing. The sobering reality hit me; I probably needed to start small if I was already doubled over thirty seconds into a light jog, gasping for air and clutching my knees. So, I set mini goals along the way. I started jogging for five minutes nonstop, then running around the track, walking one time, and running again.

Finally, after months of training, I began to jog around the entire track four times without feeling like I was about to fall over and die. Tracking my meals seemed more manageable, and I was surprised I didn't even miss indulging in the entire pint of chocolate chip cookie dough ice cream.

Six months passed in the blink of an eye, and I was now looking forward to my next progress photo. The moment the camera shuttered this time, I felt an extreme burst of energy. I couldn't wait to see how far I had come, and by the end of that year, I had lost eighty pounds. As thrilled as I was to lose the weight, the disturbing truth was that the elasticity of my skin was now a sagging mass of my previously stretched skin. I felt deformed, as though my skin was left behind like a partially empty wrapper. I was now faced with mixed feelings of ambivalence to feelings of pride, left with the aftermath of obesity and the remains of excess skin hanging from my body. Finally, I reached my goal, thinner and healthier than ever, yet disproportionate and burdened because of it.

Working out with sagging skin began to take its toll on my body. It was cumbersome; it pulled, left rashes, required special clothing and garments, and made finding clothes that hid the excess layers of skin very difficult. After spending a year changing my lifestyle and nutrition, I realized that my skin didn't regain elasticity, so I researched financing options for a surgical procedure to remove the excess skin, tighten surrounding tissue and reshape my body.

Just after my recovery, I began to build a new sense of confidence and felt empowered by achieving my goals. The surgery may have improved the shape and tone of my body, but it also allowed me to recognize the emotional resilience I developed through this journey.

I accelerated in my role as the receptionist, winning the customer service award out of over two hundred stores, three years in a row. But I was no longer just the receptionist; I became known as 'The Voice' of this leading music-inspired retail chain. I answered the phone with speed and grace, creating a magical experience for anyone who called on the phone or walked through those two large wooden medieval doors, from fashion designers, vendors, models, store managers, and stockholders to musicians and popular bands. I memorized each person's name, voice, and face, making it my goal to create a warm, personable experience, and I cherished every moment I made someone smile. I took so much pride in my position that I was recognized nationally and featured in magazine articles.

With over five years of service, I was still tickled with joy each new day, watching the company grow from two-hundred stores to five hundred, launching their new plus brand and taking the fashion world by storm.

One afternoon my supervisor called me into a private meeting, and as I walked into the large conference room, Elizabeth awaited my arrival. A feeling of impending doom washed over me, not knowing what the meeting was about, but I smiled and greeted her with a heightened, bubbly voice. As I slowly leaned in to sit beside her, my supervisor sat to my right, oddly gleaming at me with a twinkle in their eyes. Elizabeth handed me an envelope.

She said, "I've never met anyone like you, I am so proud of how much you have grown, and this is just a small token of my appreciation."

I nervously blushed and took the envelope from her but hesitated to open it. It was bonus season, so I knew there was likely a check inside. Yet a little embarrassed to open the envelope in front of her. She gently placed her hand on mine and looked me in the eyes.

Elizabeth said, "You are exceptional, and I trust you will keep this confidential."

I thanked her for believing in me and being an inspiration in my life. I had never met anyone as kind, genuine, and fierce as she was. As I stepped out of the room, I eagerly rushed to the ladies' room to privately open the envelope. I slowly lifted the fold and peeked inside. I let out a quiet scream and started hyperventilating. *Wait! This can't be. She must have given me someone else's bonus.*

I studied the name, and it was, in fact, my name, yet the numbers were beyond my imagination. The tiny box displayed the amount of ten thousand dollars. I began to drum my feet against the floor, fanning myself with the check and jumping up and down, squealing, hooting, and yelling just as my close friend and coworker walked into the bathroom to tell me she could hear me from her desk. Without thinking, I blurted out the number acting hyper, immature, and foolish as I embraced her, and we bounced up and down in the bathroom. She paused for a moment with a stoic expression.

She said, "You deserve it."

At that moment, I realized I had lost my sense of logic.

I asked, "What was your bonus?"

She said, "Oh, it's not important."

A sudden and overwhelming sensation of dread ran over me as I could feel the discord in her tone. She pretended not to care and turned to walk back to her desk. My mind was fixated on the worst-case scenario as she avoided eye contact and smugly opened the door.

I whispered, "Please don't tell anyone I told you."

She smirked and walked away. I desperately held myself against the metal stall, trying to grasp anything for stability as the panic set in. *What have I done?*

A few days passed, and I didn't hear a word. *Maybe she was my friend and didn't say anything?* She was acting rather odd and distant, but I'm sure she knew my intentions. I would never want her to feel like I was being insensitive, I genuinely care about her feelings, so I should take her to lunch and express how sorry I am.

Before I could say anything, my supervisor called me into a private room. I suddenly felt like I couldn't get enough oxygen, my heart beating out of my chest as I entered the room with my head hanging low. Elizabeth sat solemnly with her hands gripped tightly at the table as I slid down in the back of my chair. The room spun in circles as I lifted my head to focus on her words, but my ears were ringing, and my vision blurred. Then, finally, I felt my entire world crumble at my fingertips as Elizabeth explained that someone had brought it to her attention that I had broken her trust.

I leaned over the table with my head in my hands, pressing my fingers against my cheeks, and wept. I sat in humiliation as she expressed her disappointment with my behavior; before I could mutter the words, I'm sorry, she calmly stood up to leave the room. My bottom lip trembled as I tried to speak.

I asked, "Am I fired?"

Elizabeth replied, "No, but I think it would be best for you to take a few personal days to think about the impact of your actions."

I began to feel flu-like symptoms, nausea, cold sweats, and tingling in my chest as I gathered my things with an inability to look into the eyes of my peers. Self-disgust consumed my mind. *I didn't deserve that bonus; I don't deserve anything... I should have just returned it. I'm such an idiot... Why couldn't I keep my mouth shut?*

I staggered towards the exit shielding my swollen eyes, tightly gripping my bag, and glanced over my shoulder, angling away from anyone bearing witness to my shame. But instead, I noticed my friend standing in the distance with a malicious look in her eyes. In disbelief, I dropped my chin to my chest and left the lobby in tears.

Chapter 10: Broken

After months of self-deprecating thoughts, I couldn't shake the feelings of regret. Every time I entered the office, the joy that once filled my heart was exchanged for disgrace. It seemed like every glance in my direction was a reproach against my reputation. Even if these emotions were all in my head, I dreaded even looking at myself in the mirror each morning. The only thing keeping me from inflicting self-harm was my beautiful baby boy.

The seemingly small moments when he was nestled between my arms and curiously urging me to smile was the only thing driving me to press on. The unbearable truth weighed on my heart as I knew it was no one's fault but my own. I thought my strength would save me from the situation, but instead, my strength became my sickness. I masked my way through each day instead of facing the issues inside. I suppressed the shame and owned my actions, holding my head high with a fake smile and bubbly persona. I was never angry at my friend; I was mad at myself. I know there is always a reason and a purpose behind every failure, yet I couldn't see past my mistake. I tarnished my reputation and couldn't remain in that position any longer.

I was still fighting for child support as Anthony seemed to dodge every court appointment, demanding paternity tests and denying our son. In the meantime, James was kind enough to deposit five hundred dollars into my bank account each month since Adian was born because he knew I was barely making enough to buy diapers and formula. But when I tried to pay James back with the money I received from my bonus, he adamantly refused and urged me to invest in myself. Adian just turned two years old, so I decided to use the money to celebrate his birthday, invest in a college savings account, and buy a used treadmill for my apartment to maintain my weight loss.

Uncertain about where the path would lead me, I applied for several positions in the real estate industry. Finally, after a few weeks, I accepted an Information Specialist position for a new home construction company. This position never existed before and was created to support model home sales associates managing internet leads. At the same time, they focused on nurturing hundreds of families in the sales office each month. My job was to take the burden off the sales offices and the division presidents to establish a pilot program managing Internet leads seeking to buy a home online.

This was my chance to regain my confidence and increase my experience in the real estate industry. My new supervisor told me that he didn't think we could sell a home over the Internet, but he knew they were losing opportunities by not giving them the courtesy of a response. So, it was my new job to figure it out, and I was up for the challenge.

I responded to thousands of online inquiries during the first ten months of developing and launching the pilot program. Of those, one hundred and thirteen internet buyers purchased homes. I was twenty-three years old, thriving, climbing the corporate ladder, and even saving enough to buy my first home.

As my career progressed, I worked long days and late nights. Then, one evening on the way to pick up Adian from the caregiver, my aunt Elaine called and asked me to stop by.

She said, "Let's go to the county fair tonight!"

My aunt Elaine and best friend Sue were always up for an adventure. I was exhausted after the long day, still wearing business attire with Adian in my arms. He cheered excitedly, and I couldn't resist the glowing smile on his face, so I agreed.

Once we arrived at the fair, I wasn't sure how I would navigate a three-year-old in a rusty old red wagon wearing a high-waisted pencil skirt and button-up white blouse, but I was willing to do anything to make his face light up, so I trampled through the dirt in six-inch heels.

Adian was still too small to go on the rides; however, with the sound of chatter and music bustling around every corner with the smell of fresh popcorn whisking through the air, he was enchanted. I could listen to his giggles all day while pointing at all the lights with a corn dog in one hand and cotton candy in the other.

As we walked through the countless outdoor vendors, I locked eyes with a tall, handsome man with clear blue eyes and a mischievous smirk. I pretended to seem interested in what he was selling as my aunt Elaine and Sue curiously looked over my shoulder, nudging me to say something, but I shook my head, rolled my eyes, and continued walking.

The man followed me down the walkway and said, "Hey, what's your name?"

I blushed as Elaine and Sue winked obnoxiously, pushing me toward him.

I said, "I'm Serena; this is my aunt Elaine, Sue, and my son Adian."

He seemed only to have his eyes fixated on me as I pointed to each family member, so I awkwardly looked away.

He replied, "Nice to meet you all. I'm Scott!"

He seemed presumptuous, asking when he would see me again. I was flattered, although slightly skeptical. *Who would want to date a single mother?*

Scott seemed sweet and charming, so with the overzealous acts of encouragement from my two crazy aunts, I wrote my phone number on the back of a receipt paper he tore from the register.

The following week we met for dinner; I was still a little skeptical about why he would consider dating a single mother but was open to the possibilities. We shared stories of our lives, and he mentioned that he lived in the mountains with his grandmother just a few cities away from my parent's cabin. He also said he didn't have a cell phone or a car but was working on establishing himself.

Although I was slightly shocked by this information, I was humbled by my own experiences and could empathize with his situation. He was only twenty-one years old, and I was almost four years older than him, so I could see the spark of ambition in his eyes. I was cautious yet optimistic, and he was a perfect gentleman giving me a sense of comfort and safety. He didn't make any assumptions, but I felt compelled to say that I wasn't planning on having sex again until I was married. I thought that would have scared him away, but he seemed indifferent and continued asking questions curiously. Finally, I expressed that my son was my first priority.

Scott agreed, "As he should be."

My mind scrambled with disbelief. I told him about my childhood and self-proclaimed celibacy and even tried to scare him away by sharing that my son would always come first. Yet nothing phased him; he still seemed intently interested in me. So, I quickly threw my skepticism out the window and allowed myself to be vulnerable and quite impulsive.

Within a few weeks, our lives became interwoven. Everything was happening so fast, and Scott surprised me during the second month of dating.

Like every other Sunday, we attended a small Baptist church service. Adian was enrolled in the church preschool during the week and loved playing with the other children during service. I sat in the wooden pews with Scott's arm wrapped around my shoulder, listening to the Pastor share the message. The sun peeked through the stained-glass windows, with a beautiful mellow sound of piano tones articulating each note in a rich and resonating way. As the Pastor concluded his message, he shared that love is not just a biblical principle. It's the foundation of who God is, and as believers, we must apply His example of love in our lives with the people who matter most. I intently listened to his message, getting lost in the idea that someone could love me in that same way. I felt as though the Pastor had his primary focus on me at that moment, and although he was young and handsome, he was married, so I quickly directed my eyes toward Scott.

The Pastor continued, "A beautiful example of that love is a couple sitting in the midst of us."

Slightly confused, I turned my attention to the pulpit. The Pastor scanned the room, locking eyes with Scott. Scott nonchalantly withdrew his arm from around my neck and stood up. I sat upright with a sudden stiffness in my posture, uncertain where he was going. Scott excused himself to the guests sitting beside us as he shuffled around them to make his way to the center of the chapel. Scott walked straight up to the Pastor, and in unison, they asked me to stand.

My eyes widened, and my shoulders felt stiff. I casually draped my dress under my thighs, slowly rising from the bench. Scott extended his arms toward me and motioned me to step forward. I cautiously moved around the wooden pew, scrambling to meet him where he stood. I apprehensively walked toward him with sweaty palms and an uncontrollable quiver in my knees. He knelt on one knee, and the crowd began to murmur.

Scott gazed up at me in adoration and reached into his pocket, opening a small velvet jewelry box. As he lifted the top, the sanctuary pedestal lights radiated against a multi-stone diamond engagement ring, six stunning princess-cut diamonds at its center, surrounded by a sparkling halo of smaller diamonds. The band glistened with three rows of diamonds streaming down each side of the 10K white gold band.

With his voice trembling, he said, "I've never met anyone like you, and I can't imagine spending my life without you. Will you marry me?"

My mouth dropped to the floor; I pressed my hands against my cheeks; a surge of butterflies filled my stomach with a heightened sense of disbelief.

I gasped and impulsively said, "Yes!"

The crowd went wild, standing to applaud with shouts of joy. Scott lifted his knee from the floor with a burst of excitement and embraced me in his arms, lifting me off the ground and spinning in circles.

I was overwhelmed by his popping the question so soon, yet hopeful that everything in my life would be aligned. Adian and I would finally have a 'real' family. I imagined family dinners, holidays, traveling, and living harmoniously.

My stepdad, Ken, asked my mother to marry him in just a few weeks, so what if this was my fate too? I'd longed for a man to love me, just as my stepdad loves my mom, and now Adian would have a daddy. Plus, it's perfect timing! The construction of the new house I had bought was almost complete so we would have a brand-new home too!

As we picked up Adian from childcare, the church members surrounded us, asking questions, celebrating, sharing their stories, and curiously clamoring about every detail. I lifted Adian; he wrapped his legs around my waist, and with a curious look, he observed all the commotion. I buckled him in his car seat, sharing the big news, but at the young age of three, he could giggle, make funny faces, run, skip, and form sentences, but I don't think he quite understood what I was saying. Nevertheless, he smiled when I smiled, so my heart was whole.

It was a whirlwind of new experiences, engagement photos, dress shopping, cake tasting, searching for the perfect venue, invitations, flowers, and a complete checklist of plans to coordinate. Scott jumped from one job to another, trying to find his way while I balanced my career and family responsibilities and assigned him wedding tasks to complete.

Before I knew it, the wedding day arrived, and all the plans seamlessly fell into place. I was pampered all morning with Adian by my side in his adorable black tuxedo, gazing up at me with his big blue eyes. He melted my heart with his chubby cheeks and tender kisses as I prepared to walk down the aisle.

Breathtaking waterfront views surrounded the rooftop venue overlooking the Historic Queen Mary. Bistro lights swayed high above the perfectly placed white chairs, leading to a floral arch blooming with white calla lilies, and the ocean breeze flowed through the air. The wedding music played softly just as the sun was about to set, as the bridesmaids and groomsmen walked down the aisle.

Adian locked arms with the flower girl and escorted her down the aisle; he held his head high as if it was his wedding day and the flower girl was his bride-to-be.

The guests stood as I stepped forward once I heard my cue, pausing momentarily with white rose petals at my feet. My dress laid effortlessly on my body with lace and tulle delicately lining the halter neckline, the ballgown skirt boasting undeniable glamor, complimenting my hourglass silhouette.

I walked down the aisle with the rhythm of the music as I exchanged blushing smiles with each guest until I stood before my husband-to-be.

Scott watched my every move as I approached him; the prominent dimple on his chin peeked through his freshly groomed stubble as he bashfully smiled. He exuded sophistication in his timeless black three-piece slim-fit suit with a double-breasted black vest and jacket complemented by an elegant white banded collar shirt.

As we locked eyes, everything around us seemed to fade away. In a universe all our own, lost in the depths of each other's eyes. I could feel his desire for me, yet he was calm, gentle, and controlled. The evening was magical, seamlessly flowing like the champagne in our glasses as we celebrated our love for one another.

The fantasy of that night quickly faded as the reality of everyday life set in. Everything moved so fast that I hadn't fully processed my decision to marry him. I hardly knew myself, let alone took the time and patience to know him. I felt like a toddler struggling to run before I could walk. The unrealistic expectations we placed on each other stemmed from our own unresolved issues and the unreasonable desire that the other person would save us from ourselves.

I buried myself in work, and once I established the online sales position, I was promoted to Marketing Manager overseeing over twenty new home communities in the southern California division office. I wanted to "keep the peace" in my marriage, so I held onto the secrets of my heart in an effort to keep Scott and other people happy, set in their vision of our picture-perfect life together.

I hoped having a child would merge our lives, unite our family, and allow him to experience the undeniable bond that I had with my son. Scott would finally understand the depth of a parent's love. Within the first year, I was pregnant, Adian would have a baby sister, and our little family would be complete.

The night sky filled with fireworks, sporadic booms, crackling, echoes, and whistles streamed through the stars. Adian's little face lit up with excitement as the explosions illuminated the sky with radiant colors. At five years old, he was the love of my life and my mini-best friend.

By three o'clock the following day, the brisk morning air ran through my hair as we ushered through the darkness toward the car on our way to the hospital to bring our new baby girl into the world.

The birth was like a breeze as I woke up shortly after the epidural wore off, feeling slight tingling in my legs, similar to pins-and-needles, as they gently placed my precious baby girl in my arms. The moment she wrapped her tiny hand around my fingers, a tear ran down my cheek, and my love for her overflowed. We named her Nevaeh, meaning "bright" and "radiant," with a clever twist when spelled backward, Heaven. Inspired by divinity, she was a tiny piece of paradise and definitely a little firecracker.

As a mother, my soul became one with my children. Scott idolized our new baby girl, yet his blatant disregard for my son became increasingly evident. I believed that our family would band together; instead, it only divided us more.

Scott seemed complacent, allowing me to carry the weight of our financial burdens as he struggled to find stable work.

He complained, "I can't work for someone else; they don't know what they're doing."

In my new position, I reported to five Division Presidents, each with a solid A-type personality believing that the other Presidents were less important than themselves. Breathing down my neck daily, and when I tried to explain that I prioritized each one, they would reply, "Don't you know who I am?" or pressure me to focus on their projects first.

As challenging as it was, I was grateful to learn and grow, trying to balance the pressure of five different personalities, yet Scott couldn't even find one job he liked. As a result, I became increasingly distant and avoidant, shielding my heart from his reach and resentful that he wasn't willing to sacrifice, expecting me to be the provider.

I believed that time would heal the emotional baggage I carried, yet the weight only became heavier the longer I tried to hold on. I was broken, begging Scott to pull me out of the fire, but he couldn't see me through all the ashes and flames. Instead, he was desperately reliant on me, practically suffocating me while I was climbing out of my skin to get away—all the while observing as he treated my son like an inconvenience.

After Nevaeh turned one and Adian was six, we bought a larger house in a neighborhood with a better school district. Scott found a job he enjoyed, and everything seemed to fall into place. Yet it had been so long since I felt loved that I hid behind the words "I'm fine" and accepted that this was just how marriage was supposed to feel.

We were planning a road trip one day and stopped at a local gas station before getting on the highway. Scott ran inside the convenience store to buy some snacks; when he returned, he handed me two drinks, one for himself and one for me.

I curiously asked, "Did you get anything for Adian?"

He scoffed, "He doesn't always need something. He'll be fine."

My heart fell into the pit of my stomach as I looked back to see the rejection in Adian's eyes. I reached across the back seat to hand him the bottle of water.

I said, "Here you go, sugar, you can have mine."

Scott rolled his eyes and said, "You always baby him. He's fine."

I whispered to Adian, "I love you; it's okay. I want you to have it."

With his head down, Adian peeked up at me, with his sad little eyes and his tiny lips pressed firmly together, giving me a bleak smile. My stomach turned in disgust at Scott's blatant disregard, and I shifted my body toward the passenger window with a vacant stare as we drove away.

Adian yearned for Scott's attention; he wanted to be accepted by him. He spent hours coloring in picture books, drawing stick figures of our family with his blue, red, and yellow crayons, and excitedly ran toward

Scott to show him what he had made for him. But Scott would turn him away, pretending to be too busy to care.

Adian was always playful, spirited, and persistent in trying to earn Scott's affection. He wasn't like other stepchildren that snubbed a stepparent by saying things like, "You're not my dad. I don't have to do what you say." On the contrary, he did everything Scott asked and eagerly expressed his adoration for him.

As a mother, I had a deep emotional, psychological, and spiritual attachment to my children even while they were in the womb. The miraculous process of having a child and the bond between us was such a profound experience I struggled to understand Scott's resistance toward Adian. He worshiped our beautiful baby girl, and I felt torn between his overflowing love for our daughter and his undeniable animosity toward my son.

There was a constant divide; I couldn't understand why he had so much disdain towards Adian and wanted to protect my son from feeling abandoned or as though he had to fight for the slightest sense of compassion.

Every upset look, slight glance, or sharp rebuttal indicated that Scott was annoyed and irritated no matter how hard Adian tried to earn his approval. I was naive in thinking you could mash people together into the same house, call it a family, and hope everything works out. It takes a great deal of work and maturity and compassion, and time. But unfortunately, our young love was shallow and couldn't withstand the darkness we faced.

I couldn't determine if Scott was intentionally disengaged or unaware of his actions. Still, I was terrified that his behavior would cause my innocent child so much emotional and mental damage. Adian was only six years old, and I felt torn between my husband and my baby boy. I knew that the longer I allowed the dissension to seep into our family, it would significantly affect Adian. Scott seemed utterly dismissive of Adian's negative feelings and emotional needs, almost as if he wasn't important, yet idolized our daughter. He was overly critical and justified his actions by placing all the blame on Adian and positioning me to choose between them, saying things like, "I'm your husband, and it's obvious who you love more."

I felt a constant force to suppress my feelings to appease Scott so he wouldn't lash out at Adian. I would accept blame, deflecting any behavioral issues to protect him from Scott's wrath. I began to overcompensate for his disregard for Adian by being overly encouraging and shielding my son when Scott would seem agitated. I would pull Scott aside privately when I felt he would be out of line. Pleading with him to have more compassion fell on deaf ears. I felt like I couldn't reason with him, allowing him to walk all over me.

Until one afternoon, as we entertained family members, I was busy preparing food in the kitchen while Scott barbecued steaks in the backyard. The smell of wood chips and the sizzling sounds of the barbeque filled the air. Then, I heard the faint chatter of people and the little ones giggling as Scott abruptly yelled at Adian in front of everyone and sent him to his room.

The room became silent; I began glancing around uneasily with my hands shaking, embarrassed by his outburst. Before I could respond or deflect the situation, Scott's cousin pulled me aside and whispered.

She said, "How can you allow Scott to treat Adian like this? We can all see it; why can't you?"

I replied, "What do you mean?" secretly hoping she wouldn't answer me.

She said, "Serena, he favors Nevaeh and treats Adian as though he doesn't matter. I'd be embarrassed if I were you."

A sudden and incapacitating fear surged through my body; I quickly stepped back and fumbled.

I said, "I need to check on my son."

I rushed towards Adian's bedroom breathing heavily with my heart pounding. I knelt to comfort him, but he looked up at me with tears streaming down his face before I could say a word.

Adian asked, "Momma, why doesn't he love me?

I couldn't swallow as my throat swelled shut, and the realization that I could no longer justify Scott's actions shamefully weighed on my heart like a ton of bricks. My tiny human opened his heart, and I knew I couldn't create a false sense of security or provide any affirmation. I wrapped my arms around Adian as he nestled his head against my shoulder. My voice thickened with emotion.

I whispered, "You are loved more than anything in the whole wide world. Deep down inside, I know Daddy loves you, sugar. Sometimes grownups don't know how to show it."

My neck grew tense as the words fell off my lips; I closed my eyes and swayed him back and forth in my arms.

It was hard to understand why I married Scott in the first place. I was troubled with guilt, feeling like 'fate' slapped me in the face for not thinking through the repercussions of what this would do to my son; the shame of my decision was swallowing me whole.

Chapter 11: Escape

I felt like I was living in a glasshouse; everyone around me could see my life shattering through the clear glass windows while I performed and played the part of a career-driven woman, nurturing mother, and submissive wife. Yet the reality was that I felt empty, hollow, and disconnected.

After four years of marriage, the challenges never ceased, from the constant stress of fighting about the children and financial responsibilities to the lack of sexual intimacy. As a result, I felt broken and insecure, questioning if my past trauma robbed me of fully enjoying intimate experiences.

Vastly aware that he had no intention of exploring my body, I was eager to please him to end the cycle of his self-pleasure. I was still discovering my own needs and wanted so badly for him to show affection, yet each time was emotionless. Questions circulated as I lay in silence, waiting for him to finish. *Is this how marriage is supposed to be? Why doesn't he have the desire to understand my body? Am I a product of my past trauma? Am I broken?*

I couldn't find the words to communicate my sexual desires, and I became repulsed by the thought that he only cared about his needs. I wanted to escape the mess I got into and found myself wishing he would find someone else.

I distracted myself with work and the kids, suppressing my emotions and pretending everything was okay. Then, as my career progressed in the real estate industry, the market unexpectedly crashed in 2008. I was only twenty-eight years old and didn't fully comprehend how one of the most significant jolts to the global financial system would negatively impact the real estate industry. Blinded by the rising housing prices, the opportunity for short-term economic gain, and the tunnel vision of their positions, almost everyone overlooked the grave reality that it would all come to a screeching halt.

Like any other day, the sun peeked through my office window as I smirked, listening to my employee's banter. Suddenly a silence swept over the office, and the frivolous chatter was replaced with harsh yells and cries as a mass layoff occurred. The two young women reporting to me stood from their cubicles, looking at me in a state of confusion, and rushed into my office, holding the door shut behind them.

With crackling voices, they said, "What is happening?"

I was just as confused as they were, gripping the base of my neck, uncertain how to respond.

I said, "I haven't heard anything; I'm not sure what is happening. So go back to your desks, avoid eye contact, and focus on your work until I can find some answers."

I felt blindsided. The office was in an uproar of complete chaos as hundreds of employees packed their belongings into boxes, shouting and crying, begging for their jobs. Hours passed, and still no explanation; with my teeth chattering and my legs shaking, I called one of the Division Presidents, eager to find answers. Abruptly, he answered the phone before the second ring.

He said, "Your department is safe. But unfortunately, I can't talk right now."

The phone disconnected, and I was left listening to the dial tone. I sat at my desk with an open mouth struggling to comprehend the magnitude of the situation. I called my team into my office and shared what the president told me, trying to calm their nerves, but my body language spoke for itself.

A few days later, I received an even more terrifying call. The phone rang a few times, but I didn't recognize the number, so I pressed the ignore button and sent it to voicemail. Moments later, the phone rang again; I was in the middle of my workday, so I was hesitant to take the call, but the unknown caller was persistent. Finally, I answered.

I said, "Hello, this is Serena."

The caller eagerly gasped and repeated my name, seemingly excited to hear my voice. But unfortunately, I didn't recognize his voice. So, uncertain who was on the other end of the line, I skeptically waited for him to state his name.

He said, "Serena, I'm so glad you answered. It's Anthony!"

I drew in a sharp breath and asked, "Who?"

He laughed and replied in a chipper tone.

Anthony replied, "Adian's father."

Sputtering and struggling to find the right words, a rush of fire ran through my body as I felt my temperature rise. I lunged forward, stabilizing against a wall, placing my shaking hand on my forehead, squinted my eyes, and nervously rubbed my temple. I paused for a moment then, with an apprehensive tone.

I said, "Anthony? "How can I help you?"

He began rambling, sharing stories about his life over the past seven years as if we were old friends just catching up. Then, without hesitation, he continued verbalizing his thoughts and desire to meet Adian. I abruptly interrupted his chatter, asking pointed questions.

I said, "Anthony, you never wanted to be involved in his life? I fought for two years to obtain a DNA test because you denied him. I've sent you pictures, updates, and contact information; why didn't you respond?"

He replied, "I know, I'm sorry, but I'm ready now."

He continued defending his story by shifting the blame on his wife and reassuring me that it's over now; they're getting a divorce. However, after seven years of no contact, he's in the area and wants to meet 'our' son. Feeling confused, uncertain, and frustrated, I slowly slid down behind my desk until my knees hit the floor.

He asked, "What have you told him about me?"

Since Adian was a toddler, he asked many times about his father, and I always told him the same story, yet I never imagined I would be reciting it to Anthony. My chest sank, and with a deep inhale.

I said, "I told Adian that there was a tiny box when he was born. When you opened it and looked inside, you were terrified and ran away. It was a box of responsibility."

Anthony laughed, "That's a great story! I knew you would be an amazing mother."

Then quickly changing the subject, he persisted and asked when he could see Adian. I explained that my life was different now, and I needed to talk to my husband, Scott before I could make any decisions. Anthony agreed, complimenting Scott for temporarily raising his son, and asked me to call him after speaking with my husband. I ended the call with my hands shaking, hunched over on the floor, rehearsing the conversation in my mind determining how I would tell Scott.

After weeks of unexpected changes, merging offices, and managing three times my usual workload, finally, I left the company. I accepted a Sales and Marketing Director position for a senior living community.

The busy schedules, balancing work and kids, and the lack of intimacy created a vacuum, and time widened the gap between Scott and me. I craved emotional support yet continued to push him away. Every interaction became hostile and argumentative, and he began to assume that I was being unfaithful. Casting false allegations on the nights that I worked late instead of providing encouragement or appreciation for all the time I invested in supporting our family. I stopped sharing my feelings as his lack of empathy and ruthless allegations mentally exhausted me.

Yet, I still needed to have the dreadful conversation and finally mustered up the courage to tell Scott that Adian's father, Anthony, had called me. As the words carelessly fell out of my mouth, I could feel the anger rise in Scott's demeanor as he sarcastically scoffed.

He said, "Ha! Temporarily raising his son?"

I replied, "I'm sure he didn't mean it that way; he was grateful that you've been in Adian's life."

Scott deliberately raised his eyebrows tilting his head back with a smirk.

He said, "Oh, you're sure? You don't even know this man, and he's trying to insert himself into our lives. No, absolutely not."

I pleaded with Scott and begged him to, at the very least, consider it before making a final decision. Instead, he gave me a dismissive glare, shaking his head and rolling his eyes in disbelief that I would consider allowing Anthony in Adian's life.

I needed a release, so I furiously left mid-argument and told Scott I was going to the gym. My mind raced as I anxiously left the house, *what if this is the right thing to do? I want Adian to feel loved and accepted. What if Scott really doesn't love my son? How can I rob Adian of this opportunity to know his birth father?*

I walked into the fitness center; my face was flush, clenching my jaw as I vigorously worked out until I was dripping in sweat. Then, a man that I recognized approached me, interrupting my aggressive workout.

He said, "Hey, are you okay?"

I felt so lonely in my marriage that the idea of someone acknowledging my pain and showing empathy seemed oddly comforting.

I replied, "Oh, um yeah. I'm okay."

He said, "You don't look, okay?"

I said, "I'm just having a hard day."

He replied, "I'm Kyle. I've seen you often, and you always seem so radiant, but today you seemed different; if you ever need to talk, I'm a good listener."

I blushed, exhaled deeply, and looked up at his soft eyes.

I said, "I'm Serena. Thank you for being so thoughtful."

I casually walked away, sat in my car in the parking lot, laid my neck against the headrest, then leaned forward, placing my forehead on the steering wheel as I burst into tears. Kyle gently tapped on the driver's side window; I jumped quickly, wiping my tears, and trying to pull myself together, but struggled to catch my breath. Then, embarrassed that he saw me in a moment of complete vulnerability, I reluctantly rolled down the window.

He said, "Here's my number. Call me if you need anything."

I hesitantly reached for the small piece of paper as he placed it in my palm, gently squeezing my trembling hands; he smiled and walked away. As I drove home, I replayed that moment in my mind. There was something about him that struck me. *Why did he look so familiar? Where have I seen him before?*

I was already in the middle of enough chaos between Scott and Anthony, so I threw the paper in the trash before entering the house. I tried to reason with Scott, but he was still angry, so I tucked the little ones into bed and went to sleep without saying a word. I tossed and turned that night, trying to piece together the fragments of my choices, but the weight of internal conflict suffocated me with grief. I was hopeless, torn between a loveless marriage and choosing the best outcome for both of my children.

I called Anthony the following day and shared that I didn't feel it was the right time for him to come into Adian's life if he couldn't commit to being consistent. Anthony agreed that it would be challenging for him to be consistent while serving in the military. I let out a sigh of relief; I thanked him for being so honest, sat back in my chair, and felt an overwhelming release of tension lift from my chest as I hung up the phone. After that day, I never spoke about Adian's birth father with Scott again.

A few weeks passed, and I was working late in the office preparing for a Grand Opening event for the senior living community. The sun was setting, and I hadn't even noticed the time. My office phone rang, and although I found it strange for someone to call after hours, I answered. The voice on the line seemed familiar, yet I couldn't quite place it.

He said, "Hey, it's Kyle from the gym. I haven't seen you in a while and wanted to check in to see if you're, okay?"

A sudden coldness hit my core, holding still in expectation and with a shaky, soft, doubtful voice.

I said, "Oh, um, how did you get my office number?"

He charmingly replied, "Oh, I didn't realize this was your work number; I'm a fitness manager here at the gym. I was worried about you, so I called the number you had associated with your membership. I hope I didn't startle you."

I said, "It takes much more than that to scare me and thank you for checking on me."

He said, "Are you free to grab a drink tonight?"

I paused for a moment arguing with my inner voice. My mind was telling me no, as my intuition was saying yes.

I said, "Honestly, I haven't eaten all day. I shouldn't."

He quickly replied, "Well, why don't we grab dinner instead? No pressure, just as friends."

I felt like an eternity had passed as I stared blankly at the ticking clock on the wall listening to my stomach growl, trying to navigate my racing thoughts. *I knew I recognized him; he was a fitness trainer at the gym! What's the harm in a quick bite to eat? It would be nice to get away from reality for a few minutes. Wait! What am I thinking?*

I impulsively responded, "Yes!"

We agreed to meet at a little Italian cafe near my office. I expressed that I didn't have much time but needed a slight reprieve from my workload. I gathered my things and headed toward the restaurant. Approaching the cafe, I took several deep breaths in a futile effort to calm myself. Finally, I rechanneled my breath into a drawn-out sigh as I glanced around the courtyard. The moon was full, lighting up the sky with hints of pink, yellow, and orange clouds as the daylight quickly faded.

I instantly spotted his charming yet humble smirk, bashfully tilting his head down as he laughed, walking toward me. His dark brown hair was neatly trimmed and styled with a purposefully messy look. He locked his gaze on mine, not letting me look away as he approached. His fitted button-down shirt wrapped snugly around his athletic build with a lightweight fabric that formed his shoulders and chest, laying loosely around his waist. His stubble drew a perfect shadow lowlighting his sharp jawline as he smiled.

The restaurant was quaint and inviting; the low tempo of Italian music played softly in the background as the welcoming aroma coated the air with hints of garlic and basil. The uniquely textured walls created a smooth yet flowing setting with vines draping down the walls, giving the atmosphere a natural ambiance. The marble-tiled floor beneath me gave the restaurant a clean yet warm environment. We were seated at a small table near a large window overlooking an outdoor fountain; I sunk into the soft cushion seat directly across from Kyle.

The server poured a glass of deep burgundy red wine as we immersed ourselves in conversation. Like water overflowing from a river, I poured my heart out to Kyle, sharing stories of my childhood and feelings of uncertainty and loneliness in my marriage. He made me feel safe, allowing me to be vulnerable without judgment.

His eyes never swerved to the left or right but turned as the story unfolded. He followed my every word being fully present and engaged without taking notice of the distractions in the busy cafe. The sounds of dishes clattering and cutlery tapping seemed to disappear as he gazed up at me with his warm hazel eyes; it felt like he looked through me, almost as if he could see my soul. He touched my hand, and I anxiously hesitated.

He said, "Life is full of open doors. Wisdom is knowing when to walk through and when to close it behind you."

He continued by sharing, "The thing is, you don't have to be strong all the time. It's okay to be weak. It's okay to feel. It's okay to be sad. It's okay to ask for help. You don't have to be strong for everyone else when your world is crumbling beneath your feet, even if you think you do."

A moment of clarity struck me like a bolt of lightning as he inspired me with his young insight. He was only twenty-three years old, and I was twenty-nine; *how could he be so wise?* I drew in my breath, trying to process my thoughts. *I need to be strong; I'm a survivor, and I need to provide for my children. I want to give them a better life. I'm supposed to have it all together. I don't have a choice.*

He said, "The truth is, everything isn't always okay. You are allowed to mess up; you're allowed to be sad; you're allowed to struggle; you're allowed to feel broken, confused, and lost."

He continued by sharing his story that he was hurting and felt unseen. Unloved, unappreciated, and defeated. My heart sank as a tear ran down his face. I reached across the table and gently wiped his cheek; he hid his face with his hand as he looked down.

I lifted his chin and said, "It takes courage to admit you're struggling. Thank you for being so vulnerable with me."

With tears in our eyes, we giggled at ourselves for being so emotional. I was so caught up in our conversation that I lost track of time until my phone started vibrating, and I realized Scott was calling me. I immediately answered the phone, said I was on my way, and quickly hung up. Then, I motioned our server to request the check.

He said, "I already took care of it."

I glanced at him with a confused look; he smirked and said, "You always take care of everyone else. You deserve someone who is going to take care of you."

I paused in disbelief and thanked him for his kindness as I rose from my seat.

He said, "Wait! Let me walk you to your car."

I nervously clutched my bag as we walked through the courtyard. Kyle hesitated as we stood under the stars near the fountain.

I said, "Thank you for allowing me to share my story and giving me a moment of clarity."

In the shadows, his face was so close to mine that I could smell bold notes of red wine on his breath with a hint of his Prada aftershave. I merely turned to say goodbye, but before I could catch a glimpse of his face, his lips pressed against mine. So instantaneous that I found myself lost in the moment, leaning forward with a yearning desire for more. His lips were a sugar rush, like candy on my tongue.

I was startled by the vibration of my phone and jumped back.

I said, "I'm so sorry, I can't do this. I have to go."

Rushing to the parking lot, I feverishly texted Scott that I was stuck in traffic. As I drove home, my mind swirled with guilt over what I had done, yet my heart was as hollow as an empty vessel, and I didn't recognize who I had become. Scott continued to text, call, and ping my phone as I frantically dashed through the lanes on the highway. Finally, I stopped less than a block from our home and sat silently, recounting the evening discussion. I knew in the pit of my stomach what I had to do.

Chapter 12: Love Is Blind

As I approached the doorway, I felt my dry throat tighten as I was choked by fear, sending a wave of adrenaline through my body. I counted every step as I inched forward, slowly pressing the door open as I made my way inside. Scott was waiting, furious at how late I arrived home, but before he could say a word.

I blurted out, "I want a divorce."

He stood in horror as if he was surprised by my outburst. I knew that if I didn't leave him, I would carry the shame and resentment and continue down an even darker, more destructive path.

It didn't happen all at once; it was like an open wound that became infected over time. I was naive, lacking self-control, and terrified that I would sabotage the relationship or hurt Scott even more if I stayed.

I scavenged around our bedroom in a frenzy, packing my things. Scott followed, hovering over me to exert some sense of control. He was powerless against my rage as I turned to look him straight in the face.

I yelled, "I've given you everything, but it was never going to be enough. The house, the timeshare, the boat, a beautiful baby girl. Yet you couldn't have an ounce of compassion for my son or even bother to meet my needs."

Tension filled the air as he towered over me, pointing his finger so close to my face that I would feel it graze my cheek.

He yelled, "You're not taking my daughter anywhere; you will destroy these kids' lives if you leave."

The guilt of his words weighed heavy on my heart; I saw parts of him unravel as I'd never seen before. I paused and glared with my lip quivering.

I said, "You don't love me; you don't care if I stay or go. The only thing you care about is yourself."

There wasn't one big, defining moment that forced my decision. Rather, it was as if all these tiny, ignored, small moments of hurt, betrayal, and anger rose to the surface of my heart, and I knew I couldn't do this anymore. I didn't want my children to believe this was an example of love. Instead, I wanted them to experience a love that was unconditional, compassionate, patient, and understanding.

I was terrified of making the same mistakes my mother did by becoming trapped in an environment I couldn't escape. So, I unintentionally vilified Scott in my mind and couldn't see past my distorted perspective. It was no longer about me defending my position but accepting responsibility for the mess I created. I needed to find clarity and process my thoughts without allowing my emotions to impact my decision.

I said, "I will stay with my parents and be back tomorrow for the children."

I didn't want to leave my children with him, let alone my son, but I couldn't imagine separating them from each other, and I didn't have the right words to explain why I would be pulling them out of their beds. So, I left.

As I was driving to see my mother, listening to the soft tones of classical melodies playing in the background, I looked in the rearview mirror at my life. *How did I get here? I had it all together. Why can't I just put my head down and forge on?* That was when I realized I was tired of holding it together, and I needed to look inside myself to truly understand who I was, not who I was pretending to be.

I sat with my mother for hours with tears running down my face, the taste of mucus on my lips pouring out my shame. The picture of who I wanted to be and who I'd become devastated me. I wanted to live for something bigger than myself, for my children. I felt her hand holding mine, squeezing tighter as I shared; she listened attentively and encouraged me to do what I had to do, to create the life I wanted for them. I felt like a failure; I'd seen so much trouble and held my weight in shame, yet I knew I had come too far to lose myself in material things or a young marriage.

I returned home the next day. Adian was seven years old, and Nevaeh was three, so I knew they wouldn't fully understand why I felt the need to leave, so I sat them both down on the plush carpet in the living room. Scott stood behind me with tension building as I held my children close.

I said, "Just like when you make mistakes, and we give you a 'time out,' sometimes grownups make mistakes too! So, Mommy and Daddy will be taking a 'time out' so we can learn from our mistakes."

My heart fell into the pit of my stomach, I felt unloved and abandoned many times as a child, and I never intended for my children to feel like I had left them behind.

I told Scott he could have the house, the furniture, the boat, the truck, the timeshare, and the pre-paid vacation to the Caribbean. All I asked for was equal time with my baby girl. I confirmed a temporary schedule with Scott to share Nevaeh fifty percent of the time.

I had experienced more obstacles than most in my twenty-nine years, from living on the streets, sleeping on park benches, and in abandoned houses, to living in suburban neighborhoods and enjoying luxury hotels. From thriving financially, wine tasting, and fine dining to barely surviving with no income, no food, praying that I would make it through one more day. I could have spent months or years fighting over meaningless possessions in divorce court. But material things no longer mattered. I was willing to give up everything to create a loving environment for my little ones. The hundreds of hours I saved by simply walking away and my peace of mind were far more valuable than all I left behind.

As I established myself, I packed the bare necessities and found a small condo nearby to rent. It was a three-bedroom townhome overlooking a lake framed by the stunning Cleveland National Forest and near a baseball stadium that set off fireworks every Friday night. The open-concept dining and living room flowed seamlessly to a private patio. The stairs led to the main bedroom with two smaller rooms on the second floor, perfectly placed so I could be just steps away from each of their rooms. The community was peaceful and had a crystal-clear swimming pool with several young families for the kids to find new friends.

I stopped by the local grocery store one afternoon to pick up some last-minute items. Walking down the aisle from a distance, I could see Kyle; I started to walk toward him to show gratitude for giving me the courage to believe in myself.

But, as I peeked around the corner behind the cereal boxes, I noticed that he was with a woman holding a baby. I paused and observed from afar when I watched him place his arm around her lower back and lean in to kiss her. I felt a wave of nausea and quickly hid behind the other customers as I held my breath. My thoughts raced with questions; *I don't remember him saying he was married. How could this be? Maybe that's his sister, but who kisses their sister? I must be an idiot for thinking he genuinely cared for me.*

I felt humiliated and disgusted with myself for even allowing him to kiss me. I was so wrapped in the connection between us that I didn't even consider asking if he was married, let alone realize he had a baby boy. My stomach turned as I waited for him and his family to exit the store.

The following day, I intentionally waited until I knew he had started working and sent him a text message.

> Please don't ever contact me again.

I received no response and took that as he understood my request.

Several weeks later, it was a beautiful day. I was in my office making phone calls and scheduling meetings. The sun shined against my office window, and I took a moment to sit back in my chair, listening to the birds chirping with the slight murmur of office chatter. The receptionist called my office and transferred an unknown caller. I answered the phone and repeated my name, but no one replied, just as I was about to hang up. I heard the strumming of an acoustic guitar loosely playing a series of basic chords with the same rhythm. I listened intently, asking again who was on the line, but the caller began to sing before I could say another word.

"The strands in your eyes that color them wonderful... you steal my breath... Tell me that we belong together... and I will be better when I'm older. I'll be the greatest fan of your life."

My breath began to quicken in slow increments as I leaned over my desk, sharply inhaling.

Then, finally, I said, "Kyle?"

He continued singing, "I'll be better when I'm older."

I tried to hold the tears back, but they flowed down my cheeks in a flood of emotion. He silently demanded my undivided attention as he finished strumming his guitar, then with his voice trembling.

He said, "Serena, forgive me. I should have told you. Since we met, you haven't left my mind, and I can't go another day without you."

I froze in my seat, closed my eyes, and took a deep breath trying to control my emotions. I was having difficulty formulating my thoughts. I wanted to pretend Kyle wasn't drawing me in with his charm, but he had come in like a thief in the night and stolen my heart.

I replied, "That was beautiful; I don't know what to say."

He said, "Can I see you?"

I hesitated, wavering back and forth, yet the words fluttered off my tongue.

I said, "Yes, but only to talk. You can stop by my new place after the little ones go to bed."

That evening when he arrived, the children were fast asleep in their beds upstairs, and we sat on the loveseat in the living room below. We caught up on the changes in our lives since we last spoke. He apologized for not telling me about his wife and explained that the only reason he tried to make things work was for their six-month-old son, Ashton. He seemed genuine and vulnerable, sharing that his marriage was a magnet for negativity; they were married shortly after he found out she was pregnant, but he felt trapped, unimportant, and devalued.

I was listening intently, but my phone kept vibrating. Scott called me repeatedly, so I excused myself to take the call. I could sense that he wasn't himself; he was belligerent, demanding to talk to our daughter. I explained that she was asleep, and he abruptly hung up. I looked at Kyle shaking my head, pressing my lips into a fine line with raised eyebrows.

I said, "That was weird."

Within moments there was a knock at my door. Kyle glanced at me with a concerned look.

I said, "I'm sure it's fine, don't worry."

Scott stood over me aggressively as I opened the door, outraged by seeing Kyle's car parked near the garage. The smell of alcohol oozed from his breath as he tried to force his way around me while I blocked the door. The living room was tucked away from the direct view of the entryway, so I strategically positioned myself to block Scott from seeing Kyle.

I said, "Scott! The kids are sleeping; you need to leave."

He demanded, "I want to see my daughter now!"

I tried to block the entryway backing him onto the porch, but at only 5'1, his six-foot body towered over me. He stumbled back, leaning his arm against the door frame to stabilize himself, tilting his head down, and raising his eyebrows with an evil smirk. He rolled his eyes with a passive-aggressive tone.

He said, "What are you hiding?"

I responded, "You've been drinking. You need to leave now."

Scott scoffed sarcastically as I closed the door, leaving him on the doorstep. Kyle quietly sat in the living room, listening to the commotion.

Kyle said, "Are you okay? Should I move my car, so he doesn't get any bright ideas?"

I responded, "I've never seen him like this; that might be a good idea."

Just as Kyle opened the garage door to pull into the driveway, I stood in the doorway and saw Scott running full speed ahead in my direction from a distance. Scott pushed me to the side like a rag doll knocking the wind out of me as he passed through the entryway and sprinted up the stairs toward the kid's bedrooms. I scrambled up the stairs behind him.

Yelling, "Scott, stop!"

My words were lost in the shuffle as he had already ripped Nevaeh out of her bed. She screamed and cried because of all the commotion. I stood in the stairwell, desperate to stop Scott, but his strength overpowered me as I fell backward down the stairs, quickly rising back up, wrestling to protect my baby girl.

Pleading, "Scott, stop! You're scaring her."

He paid no attention to my attempts to stop him, strong-arming me and pushing my body out of the way as I slid down the stairs. I ran into the parking lot after Scott, pleading for him to let our daughter go. I used my body to block him from opening the passenger door, and in a moment of extreme chaos, everything stopped as he looked me dead in the face.

He said, "Get out of my way."

With our three-year-old daughter in one arm, he used his other hand to grab me by the throat and lifted me against the side of the truck, my toes barely touching the pavement as he pressed my head against the passenger window.

Then, in a split second, everything stopped; it was as though Scott had a moment to recognize what he was doing and slowly removed his hand from my throat as I slid down the truck door, repositioning my bare feet on the asphalt. Then, finally, Scott paused, and with a terrified look in his eyes, he placed our baby girl in my arms, then cautiously stepped back with his head down; Scott walked around the truck, got inside without saying a word, and drove away.

Gripping Nevaeh tightly in my arms, I ran towards the house and slammed the door behind us. I laid Nevaeh in my bed and prayed over my children, then kissed them on the forehead and reassured them that I would return shortly to sleep beside them.

I paused for a moment to collect myself before entering the living room. Kyle urgently jumped from his seat with a concerned tone.

He said, "What happened? Are you and the kids, okay?"

I touched his hand, leading him to sit beside me on the loveseat, sitting together so close that our legs intertwined, explaining what had happened. I shared that I had never seen Scott act like that before; it was out of character, as though something took over him, and within moments he snapped out of it and left.

Kyle asked, "Are you going to call the police?"

I replied, "No, I don't want to make the situation more complicated than it already is, so I'd rather move on and not create more chaos. But I think it's best if you leave; I need to be with my children."

Kyle noticed my hands shaking and gently placed his arms around my shoulders, pulling me closer; I laid my head on his broad shoulder. He softly grazed his fingertips through my hair, wrapping the strand that covered my eyes behind my ear; he paused, gazing into my soul—speaking in a calm, comforting tone.

He said, "Serena, you are strong and beautiful; you have been through so much and deserve someone who will protect your heart."

I was lost in his hazel green eyes, concentrating on every word that fell from his lips. He was warm and gentle, genuinely nurturing and caring for me, yet I was conflicted and overwhelmed by the events of the evening. I melted in his muscular arms as he cradled his hand under my chin, lifted my head, positioned his finger over my mouth with a soft stroke, drew his attention to my lips, and hushed me before speaking. I closed my eyes as a tear grazed my cheek. He leaned in closer, brushing his lips against mine. A tingling feeling rushed through my body as the tension in my neck and shoulders disappeared; the smell of his Prada aftershave tickled my nose as I became putty in his arms, fully submerged in the moment.

Suddenly, I heard a small voice from upstairs calling me.

Nevaeh curiously said, "Mommy?"

I quickly positioned myself away from Kyle and whispered, "You have to go."

I tiptoed up the stairs to comfort Nevaeh, lifting her from the top of the staircase and tenderly lying beside her on my bed as I heard Kyle quietly leave, gently closing the door below.

Chapter 13: Uphill Battle

After that night, Scott's wrath and resentment toward me became sharper and more powerful than a double-edged sword. He would move mountains to ensure I endured the same suffering I caused him. My confidence in my decision to leave him became even stronger as I saw the hatred filling his heart. I felt his piercing pain through every interaction, my intention was never to hurt him, yet he went to great lengths to punish me.

I accepted a new position as a Vice President of Marketing for a company specializing in organizational culture and accountability training. Unfortunately, as I excelled in my career, I didn't realize its impact on my financial stability, and Scott was determined to use that to his advantage.

Our mediation date had finally arrived; I waited patiently in the parking lot in the early morning hours, practicing breathing exercises before entering the courthouse. My stomach grew nauseous as I walked up the cement stairs leading to the security agent, wearing a charcoal gray double-knit pinstripe blazer with a matching pencil skirt and white blouse complimented by my freshly highlighted and trimmed blonde A-line hairstyle.

The security guard said, "Are you sure you're not a lawyer?"

I smiled nervously as I passed through security, navigating to the check-in area for mediation. The court attendants directed me to wait in the gallery until both parties arrived. I shuffled through the piles of court forms to confirm they were in perfect order. I quietly observed the lawyers, witnesses, judges, and families interacting, with the sounds of chains rattling, people whispering, and papers ruffling in the background.

Young children squirmed on the hard wooden benches, and babies cried in their mother's arms. The courthouse smelled musty, and I could barely feel the air conditioning as the sweat slowly seeped through my white dress shirt.

I quickly dropped my head down as I saw Scott enter the room; my breath became short and fast, and my heart rate increased. He sat across the waiting area, pretending not to notice me. He wore a black polo shirt with an embroidered logo I designed for his newly established audio-video business. We used our entire savings account to fund his business before we separated. I sighed in disbelief that I had invested in his company, and he still wanted more from me.

Finally, the mediator called our names, and we stood up simultaneously, walking toward her. I allowed Scott to proceed first as he sat across from the mediator's desk and pulled my chair a few feet away before I sat beside him. He demanded primary residence for our daughter, the house, the truck, and the timeshare; he also requested that I pay him child support and alimony. I was appalled that he could be so unreasonable, as I didn't ask him for child support or alimony, yet I sat in silence observing his behavior. After he finished barking his demands in a curious tone, I asked the mediator.

I said, "What about his business? Do I own half of that too?"

Scott lashed out in anger, laughing sarcastically at my question, saying, "Absolutely not!"

The mediator replied, "Yes, in fact, you do."

I glanced over the documents, reviewed his demands again, sat upright in my chair, crossed my legs, and leaned forward with my hands clasped, interlacing my fingers on the edge of her desk.

In an assertive tone, I said, "I will give him the business if he retracts his request for child support and alimony."

Scott scoffed and said, "You can't do that."

The mediator quickly interjected, "Mr. Elliott, yes, she can. How would you like to proceed?"

Scott proceeded to banter with the mediator as I sat quietly, waiting for his decision. Finally, he leaned back in his chair, glaring at me with disgust, and took a moment of silence as he processed his thoughts.

He replied, "Fine. I'll retract the alimony and child support request as long as she has zero ownership in my business."

I felt relief but pretended it didn't faze me as I confidently adjusted my posture.

I said, "Yes, I agree."

I sat restlessly, picking at my fingernails as the mediator finalized the documents; she set the forms in front of us and asked for our signatures. The moment Scott's pen hit the paper, I exhaled deeply and felt an unexpected release of all tension in my stomach. I quickly followed suit in signing each document and practically skipped out of the courtroom, celebrating my small win.

I needed to get away for a few hours the following day, so Kyle offered to join me and said he had a special place in mind. I was still apprehensive about his situation, but he assured me that it was over and not to worry. Kyle was charming, insightful, and engaging, always making me smile. Kyle had such a magnetic personality; I felt like he knew my heart and looked at me like no one else ever had. His love was the kind that awakens the soul, igniting a fire in our hearts yet bringing a sense of peace when we are together.

We drove for a few hours being silly and singing cover songs in unison, with the melody of the radio vibrating through the car speakers until we arrived at Thousand Steps Beach. Kyle held my hand as he led me down a plant-shrouded staircase that ended where the ocean met the sand. All around me was a symphony of sounds, waves crashing against the rocks, rushing in with the tide, then gently drifting away. The sun bathed my body as I basked in the breathtaking views of the sea spraying against the sandstone cliffs, saltwater-filled tide pools with sand bottoms carved in rock, and unique moss-covered rocky ledges bridged from the sea caves to the ocean waves.

Kyle said, "This is my favorite place. I wanted to share it with you."

He enchanted me with his charm while exploring the rock formations with the warm sand tickling our toes. Surrounded by such beauty, yet my eyes were solely fixated on him. He playfully nudged me towards the incoming waves and splashed the water near me, giggling and laughing with a mischievous smile. I wasn't quite prepared for the beach, wearing a simple white tube top wrapped snugly around my waist with distressed denim jeans and flip-flops. As the water splashed in my direction, I removed my sandals and ran in the opposite direction. He quickly followed behind, wrapping his arms around me, and we tumbled to the ground. We playfully wrestled in the sand, interlaced in each other's arms; he angled his body closer, pulled me in, and stole a kiss. It was as if the symphony of sounds silenced when his lips touched mine.

Affectionately squeezing my hand, he pulled me up from the sandstorm we had created. Kyle left me with a compelling sense of curiosity as his flirtatious smile persuaded me to follow him. I was slightly hesitant as he led us to the rock formations. Kyle insisted we get closer to the "secret" blowholes, a marine geyser formed near the sea caves. The blowholes are tube-like holes inside the rocks that create a bridge from the shore to the ocean and expel pressurized water into the air as the waves crash.

While the idea seemed alluring, the rocks were uneven, slippery, and treacherous when balancing on the dry areas wearing flip-flops. Yet I was so transfixed on Kyle's face that I didn't realize how far we wandered until a giant wave splashed against us. He held my hand to stabilize me as I regained control of my stance and then navigated me around the blowhole further away from the shore.

It was like seeing a whale in the sea; the marine geysers were magical, expelling fifteen-foot streams of water in the sky. I curled my toes tightly around my sandals, gripping the surface, and captured Kyle's attention by letting go of his hand.

I said, "I think that's as far as I can go. Let's go back to shore."

I saw an adventurous twinkle in his eye, but I was terrified, so I turned my back to the ocean and began walking toward the shore. Just as I took one step forward, I felt the overspray of seawater against the back of my neck. Before I could turn around, an unexpected wave came up over my head and launched me into the four-foot-wide blowhole, lodging me inside a ten-foot-deep crevasse. The whirlpool of water submerged my entire body inside the blowhole like a vacuum suction. I tried to grip the jagged rocks in a surge of adrenaline, but the force was too powerful; ocean water filled my lungs, and my feet sank deeper into the hole. I heard the muffled sounds of Kyle's voice and felt his strong arms slide around my waist as he laid his body against the ground, reaching through the whirlpool, trying to keep my head above water.

He yelled, "I got you. Hold on!"

Suddenly, I felt the pressure rising under my feet combined with intense bursts of wind, causing the trapped water to shoot up and propel my entire body out of the port with a powerful force launching me into the air. Just as gravity caught the wind, I immediately fell to the ground. We lunged forward, skidding our bare skin on the razor rock towards the shore, twisted in each other's arms. We jumped up, running toward the beach until our feet touched the sand, leaning forward, coughing, and gasping for air.

As I leaned over with my hands propped against my knees, I inhaled deeply and noticed my tube top twisted around my waist, exposing my breast. I quickly unraveled my top, pulling it up to cover myself, and slowly turned my attention to the several onlookers frozen in shock staring in our direction. Kyle comforted me as I regained my composure, gently brushing the wet hair away from my face with his fingers; he laughed nervously and turned toward the spectators, still staring in confusion. Kyle waved in their direction.

He yelled, "Don't worry, we're okay."

Standing silent in a state of disbelief, I began to scan his drenched body and realized that the sharp rocks had sliced several deep cuts on his arms and legs, dripping blood onto the sand. I panicked, examining my body, yet I only had minor scrapes and scratches. Then, without realizing Kyle was observing me, he placed his fingers on my chin, lifting my head as he gazed into my eyes.

He said, "I will always protect you."

He wrapped a towel around me, rubbing my arms and drying my body, using the towel as a sling to pull me into his chest.

He led me to a private cove away from the spectators, wrapping his strong arms and broad shoulders around me, holding me close as his body heat warmed my body.

The chemistry between us was deep and passionate. Kyle grazed my arms with his hands, sending a surge of goosebumps from the top of my head down to the tips of my toes, exploring my body with his fingertips, kissing my neck while he made his way around my waist, slowly unbuttoning my jeans. The ocean breeze sent chills down my spine as he gently laid my back against the warm sand, pressing his chest against mine, passionately kissing my lips as I melted in his arms.

He navigated every angle of my body as if it was his wonderland. I gazed into his hazel green eyes as his pupils dilated and his rising body temperature ignited like wildfire. I couldn't contain my hands as they wandered feverishly through every muscle on his shoulders, arms, chest, and back; my fingers followed the path down his spine, pressing his body deeper into mine.

We paused momentarily, turning our heads in each direction to ensure we were in a secluded place shielded from bypassers walking on the beach. Then, as the sun began to set, the sky transformed into vibrant hues, pink, orange, yellow, and blue; the rising tide echo hushed the birds fluttering above the ocean water.

He scooped his arms beneath my thighs and lifted me up, placing my legs around his waist; I gripped his shoulders tightly as he positioned our bodies into a shallow cave between the rocks.

The skin on my face and throat was hot, but my fingertips were cold on my legs as I quickly removed my jeans. Kyle gripped my thighs, thrusting my body under his, kissing me passionately, breathing deeply as our bodies merged as one. It was like a magnetic force pulling me in; I could feel light drops of sweat gently graze my stomach as we rolled in the sand craving each other's touch.

He drew me in like a moth to a flame. We had electric energy that was impossible to ignore, and I realized then that our magnetic attraction was so intense it felt like the universe was pulling us together.

In the following days, Kyle sent me sweet messages and videos of him singing cover songs and strumming his acoustic guitar, playfully sneaking my name into each melody, sweeping me off my feet with every interaction.

One Saturday afternoon, I received a call from an unknown number; I ignored it as I was busy cleaning the house and doing laundry with my little ones. However, the mysterious unknown caller was persistent, so finally, I answered the phone. The woman's voice seemed agitated as she abruptly said my name. I curiously asked who was on the line.

She said, "This is Kyle's wife."

In a frenzy of disarray, I motioned to my children that I would be right back as I rushed into a separate room. I leaned against the wall to brace myself, and with a sharp inhale, I tried to catch my breath but was shaking uncontrollably.

She asked, "Are you sleeping with my husband?"

I was at a loss for words; I clenched my jaw, pacing the room, terrified as I tried to formulate a response. I was replaying the conversations between Kyle and me in my mind. I was shocked in a whirlwind of humiliation and guilt. I had never intended to become 'the other' woman let alone be responsible for tearing a family apart; the shame and self-deprecating thoughts twisted my stomach in knots. *How could I have been so stupid? Why didn't I ask more questions? He made it seem like his marriage had ended, and I was the only one. God, how could I be so blind?* He painted this picture that she was a monster and that he never loved her, but she didn't seem like any of those things. Instead, she sounded like an angry wife with a broken heart. Confused and struggling to respond, I couldn't seem to understand what was happening; I was frozen in shock and exhaled to calm my nerves.

I replied, "I think you need to have this conversation with him."

She insisted and continued asking me the same question, demanding an answer. All I could hear was the ringing in my ears and the sound of my teeth grinding. I stopped pacing and inhaled sharply. The silence seemed almost as devastating as her question. Uncertain of how to proceed, I composed myself, stood upright, and restated my response. Just before I could say another word, she hung up the phone.

I felt a piercing pain in my chest, staring blankly at the cell phone screen, rubbing the tension in my neck. I tried calling Kyle to figure out what was happening, but his phone went straight to voicemail, I called again, and it went to voicemail again. Finally, leaning forward with a stiff neck, I texted him, asking for answers, but he didn't respond. The tears began streaming down my face as I fell to my knees with my head in my hands. I heard Adian and Nevaeh approaching, so I urgently wiped my tears.

Adian said, "Momma, what's the matter?"

In a nervous tone, I laughed and said, "Mommy is okay sugar. I just got something in my eyes."

Nevaeh reached her arms in the air, nudging me to pick her up, and Adian curiously clenched my hand. I lifted Nevaeh, holding her around my waist, and guided them back to our chores. I began making silly jokes to divert their attention from asking more questions. A few hours later, after I tucked the kids into bed, I sat silently on the loveseat in the living room. Suddenly, there was a knock at the door; my intense thoughts stopped as I hesitantly walked toward the front entrance peeking through the blinds. Kyle stood solemnly at the doorstep; his face was flushed and blotchy with swollen eyes; he tilted his head down, staring at the ground with a duffle bag hanging from his shoulder and a large box filled with clothes in his arms. I was hurt, angry, and confused, but I couldn't leave him standing in the cold. My eyes welled up with tears as I slowly opened the door.

As he lifted his head, I saw a broken man approaching me. I couldn't raise my voice or lash out in anger. Instead, I was empathetic; I could feel the pain weighing heavy on his heart. I opened my arms, and he fell into my chest with tears flooding down his face; with his voice shuddering in a raspy tired tone, Kyle apologized for all the pain he had caused. I acknowledged his mistake, extended grace, and compassion, holding him in my arms and gently wiping the tears dripping down his chin.

Kyle set his belongings by the stairs, and we sat on the loveseat with our knees pressed against each other. His voice trembled.

He said, "The depth of love I have for you far exceeds anything I have ever felt. You make me feel alive. There is no excuse for the damage I have caused, but I can't deny my love for you. I am so sorry for hurting you, and I promise to protect your heart."

Kyle continued repeating how sorry he was, so I softly pressed my finger against his lips to quiet his chatter and laid his head on my lap, gliding my fingers through his hair until he fell asleep.

Kyle enraptured me with his charm and adoration for me despite my intuition. Yet, an unsettling feeling lingered, making me question who he was or claimed to be. He said he never loved her and couldn't live without me. What if he's lying? If I trust him, will he do the same thing to me? But maybe I'm different; perhaps this was meant to bring us closer together.

I put his faults aside, embracing, believing, and behaving as if he was perfect, wonderful, and flawless. Falling in love with Kyle was effortless; he was a dreamer with ambitions that overflowed beyond what I ever thought possible. Our emotional and sexual intimacy was exhilarating and exceeded my wildest imagination; our connection and conversations were expansive, making time non-existent. He made me feel like the world was our oyster and we could overcome anything together. I knew we were entering uncharted territory, yet I believed we could conquer the world, and I was willing to walk through the fire with him.

The following day, I awoke to the sounds of little feet running around upstairs, playing and giggling. Kyle and I had fallen asleep on the loveseat in the same position as the night before. Even though my children had met Kyle before, I wasn't quite ready to tell them he had stayed the night. So instead, I gently nudged Kyle; he wiped his eyes and gazed at me with a glowing smile.

I said, "You have to go! I don't want the kids to know you spent the night."

He replied, "I have an idea!"

Kyle jumped to his feet, tiptoeing towards the front door, lifting his finger against his lips, and shushing me as he snuck out the door. I raised my eyebrows curiously, wondering what he was up to, giggling, uncertain what to expect. Then, finally, I heard the little ones calling mommy and stomping down the stairs.

I said, "Good morning, my rays of sunshine!"

Just then, there was a knock at the door, and Adian and Nevaeh ran towards the entry opening the door before I could reach them. Kyle stood in the doorway with a beaming expression, glowing cheeks, and a playful smile; he lowered down, scooping the kids in each arm, twirling them around.

He said, "Good morning, guys! I couldn't wait to see you, so I got here as soon as the sun came up."

I shook my head with a soft, partly suppressed laugh; I knew he was clever, but that melted my heart. The kids squealed with excitement, jumping up and down, fighting for his attention as they wrestled around, rolling to the floor. They climbed on his back, taking turns riding piggyback while I prepared breakfast, giggling to myself with an endless smirk.

For the next several months, that became our morning routine. Kyle would come over after the kids fell asleep, spend the night, wake up bright and early before the little ones opened their eyes, wait on the front porch until he heard their footsteps, knock on the door, and greet them with hugs and kisses. Kyle had an endearing way of captivating their attention; he was playful and fun, and their faces lit up every time they heard the daily knock on the door.

Chapter 14: Baggage Reclaim

As the dust settled, Kyle introduced his six-month-old son, Ashton, into our lives, and we began to merge our little families. Adian was seven, and Nevaeh was three years old; they adored Ashton, calling him their baby brother and fighting over his attention.

The five of us spent every waking moment together, having family sleepovers, building forts in the living room, beach days playing in the sand for hours, taking road trips, and creating special memories wherever we went. We lived in a bubble of our own, and all our worries disappeared when we were together. Yet the struggle was very real as Kyle and I fought for our love against all odds, navigating through the trenches of child custody, divorce, and blending our new family.

Kyle's family was apprehensive and reluctant to meet me, so I recognized my place behind the scenes and patiently waited for an opportunity to arise. Unfortunately, I was perceived as the 'other woman' who destroyed his marriage. It weighed heavily on my heart as I yearned to be accepted and show them my unwavering love for their son. Kyle was angry that his family didn't support him, driving a wedge between them. Ashton's mother moved in with Kyle's parents temporarily until she got back on her feet, causing an uproar of arguments between him and his parents, leaving them without communication and further dividing their relationship. Kyle felt abandoned and defeated, yet his determination to earn their approval never ceased.

After a year together enduring an uphill battle of navigating co-parenting challenges, divorce hearings, blending our family, and feeling estranged from Kyle's parents, we finally started to find our cadence. Kyle and I sat in the living room deep in conversation, planning our future one

Saturday morning. Kyle shared that he wanted to find a larger home so the kids would have a yard to play in, to make more money so we could have a better life, and wanted us to travel, describing our future family vacations. Just as I tried to determine how we could afford all our desires logically, he paused to capture my attention, staring at me with an endearing expression and a twinkle in his eyes.

He said, "I want to spend the rest of my life with you."

I blushed, looking down as I felt the heat on my face rising. It was as though he was reminding me of our unspoken commitment to be together forever. Kyle knew I was terrified of getting married again because of all the pain I had endured. Yet, the heart wants what it wants, no matter how much you try to tame it. As I leaned forward to kiss him, my gaze was locked in his. Kyle placed his hand under my chin to draw me closer, then paused.

He said, "Serena, you are such an incredible mother; you have overcome so much and never given up. You are compassionate, vulnerable, empathetic, intelligent, and strong. I don't know how I managed to win your heart, but I will continue to prove my love to you every day for the rest of our lives, and I will do whatever it takes to give you the life you deserve."

Kyle had a particular way of making even the little moments unforgettable; I followed every word that fell from his lips. Although I was fully transparent in expressing my concerns and desire to wait before we took the next step, he intentionally reminded me of his unwavering love and adoration. With every ounce of my being, I knew that he was my soulmate, best friend, and the love of my life. Yet I wanted our healing process to unfold so we could be whole individually before uniting as one.

I found my mind wandering as I was lost in his words, daydreaming, and fantasizing about our future together, but the moment he touched my skin, he reminded me that he was real. I felt undeserving of his love and couldn't imagine someone sacrificing so much for me. My self-limiting beliefs were more prevalent after I left Scott, and I didn't fully see my worth. Yet, even when I doubted myself, he didn't waiver and continued professing his love for me, acknowledging every quality he saw in me.

Kyle sat forward on the loveseat and continued the conversation by expressing the agony he felt about his parents not accepting his decision to leave his former wife and our relationship and began leaning over, placing his head in his hands.

He said, "I haven't spoken to them in over a year since they let my ex-wife live with them, and if they don't want to accept me for who I am, then I don't want them in our lives."

I placed my hand on his knee and leaned forward to wrap my arms around him; he looked toward me and nestled his head against my shoulder.

I replied, "How can you ask them to accept you if you haven't fully accepted them?"

Kyle sat up with a curious expression and in a confused tone.

He said, "What do you mean?"

I said, "You never accepted their decision to have Ashton and his mother live with them, you haven't considered how our choices have impacted their lives, and you haven't allowed them to be a part of our life. So how can you ask them for unconditional love and acceptance when you haven't displayed it in your actions?"

Kyle sat in silence as he pondered my question and leaned his back against the sofa, his neck tilted up, staring at the ceiling. Several minutes passed until he repositioned his posture and sat straight up in a moment of clarity.

He said, "You're right. I never thought about it that way. I'm going to call them right now and apologize."

Stunned by his sense of urgency, I nervously clenched his hand. I encouraged him to let go of any expectations and approach the conversation with humility, accountability, and acceptance, no matter the outcome. Kyle took a sharp breath and agreed; then, with his hands shaking, he reached for the phone to call his parents. I could hear the phone ringing as I pressed in closer, wrapping my arms around him as I could feel his heart pumping out of his chest.

His father answered the phone, and with a trembling voice, Kyle began to speak. I quietly left the room, giving him space as I knew he needed to face them alone. It felt like hours had passed, and I heard the occasional sounds of tears, soon turning into laughter until finally, I heard Kyle say goodbye. I eagerly ran downstairs to see how he was feeling, and just as I peeked my head around the corner, Kyle jumped up with tears of joy.

He said, "Thank you for giving me the courage to talk to my parents."

I replied, "I didn't give you the courage, my love; I simply reminded you that it was there all along."

His face was glowing with excitement as he began to share the details of their conversation. It was as though an enormous weight was lifted off his shoulders as he floated around the living room, replaying the conversation.

He said, "They're ready to meet you."

My heart dropped into my stomach, and moving back slightly, I gulped.

I said, "Are you sure?"

I tried to control my breathing to calm my nerves and suggested he spend some time alone with his parents before introducing the kids and me. He was adamant and insisted that we were in this together. I reminded him that when he introduced me to his older sister, she wasn't ready to accept our relationship fully, and our visit ended in uncomfortable silence.

He said, "This will be different; you'll see. We're going to my parent's house tomorrow; the whole family will be there. They'll love you!"

I tried to swallow, but it felt like my throat swelled shut. I was worried that Kyle's ex-wife would be there, let alone my concern if his family could ever forgive me for the chaos I created. Then, negative scenarios began swirling through my mind as I imagined every possible outcome.

However, my worries quickly disappeared when I met his family the following day; they were warm, friendly, and a little on the wild side. Kyle's dad had long dark hair with strands of gray left unbound to tumble down his shoulders, a smile that could light up the room, with a boisterous personality and classic rock apparel. His mom was highly affectionate and nurturing, with ash blonde hair cascading down her back with a cozy outfit and a vibrant personality. Kyle's parents didn't seem as unreasonable as he made them out to be they were fun and inviting. His dad even pulled out the electric guitar, and the whole family burst out in song as he played.

 Aunts, uncles, siblings, cousins, and grandparents gathered around the house, shared stories, and raised their glasses. It was an unusually chilly day in California. As I listened to the kids playing outside, I overheard them bursting with excitement as the weather quickly changed, and it began to snow. The wind whispered through the trees just after a storm had passed the night before, the clouds covered the sun with dimly lit highlights sweeping through the sky, and suddenly, flakes of white snow sprinkled the ground. Kyle's entire family gathered in the front yard, singing, dancing in circles, embracing each other, and taking photos of memories that would last a lifetime.

 A few weeks later, I had a business trip in Chicago; I dreaded the idea of being away from Kyle and the kids. The company prepared my travel schedule for only a few days; however, my parents decided to take the kids on a summer road trip. Kyle called me every day while I was away. Each morning I would receive a message from Kyle, saying how proud he was of me for growing in my career, and every night, he would call me strumming his guitar and singing.

 He stole my heart with every word that fell from his lips. Then, when he finished singing, I could hear his soft chuckle as I nestled my head into the hotel pillow.

 Kyle said, "You are perfect in every way, and I can't imagine one more day without you. I'm counting the minutes until I can see you again."

 I rolled over, laying on my back, playing with my hair with a soft grin as I stared at the ceiling listening to his angelic voice.

I asked, "Please play another song until I fall asleep."

Kyle was endearing; with his bright hazel-green eyes and bashful smile, I could feel his energy through the phone. Imagining his fresh twenty-four-year-old masculine yet youthful face lightly dusted with stubble and his gentle spirit as he continued singing with a pure and tender tone until I fell asleep.

I arrived home the following evening to Kyle ushering me around the condo with a wide grin and a gleam in his eyes.

Kyle said, "Close your eyes; I made something for you."

He placed his hands over my eyes as he walked behind me, guiding me toward the kitchen.

He said, "Okay, now open your eyes."

As I scanned the kitchen, I noticed the back of a large 24" x 30" white canvas. I curiously studied Kyle's expression as he lifted the canvas and turned it toward me. My face lit up with excitement as I placed my hands over my mouth and gasped.

He said, "I couldn't stand another moment without seeing your beautiful face, so I painted a portrait of you."

The white canvas was a lustrous shadowy painting of my side profile using spray paint as the medium in charcoal, gray, and white shades. The monochromatic use of extreme lights and darks with a slight mist of tiny particles gave the contour of my silhouette a contemporary yet sophisticated look. The image Kyle used to sketch the outline was a photo of me looking down with my head tilted slightly forward, using shades of white to highlight the thick strands of hair that veiled my expression. He used stencils to shade the dimensions of my cheekbones with soft gray tones allowing the shadows to drift down to the edge of my chin. The natural light from the kitchen window displayed the layers of dark gray and charcoal, distinguishing my features with a soft glossy tone that sealed his masterpiece.

He said, "This symbolizes my love for you."

I stood in awe of his limitless talent, examining every detail of his exquisite work of art. I lightly skimmed my fingertips against the canvas, feeling each outline's texture with the smell of fresh paint lingering in the air. Just as I attempted to speak, my lips quivered, gazing up at him in adoration, fixated on his blushing grin. I closed my eyes to savor the experience as a tear glided down my cheek.

I said, "Nobody has ever done anything like this for me before."

He replied, "Words cannot express my love for you; my love for you runs deep into my soul, and this painting symbolizes my love for you."

A flood of heat fueled my body with an overwhelming desire to pull him closer, to feel his body pressed against mine. I lunged toward him, wrapping my arms around his neck, kissing him with a fierce passion, running my fingers through his thick hair as I moved rhythmically around his body, removing the canvas between us and gently setting it aside. He lifted me, placing my legs around his waist with our lips pressed firmly together as he led me into the bedroom.

Twisted in each other's arms with heavy breathing, rocking from side to side as we quickly tore off our clothes, I moaned, pulling his body tightly against mine. The taste of his tongue, and the weight of his muscular chest, pressed me deeper into the mattress, clenching the soft sheets into knots with my hands on each side as he devoured my body. My legs flexed against his back, urging him closer, wrapping my hands behind his neck to hold him steady as I rocked into him. The sweat dripped off his chest onto mine as we tangled ourselves in the sheets making love for hours until our bodies became too weak to move.

I leaned over, laying my head on his chest, listening to his heartbeat as we both panted for air, allowing our bodies to recover from the intense passion. I lifted my head and whispered in his ear.

I said, "Thank you for loving me. I will cherish your painting forever."

He gently laid my head against his chest and softly kissed my forehead.

He said, "I will cherish you forever."

A tear shed from the corner of my eye as I would never have imagined anyone loving me the way he did. I felt seen in his presence, almost as if he could see my soul. I nestled deeper into his chest, and we fell asleep entangled in each other's arms. Our love grew more profound, and after being together for just over a year, Kyle found the perfect home for our blended family. He handed me the keys with a smile from ear to ear.

He said, "I'm giving you a private tour before we surprise the kids."

A little apprehensive, I gave him a concerned look as he rushed me to the car. When we parked in front of the house, my eyes widened, and I couldn't grasp how we could afford something this extravagant.

The exterior elevation was a Colonial-style house with white trim and shutters, accented with a neutral color scheme, chestnut roof tiles, expansive symmetrical windows surrounded by lush trees and plush grass with breathtaking views of rolling hills and mountain sides tucked away in a quiet suburban neighborhood.

I said, "We're moving out of our tiny three-bedroom condo into a massive two-story house?"

Kyle replied, "Just wait until you see inside."

He opened the double door entry and described the house in more detail, saying there are five bedrooms and five bathrooms with over four thousand square feet of living space. I gasped as Kyle opened the front door to give me a sneak preview; his voice faded in the background as I slowly stepped through the doorway in utter disbelief.

I said, "I don't think we can afford this, love?"

Kyle chuckled with a mischievous grin; he reached for my hand.

He said, "I already negotiated a price we could afford. So, you have nothing to worry about; it's only a few hundred dollars more than we pay for the condo."

Slightly reluctant, I stepped back to take it all in. Kyle had an astounding sales ability; he was extremely smooth, charming, and persuasive, such that he could effortlessly talk his way through just about anything. He even made frivolous jokes about 'selling me' on his charm, bragging that I was the biggest deal he had ever closed, which never failed to make me blush. Yet this seemed impossible.

I asked, "What do you mean a 'few' hundred more?"

He replied, "The owners are going through an ugly divorce and can't agree on selling the property. They want a family who will care for their home and take over the mortgage for the next few years until they can come to an agreement. They even offered a lease with an option to buy when they're ready."

My mouth dropped as Kyle escorted me on the grand tour. An elegant staircase centered the grand entrance with white spindles and a dark stained wood banister that split elegantly into two landings at the top. The foyer led to an open space plan with soaring twenty-foot-high cathedral ceilings, a formal living and dining area, a family room, a breakfast nook, and a guest suite. Granite counters and backsplash bordered the expansive kitchen, with an oversized center island, breakfast counter, and bar seating. The grand staircase led to a master suite and three spacious bedrooms with a loft and bonus room. We explored every inch of the house, imagining our furniture and choosing which rooms the kids would have.

Finally, Kyle guided me back to the main suite, and we climbed into the oversized jacuzzi tub with our clothes on to make sure we both fit inside. Kyle reached for my hand before we finished our exclusive tour, lifting me out of the jacuzzi tub with a mischievous smirk and persuading me to follow him. Slightly skeptical of his expression, I curiously followed him to the master retreat as he escorted me through the French doors leading to a private balcony.

We stood holding hands, taking in the majestic view of a private lake nearby; he turned toward me, gazing intently in my direction; just as I leaned in for a kiss, Kyle knelt on one knee. He opened a little black box centered with a beautifully crafted white gold vintage diamond ring surrounded by a row of smaller pavé-set diamonds creating a border around the central stone. It was elegant, bold, geometric, unapologetically dramatic, timeless, and sophisticated.

He said, "You are the best thing that has ever happened to me. I can't express the depth of my love for you. You are my soulmate; I couldn't imagine spending the rest of my life with anyone else. Anything is possible when we're together. Will you marry me?"

It felt like time had stopped, and all I could hear was the wind whistling through the trees. This man kneeling before me was what I had dreamed of all my life. I nodded as he spoke, and my voice cracked with emotion.

His eyes welled up with tears as he smiled nervously, anticipating my response.

I said, "Yes! Yes!

Kyle jumped to his feet and kissed me with such passion that I surrendered in his arms. He paused, placed his hands on my cheeks, and admired the curves of my face with his fingers, softly caressing my hair.

Kyle replied, "I love you, Serena. I want this house to be our home, where our next chapter begins."

Within just a few weeks, we moved into our dream home. Adian, Nevaeh, and Ashton ran around our new house with smiles from ear to ear, unpacking and decorating their rooms enthusiastically. It was the fresh start we needed with the support of our loved ones. I was thriving in my career, Kyle accepted a position as a fitness manager at a local gym, and the kids were in school and sports programs. In addition to planning a destination wedding in Napa, California, with our immediate family, my parents moved into the guest suite to help with the kids. It finally seemed like everything was falling into place.

Chapter 15: I'm Not Enough

 Kyle continued to surprise me with his endless good qualities. He was not only the man of my dreams but also an incredible father and role model in our children's lives. He spent hours teaching Adian how to play the guitar, took Nevaeh on weekly date nights, and sometimes even got pedicures together; and Kyle even taught little Ashton how to help him change a tire when he was just two years old.

 One morning Kyle woke all the kids up extra early and wouldn't tell us where we were going but made sure to pack jackets and snacks. The little ones waited anxiously in the back seat, trying to guess our destination, but Kyle wouldn't budge. I've never experienced someone loving my kids as much as Kyle did; he treated them like his own. We even made a family rule never to use the word "step" because we wanted each child to feel inclusive, so we fostered an environment where everyone was loved unconditionally as one family. I even teased that Ashton came out of my belly button.

 Finally, we arrived at the surprise destination, pulling up to tall gates that opened to an expansive parking lot with an arched sign overhead. The kids squealed with excitement bouncing up and down in the back seat.

 Adian yelled, "DISNEYLAND?!"

 Although Nevaeh and Ashton had never been before, they followed Adian's lead by chanting with their big brother in unison. My heart melted as I glanced over at Kyle's endearing grin.

 Kyle said, "Surprise! We're going to the happiest place on earth."

The day was filled with giggles, roller coasters, cotton candy, silly photos, and souvenirs and ended with the three little ones fast asleep in the back seat leaning their heads against one another. I couldn't believe Kyle went out of his way, managing all the little details to surprise the kids without saying a word. To say he swept me off my feet would be an understatement; I floated on the clouds when we were together.

As the wedding planning began in the following weeks, Kyle and I were lying in bed one morning looking at wedding ideas and photos. Kyle quickly sat up against the headboard with an inward gaze as his expression perked with a bright idea.

Kyle said, "We should do a fitness competition before the wedding!"

Kyle was thriving in the fitness industry and always wanted to do a competition, we were both active at the gym, and I had made so much progress in my weight loss journey; I looked up, contemplating his idea while staring at the ceiling. *I don't look anything like a fitness model, let alone have the body type to compete on stage with several women half my age who've never had kids. I'll be humiliated.* I wanted to support him, knowing that it would mean the world to him if I agreed. However, my thoughts continued racing; *Kyle is six years younger than me and already has an incredible physique with broad shoulders, muscular arms, full muscle definition, and six-pack abs. I'm thirty years old, I've had two children, my body is curvy, and there is no way I could do a fitness competition. How will I balance a demanding career, three kids, an intense workout routine, and plan a wedding? This is crazy!*

I sat up next to him against the headboard with a puzzled look.

I said, "I wouldn't even know where to begin. I know you can do it, my love, but I'm unsure I can. I have too much on my plate."

Kyle turned toward me, noticing the discouragement in my tone; he gently placed his fingers under my chin and guided my head in his direction. He observed me closely, gazing into my eyes.

He said, "Your body is perfect in every way, believe me, I can barely keep my hands off it. I know you're concerned, but I've wanted to do this for a long time. I want to do this with you because I know we can do anything together. Plus, we will be the hottest bride and groom ever!"

I tilted my head down and blushingly smiled. This man could talk me into just about anything, yet I didn't feel like I was skinny enough, strong enough, or even mentally capable of accomplishing something of this magnitude.

He said, "I know several fitness trainers that coach competitors. We can get a coach and work out together. We can do this: it'll be a memorable experience. I bet we'll even tell our grandkids about it when we get old."

I chuckled softly, nodding my head from side to side. He knew exactly how to tug at my heartstrings; I craved new memories and experiences over anything else, so I agreed to his crazy idea without another thought.

When I arrived home from work that evening, the smell of roasted chicken, steamed rice, and grilled fish filled the air. I skeptically walked through the entryway listening to the sounds of clinking pans and rustling dishes and vegetables sizzling over the fire, peeking my head into the kitchen. Just as I stepped forward, curious to see all the commotion, I noticed our entire kitchen island stacked with mounds of Tupperware. Kyle hovered over the stove top, wearing my pink and white apron with a perfect bow around his waist, cooking a feast for an entire army.

He greeted me with wide open arms and a big kiss when he noticed me.

He said, "Welcome home! I spent the entire day grocery shopping, buying Tupperware, and preparing meals for our new nutrition plan."

I inhaled sharply, nervously looking at the pile of pots and pans filling the sink. Then, with a gleaming smile, Kyle raised his eyebrows and opened the refrigerator to display a mountain of neatly stacked Tupperware labeled with little yellow sticky notes organized by name breakfast, lunch, and dinner with little hearts and smiley faces. Then leaping into motion, he guided me to the pantry, where he measured and pre-packaged almonds, rice cakes, oatmeal, and healthy snacks. Kyle's eyes lit up with excitement; reaching for my phone and logging into my calendar to create daily reminders for me to eat every two hours.

Then, without skipping a beat, he shouted, "Guess what? I even scheduled our first training session for tomorrow!"

I wandered in circles around the kitchen island, with my mouth falling slightly open, fascinated by everything he had prepared. Kyle thought of every little detail, investing hours of his day planning, shopping, and cooking, and he even picked up the kids from three different schools. I paused in awe of his presence with a euphoric expression, not wishing to interrupt the surreal moment.

I said, "I can't believe you did all this for me. Thank you so much, my love. It's incredible. You're incredible."

He replied, "You do so much for everyone else; the least I could do is make your life a little easier. I love you."

Kyle had a funny way of knowing exactly what I needed. He inspired me and made me feel like I could accomplish anything. His attention to detail and preparation diminished my uncertainty about the competition. I knew when we were together, anything was possible. Kyle's excitement and determination inspired me. I even questioned myself sometimes, *how did I get so lucky?*

Progress photos, rice cakes, three hours of daily fitness training, juggling the children's schedules, planning a destination wedding, and long hours at the office filled the following months. Yet, even the most stressful times seemed to float away in the wind with Kyle by my side, encouraging me every step of the way.

The fitness competition was just a few days before our wedding date. I lost several inches; however, I was concerned that I hadn't made enough progress to compete on stage in front of hundreds of people. I had an hourglass figure with a smaller waist and developed tight glutes, with definition in my quads and shoulders.

However, the judges divide bikini competitors into groups based on height and body fat percentage. Being 5'1 and 130 lbs. (on a good day) with a 17% body fat percentage, whereas most of my class had a 10-14% body fat percentage, my coaches expressed that they didn't think I was ready and suggested I reconsider competing.

That evening after Kyle and I tucked the little ones in bed, I told Kyle I would join him downstairs in a few minutes. I walked into our bedroom, quietly pressing the door closed behind me because I didn't want to let him down, but I was discouraged and defeated. I began undressing each layer of clothing with a somber expression as I stood naked in front of the full-length mirror. The dimly lit lights above the vanity highlighted every imperfection as I examined each crease and dimple on my body. Thick strands of blonde hair cascaded over my face absorbing the tears rolling down my cheeks. Scanning each angle, I glided each finger against my exposed body, inhaling deeply to hold my breath as my stomach expanded in and out. Again, self-doubt consumed my mind. *I worked so hard, but it wasn't enough. What was I thinking? I can't do this. I'm going to embarrass myself if I go through with this.*

Emotionally, physically, and mentally drained, my body couldn't withstand this extraneous routine for much longer. I heard the door slowly creep open and quickly wiped my tears. Kyle stood behind me, observing our reflection in the mirror, wrapping his arms around my bare skin, caressing each curve as he whispered in my ear.

He said, "You are flawless."

My heart sank into my chest as I expressed my concerns about what the fitness coach had said. Kyle repositioned himself between the mirror and my body, placing his hands on my waist, pulling me closer, and looking into my eyes.

He said, "I don't care what the coaches said, and I don't care what the judges say. We are doing this together, and you will stand on the stage with your head held high and prove everyone wrong. You are the most beautiful woman in the world. I won't let anything stop you from believing in yourself because I believe in you."

Kyle made me feel like I was capable, worthy, and irresistible. I inhaled sharply as I melted into his arms; my body merged into his. He grazed the hair from the top of my head down my neck.

I said, "I can do this, and I will, thank you for believing in me. I love you."

The next day, Kyle walked me through the strategy of depleting water before we went on stage. This process is not for the faint at heart; it's not sustainable and should only be used to dehydrate our bodies before the competition. I was concerned and discouraged because I didn't feel like my body was ready for the competition, yet I trusted him, confident that he was the expert, so I followed his lead. He explained that by reducing the volume of excess water stored in the body, we're effectively reducing the distance between the skin and muscle, giving the appearance of larger muscles, and making our progress more visible. Within a week, I lost an additional ten pounds of water weight, finally preparing my body for the competition.

The following morning was the big day; we woke up extra early, eating dried chicken breast for breakfast with no water until we left the stage. As we arrived at the venue, before we went backstage to the private locker rooms, Kyle grabbed my hand and spun me around, placing his palms on my cheeks and looking straight into my eyes.

He said, "I don't care what happens today; you are the most beautiful woman in the room, and I am so proud of you. Thank you for doing this with me."

Kyle kissed me passionately, then, with a deep exhale, I made my way behind the stage. Each contestant received a numbered pin to attach to our bikinis; as I turned to see the other competitors in my class, I realized that most of the other women were no older than twenty-five years old. As intimidating as this may have been, it didn't faze me. I encouraged every one of them before it was their turn to enter the stage, knowing that no matter how beautiful each woman was, we all had insecurities, so I embraced them and reminded them of how hard we worked to get here.

The moment I saw my cue to enter the stage, I held my head high with a glowing smile and confidence. I owned the stage without a care in the world, and although I didn't place as high as I had hoped, I was proud of myself.

Now that the competition was behind us, the wedding was fast approaching, just a few days away. Our lives were a whirlwind of preparation, between waxing, manicures, pedicures, hair, makeup, packing, and traveling to Napa with the kids. The night before our special day, we stayed in separate hotel rooms. When I woke up the following day, I looked at my reflection in the mirror. I realized I was allergic to the wax applied to my face and had a rash with giant red and white bumps above my upper lip. In addition, my eyes were swollen due to dehydration before the competition because my body retained all the water I consumed after the show, causing extreme inflammation.

Meanwhile, Adian was feeling unwell. I froze in disbelief, reaching my arms around my son and comforting him. My mother overheard the commotion, ran into the bathroom to care for Adian, and rushed me out the door to get my hair and makeup done. My soon-to-be sister-in-law sat me down in an oversized chair to do my hair and makeup; she calmed my nerves by reassuring me that she would magically make everything disappear, and she did.

We arrived at our venue, a luxury hotel and resort surrounded by panoramic vista views as our backdrop overlooking illustrious vineyards with the Mayacamas Mountains in the distance. The outdoor terrace and ceremony deck overlooked a stunning view of lush trees and blooming vines giving our guests a slice of tranquility in Napa Valley. Mahogany Chiavari chairs with ivory cushions lined each side of the dramatic aisle as my stepdad, Ken, stood at the forefront of the terrace in preparation for officiating our union.

Kyle strummed his guitar wearing a timeless gray suit with a rich textured appearance draping perfectly over his broad shoulders, a white pearl vest with a crisp white shirt slightly unbuttoned around his collar. At the same time, Adian sat beside him in a complimenting charcoal gray suit and vest with a matching crisp white dress shirt and pearl white tie tucked neatly in his blazer playing the cajon drum. Kyle handmade all the floral boutonnières and the bouquet I was holding. Together, Kyle and Adian entertained our guests as I prepared to enter the private terrace through the French doors.

Nevaeh stood to my right with her long blonde curls swirled over her camisole shoulder straps as her champagne silk dress laid perfectly on her tiny five-year-old frame. Pleated taffeta ruffled at her hips and matching fabric sash with matching ballerina shoes and a sequined purse over her shoulder with a basket of white rose petals in her hands. Three-year-old Ashton stood to my left with his charcoal gray suit and vest perfectly matching his big brother with tiny black oxford dress shoes holding a black velvet box with the wedding rings tucked inside. They skipped toward the French doors until they noticed the rows of guests, then paused, refusing to step forward without holding my hands.

As the French doors panned open, Kyle and Adian began to play the rhythm of *I'll Be* by Edwin McCain, the song Kyle sang to me the night he called my office. I paused at the base of the terrace in a sophisticated strapless fit-and-flare wedding gown with an asymmetrical bodice complimenting my hourglass figure with a subtle sweetheart neckline. The elegant champagne gown draped around my waist highlighted shades of pompous gold, sweet vanilla, and neutral beige. Nevaeh and Ashton interlaced their tiny fingers between mine as we walked down the aisle together. Kyle gazed in my direction with tears in his eyes as we approached the altar; his voice began to crack as he struggled to sing the words. Then, he stood to accept my hand as all three children circled us. First, we presented each child with a handmade gift with the inscription "Love Never Fails," binding our family together and making each child feel inclusive during the ceremony. Next, Ken led us into a sand ceremony inviting each child to hold a glass bottle filled with colored sand. He explained that pouring these individual containers of sand into one vessel represents each of you; all that you are and will ever be, will bind you as a family together forever.

The cool summer breeze whispered through the trees as my curls pressed softly against my cheekbones. As our guests witnessed our union, I recited my vows, gazing into Kyle's hazel eyes.

I said, "I promise to be intentional in all I do and express grace, patience, mercy, and unconditional love. I promise to give you the freedom to be yourself, give you all my trust, and discover new adventures together as a family. I will listen to you with compassion and understanding and speak with thoughtfulness and complete transparency. I will cherish you, respect you, appreciate you, and empower you to be the man God has created you to be."

Kyle recited his vows with tears streaming down his cheeks as we exchanged rings. As my dad cheerfully announced, "You may kiss the bride," We leaned toward one another. Nevaeh and Ashton covered their eyes as Kyle's lips met mine, and the crowd cheered in celebration of our union as husband and wife.

The festivities began as we invited our close friends and family to caravan through the Napa Valley wine tasting at our favorite wineries. Each guest bought us a bottle of wine from every stop, and we ended the evening at a tiny French bistro that Kyle and I fell in love with on a previous visit. Magical moments filled the evening with an outpour of love from all those who joined us on our special day.

We wanted to include our little ones in every aspect of our experience, so they joined us on our honeymoon, a road trip on the coast, touring every attraction on our journey home, and creating memories the entire way.

After we arrived home, we finally had the life we dreamed about, the kids were back in school, and our routine seamlessly continued; everything seemed to fall into place as we started our lives as one family.

Within a few days, I returned to the office. I had been in my role as a V.P. of Marketing for almost two years and it was grueling; the stress at times seemed unbearable, and although I was growing and evolving in my career, it was not without sacrifice. The nights seemed endless with unreasonable deadlines, and the CEO micromanaged my every move, hovering over my shoulder. Even when he traveled, he would call my office hourly to assign new priorities and request a status on the tasks assigned just hours before.

On this particular day, I worked through my lunch to catch up on urgent projects demanding my attention after returning from our honeymoon. The corporate office had two suites; each guest was greeted by a receptionist in the central area, with several department managers and employees circulating throughout. My office was tucked away in a private executive suite with only a few large offices, where most of the C-Level Leaders worked strategically positioned away from daily distractions.

I focused intently on the glowing computer screen as all the other executives left for lunch. The office was peaceful, with only the sound of the ticking clock and the vibration of muted telephones directing calls to voicemail. Within moments, I heard the main door creep open as someone entered the executive suite; I curiously tilted my head to observe the person who walked in. As I looked toward the suite entrance, a woman with a pale complexion, puffy eyes, and long dark hair stood upright, seemingly tense in her arms and shoulders. She hesitated at the entrance, scanning the area suspiciously, then paused as she stared in my direction stoically.

She said, "Serena?"

I didn't recognize her, yet she seemed to know who I was. The woman urgently walked toward my office, closed the door behind her, and sat directly across from my desk, pulling the chair in closely, demanding my full attention. Confused by her assertiveness and questioning how she knew my name, the woman stared blankly at me. Her presence brought an unsettling energy into the air as I observed the distress in her body language. Finally, after a few moments of silence, looking down, shaking her head, she reluctantly began to speak; her voice trembled.

She said, "My name is Angela, and I need to talk to you about your husband, Kyle."

I sat upright in my chair and felt a heaviness in my stomach; a vile taste entered my mouth, and I grew nauseous as Angela began stuttering over her words. I leaned forward with my elbows against the desk, holding my head from collapsing against the surface as I had a gut-wrenching feeling that my entire world was about to spiral out of control.

Chapter 16: Spiral of Lies

A ray of light leaked into my office through a small gap between the window blinds. Yet the room grew dark as Angela began to describe my home in grave detail. I observed her, my eyes glazed over, slowly yet forcibly expelling my breath, trying to process what she was saying.

She said, "I apologize for disturbing you in your office, but I felt compelled to tell you that I have been with Kyle for over a year. I was recently pregnant with his child and gave birth just a few weeks ago."

Angela sat up in her chair, lifted her shirt above her waist, and, with her hands shaking, pinched the loose skin between her fingers as she presented her stretch marks to me.

She continued, "We decided to give the baby up for adoption due to the circumstances, but I wanted you to know the truth."

The sound of a sharp ringing in my ears diluted her voice. I could feel the color drain from my face; I was frozen in shock, disorientated, and light-headed as the room spun in slow motion, swaying in circles. My chest tightened, and my breath was briefly trapped in my lungs as I sat silently, clinging to every word she said. I tried to speak, but I couldn't articulate my thoughts.

She said, "Kyle will deny everything and tell you I'm crazy, but Serena, I have proof."

Angela reached for my business card sitting on the desk and placed it in her pocket.

She continued, "I saved all our messages, photos, and videos over the past year. I will send them all to you. You deserve to know the truth."

Suddenly I heard the main entrance door open as several executives returned from lunch. A surge of adrenaline rushed through my body; I quickly stood up, motioning Angela to follow me out of my office. My voice cracked as I whispered.

I said, "Follow me. We can't have this conversation here. There is a restaurant just outside the building."

I could barely stand as my legs began to buckle, yet I had no choice; I couldn't take the chance of anyone overhearing our conversation. She followed closely behind me as I rushed through the building and down the walkway, struggling to keep my balance as we approached the restaurant. Finally, I reached for a chair outside the restaurant to hold myself up, inhaled sharply, then sat across from her at a table on the patio.

My head was heavy, dragging my gaze to the floor, I couldn't formulate words, yet I could feel my body absorbing all her emotions, making it impossible for me to comprehend my own feelings. As tears fell from her face, I reached across the table, touched her hand, and comforted her. Angela's body trembled in anguish as if her heart was being ripped open. I could sense and feel every emotion she experienced, listening intently with empathy as she described intimate details about her relationship with my husband. A cold breeze brushed against my face in a moment of complete confusion.

I asked, "Where is the baby?"

She replied, "I met a family at church and gave our baby to them."

A deep and painful sorrow filled my soul, and I could no longer process her words. Angela continued speaking, yet my mind was fixated on finding this poor baby. Then, finally, she noticed my trepidation, began to panic, and quickly reverted my attention.

She said, "The only way Kyle will tell the truth is if we confront him together."

I couldn't see straight, process information, or grasp what was happening. I aimlessly followed Angela through the parking lot to our vehicles.

She insisted, "Follow me."

Submerged in a cloud of confusion, I complied without question, entirely outside of my body. Angela parked behind Kyle's car in the back alley near the employee entrance as we approached the fitness center. She motioned me to get out of my car, then in an assertive tone.

She said, "Text him to let him know you are here and need something out of his car."

I felt like I was in someone else's nightmare, and without rebuttal, I did what she said. The sounds of cars passing and engines revving from the main street drowned my thoughts, with the faint smell of garbage from the bins stacked behind the building. I was nauseous, and my entire body trembled as I stood beside her, waiting for Kyle to open the door.

I stared blankly at the door handle as it began to turn, the large metal door slowly crept open. Angela abruptly grabbed my hand just as I felt my knees buckle; she held my hand so tight that I could feel the flood of adrenaline rushing through her pulse. When Kyle locked eyes with me, he wailed and fell to his knees, screaming at Angela.

Kyle yelled, "You fucking ruined my life! I hate you!"

Kyle swayed back and forth on his knees, hunched over on the pavement digging his fingernails into the ground with tears rolling down his face. It was as though I fell into the crosshairs of their love affair, trapped between them as they screamed.

Angela yelled, "You told me that you loved me! You're a fucking liar!"

Kyle screamed, "I never loved you! I told you to leave my family and me alone, you psycho bitch!"

I stood in silence, absorbed by the intense energy between them, with my eyes glazed over, lost in the uproar of screams. My mind was utterly disconnected from my body, as though I was outside of myself, immersed in someone else's story. My throat began to tighten as I struggled to breathe, with a dark, cold numbness running through my body. The heaviness of my limbs was the only thing holding me up from collapsing on the asphalt as their lies began to unravel before me.

I was trapped in the crossfire between them, unknowingly giving her complete control as she stood over him with a sense of dominance screaming in his face. Kyle glared at her with bloodshot eyes, a tightened jaw, and clenched fists as his knees dug deeper into the pavement.

I trembled in terror as I watched my entire world unfold. I'd never seen a man weep like this before. I couldn't comprehend the magnitude of the situation and slowly turned, walking toward my car. My only thought was to flee.

Kyle saw me walking away amid the chaos and jumped to his feet, pleading with me to stop. I couldn't hear his cries through the tunnel of sharp ringing in my ears, and the shock was so severe that his voice became unintelligible as I got into my vehicle and drove away.

I reached the stop light in a daze of confusion and slowly pulled to the side of the road just a few blocks away, shifted the car into park, and sobbed uncontrollably. I threw my head back against the seat, then abruptly thrust forward, catching my head in my hands before it hit the steering wheel, rocking back and forth, trying to catch my breath. The mucus and tears saturated my face as the crippling reality of their love affair registered in my mind.

I screamed, "Noooooo! This can't be happening. Why God? Why me?"

My voice deepened to a raspy tone as my screams diluted the sounds of the busy highway. I shook my head in denial while trying to piece together a timeline of the earth-shattering details. My cries transformed into sporadic wails of disgust as I replayed the intimate details she shared about their sexual relationship.

I heard a vehicle approaching behind me, so I frantically searched for something to wipe my face. Kyle tapped on the passenger window, begging me to unlock the door; the shock quickly set in again as my gaze became dull with a hollow expression. I opened the car door, and he leaned in, begging me to pull into a nearby parking lot away from the main road.

I hadn't even noticed the traffic racing past my vehicle, so I drove forward, turned into a shopping center, and parked behind the retail store to hide while I removed the black streaks of mascara running down my face. Kyle parked behind me and got into the passenger side of my vehicle. I slid down, slumping into the driver's seat with my back turned against him. I couldn't stomach looking in his direction, so I leaned against the window as the tears dripped off the end of my nose, splattering on the door panel.

He attempted to touch my arm, and I flinched, pulling my entire body away from his reach. I was revolted by the thought of him even being in the same vehicle, let alone grazing my arm. We sat in silence for several minutes; I could hear him whimpering beside me as the devastation of shattered dreams filled the air. A slow, piercing pain twisted in my stomach while explicit visuals of them together poisoned my mind. Kyle began to hyperventilate, attempting to formulate words into a coherent sentence, pleading for my forgiveness and muttering his thoughts of self-harm.

He sputtered, "I hate myself; I'm so sorry, I'm so sorry, I just want to die. I don't deserve you. I don't deserve to live."

I turned and interjected, "Don't you ever say that again! Do you think you'll save me from the pain by taking your life? Are you kidding? That would only cause more pain. Don't you dare threaten to hurt yourself; just because you hurt me doesn't mean you have permission to hurt yourself. You need to own your actions like a man and fight for your family."

Kyle hunched forward in a ball, moaning and groaning, then the pitch of his cries turned to a deep bellow.

He cried, "I can't live with myself for hurting you, Serena. You are my whole world, and I don't know what I would do without you. I just want to die."

I realized he was going down a dark path, and I couldn't live with myself if he spiraled out of control. I was deeply wounded, angry, and hurt, but I was unwilling to give up on him (on us) this quickly. We made amends with his parents, blended our families, completed a fitness competition, celebrated our wedding, and spent the last two years building our lives together. As shocked and overwhelmed as I was at this moment, I was determined to set aside my pain to protect him. I inhaled deeply, sat straight up in my seat, pulled him toward me, wrapped my arms around him, and wept together.

I knew it would take courage to stay, just as it would take courage to walk away. I truly believed that love never fails, and I realized at this moment that people do. Yet the purpose of love was not the absence of failure; instead, it was accepting that failure was a part of the process. I just never realized that I would be facing insurmountable pain only a few weeks after our wedding day.

The following day I returned to work; as I approached my office that morning, I relived the trauma that had occurred the day before, yet I had no choice but to hide my pain and pretend everything was okay.

Kyle sent me a message saying he couldn't face the day and was going home early after being at the gym for only a few hours. Instead of focusing on the pressing projects in my inbox, I reviewed every message, photo, and video Angela sent. The conversations were filled with professions of their love for one another, nude pictures, and explicit discussions detailing what they would do to each other the next time they were together. My stomach felt nauseous, yet I couldn't stop reading every message. I noticed that some of the videos he sent her were videos I took of him singing and playing the guitar to me. I could feel the anger rising in my blood, yet I kept going. The following message I saw was about me; several months prior, I was in our master bathroom and noticed a strain of long black hair on the tile; I picked it up and curiously asked Kyle where it came from as I tossed it aside. I remember him laughing and suggesting that it probably was from one of his sisters the last time they visited. However, in the messages between him and Angela, he scoffed while sharing the story with her and was proud that he conned me into thinking it was from someone else.

I couldn't hold back the tears as I quickly closed my office door. Just as I turned toward my desk, I received a call from Kyle and hesitantly answered. Kyle was slurring and begging me to come home.

He cried, "Please, baby, come home. I don't know what I will do if I'm here alone, and I need you with me."

I replied, "Have you been drinking?"

Kyle continued to slur his words together between gasps and heavy wails, pleading for me to come home. I tried to calm him down by encouraging him to breathe, but his cries kept getting louder and more uncontrollable. The children were in school, and my parents, who were living with us at the time, had been away for the day, so I knew he was home alone. I hadn't told anyone what had happened, and I knew I needed to check on him during my lunch hour. I asked Kyle to rest and reassured him I would be there soon.

As I approached the house, I felt a nervous energy; my stomach was already in knots as I rushed up the stairs to our bedroom. Kyle was lying on the floor with his arms and legs sprawled on the carpet. I scanned the room and noticed an empty handle of Vodka and an open bottle of pills tipped over beside him. I panicked, trying to wake him up, shaking him from side to side, but his body was limp. He wasn't responding to my voice; I straddled my legs around him, holding his head up in my hands, trying to get a response, but nothing. Finally, I screamed his name, yet his face was pale, and his body was fully submerged in the carpet. I jumped up to grab my phone, frantically calling the police, tears streaming down my face and my voice shuttering.

I cried, "Please, I need an ambulance! I think my husband has overdosed, and he's not responding. Please hurry!"

The dispatching operator tried to calm me down and walk me through taking his pulse, but I was crying uncontrollably and couldn't find his pulse. Within minutes there was a knock at the door; I ran toward the stairs sliding down frantically to let the paramedics in, and when I approached the door, there were two police officers.

I was stumbling over my words to explain the situation, then suddenly, Kyle ran down the stairs behind me, out the back door, and fled from the police. The officers turned to chase him, demanding that I stay in the house. I was beside myself, spinning in circles, and couldn't grasp what had occurred. I climbed onto the loveseat in the formal living room peeking through the blinds and watching as the police officers chased my husband down the residential street. They quickly disappeared in the distance, and I knelt over with my head between my knees, weeping.

I pleaded with God, "Why God? Why? Why is this happening? Please bring him home safely. Please, God! Please."

Several minutes passed, and I heard someone approaching; I wiped my tears, running toward the entry. My parents returned home from running errands, my mind started racing. *Oh no! What should I say? There is a police car in our driveway. Shit! Shit! Shit. Shit. Shit. I have to tell the truth; I can't hide this from them.*

With mascara running down my face, I rushed toward them and quickly blurted out everything that had happened. My mom and dad paused in shock, then reached their arms around me once they realized how broken I was—reassuring me that everything would be okay and holding me tightly as I fell into their arms. The two officers finally returned, approaching my parents and me letting us know that they couldn't keep up with Kyle and that he had disappeared a few blocks away. They handed me their card and said to call them if he returned.

My parents offered to pick up the children from school and take them out for a few hours, so I could search for Kyle, promising me that this would stay between us and encouraging me to take the rest of the week off work so I could process everything. I knew they were right; I could barely focus and called the CEO to whom I reported and informed him of a family emergency, expressing that I needed to take a few days off. He seemed skeptical as I recently returned from my honeymoon, yet he approved my request.

I wandered the streets around our neighborhood, calling Kyle's name, knocking on doors, searching behind hedges, peeking over fences; and as the sun began to set, so did my defeat, and with my head down, lowering my chin to my chest, I hopelessly walked home. Then, finally, I saw the headlights of my parent's car as they pulled into the driveway with the excitement of the little voices calling out, "Mommy!" as they jumped out of the backseat showering me in hugs and kisses. I ushered them upstairs, dodging their questions about where Kyle was, and eagerly rushed them through their baths, saying our nightly prayers and tucking them into bed.

    I sat alone in our bedroom with my eyes glazed over, fluttering around the room, never settling on a specific object yet vacantly staring at the wall, exhausted from the flood of emotions wholly dissociated from any logical thoughts. Then, finally, I heard the front door open and close, so I jumped up, rushing toward the stairs. I paused at the top banister to observe Kyle as he quietly stood with a gaunt appearance, lethargic and in a state of withdrawal; he looked up at me with bloodshot eyes and a hollow expression.

    There was a knock at the door, Kyle turned slowly to open it, and the police officers were waiting to arrest him. I stumbled down the stairs frantically to stop them; time and space stood still as the room began to spin in slow motion. My parents rushed into the entryway, confused by all the commotion.

    I yelled, "No! Please stop! He's safe now."

    The officers demanded to take him in and turned Kyle toward the wall while they handcuffed him, escorting him out of the house. Adian woke up, ran toward the stairs, and saw the police handcuffing Kyle.

    I held Adian in my arms, swaying back and forth at the staircase's top landing. I placed my hands over Adian's ears so he wouldn't hear the officers explaining to my parents that they were detaining Kyle for a fifty-one-fifty and admitting him to a psychiatric institution for a seventy-two-hour hold to assess his mental health. Then, as the door shut behind them and they drove away, the voices around me became inaudible, with only the sharp sound of ringing in my ears.

I was brought to my knees and couldn't find the strength to pull myself up. My mother guided us to the main bedroom and tucked us into bed. I was lying motionless, watching my son sleep as the tears soaked my pillow.

The next seventy-two hours seemed like an eternity. Angela continued sending me messages, and I became obsessed with uncovering the truth. I searched the internet desperately, seeking answers, and it revealed more than I had anticipated. I found Kyle's profile on a dating app and found several aliases for Angela; her real name was Jessica, and she posted several classified advertisements soliciting sexual favors for men with money or what they referred to as sugar daddies. She had two small children and was previously married, losing her rights as a mother during the divorce. Jessica also frequented the gym where Kyle was employed, and she was a bartender at a dive bar in a run-down neighborhood nearby and rented a room just minutes from our house. I found her former husband on a social media website, mustered up the courage to introduce myself, and asked if he would be willing to help me piece the truth together to find clarity. Instead, his new wife responded to my message, expressing her remorse for my situation, and sharing that she knew Kyle and had met him with Jessica a few times. She verified that Jessica was never pregnant but validated that all the remaining information was accurate. I felt an odd sense of peace knowing they didn't have a child together, yet with the timeline of events provided; I realized that Kyle and Jessica had been together for over a year, even during my trip to Chicago.

The dreadful day finally came as I drove to the psychiatric facility where Kyle was being discharged. The lobby was sterile with bare walls, an analog clock ticking loudly, diluting the sounds of patients mumbling amongst themselves, and black marks stained the linoleum floors as a silent memory of those who tried to retreat.

As I waited for Kyle to be escorted to the lobby, I observed the fluorescent lights flickering down the dimly lit hall, windowless rooms, and concrete walls, each with a bare mattress and stainless-steel toilet. The environment was an obviously constructed metaphor for emotional indifference. I struggled to swallow as he approached; his skin was pale, and darkness circled his eyes with an expression that could strike a knife through my heart. We drove away in silence as I could feel his animosity with his back turned against me. Finally, in a monotone voice, he began to speak.

He said, "Where do we go from here?"

I parked the car a few blocks from our house and asked that he turn to look at me, he refused, and I asked again.

I said, "Kyle, I have never loved anyone the way I love you, and what you did tore my heart out of my chest, but I will not give up on you."

Kyle slowly turned to face me, and with tears streaming down his face, he broke down and cried in my arms.

I said, "We will overcome this together."

I knew with every ounce of my being that this would be a treacherous journey, yet I was willing to stand beside him despite the pain he had caused. I was determined to prove my worth.

Shortly after the dust settled from all the commotion, life slowly returned to our usual routine. Oddly, Kyle insisted on getting a vasectomy. I couldn't quite grasp why he was so adamant about having the procedure; after all that we had been through. I reluctantly agreed, but my heart never fully settled on his decision, and I was too broken to fight another battle. First, Kyle scheduled the procedure without communicating with me; then, when he confirmed the appointment, he told me he needed me to drive him home. I had a foreboding feeling in my gut, and with a silent resentment, I agreed. Finally, the day arrived, and Kyle seemed almost relieved, only furthering my suspicions. *Why does he feel the need to do this now? Why is he being so persistent?*

I sat quietly beside Kyle in the waiting room, weighing unanswered questions. *Why did he set the appointment so soon after I found out about Angela? What else is he hiding?*

The nurse called Kyle's name, he grabbed my hand, and I followed closely behind him as the nurse escorted us to a small cold operating room. Kyle undressed from the waist down, wrapped a gown around his exposed body, and sat on the edge of the exam table. I looked to the left and noticed a stainless-steel tray slightly covered with several surgical tools. My stomach turned in knots as the nurses prepared Kyle for the procedure. They cleaned and shaved around the area, taped his stomach, and explained the following steps as the doctor came in. The doctor calmly described the procedure and administered a local anesthetic through an injection to numb the area. Kyle squeezed my hand tightly while I silently wished he would feel the pain. After a few minutes, the anesthetic set in, and the doctor began. I curiously peeked through Kyle's gown while the doctor took a scalpel and made a small incision. Kyle's heart rate increased, and he breathed heavily to calm his nerves. After the cutting and tugging, the doctor cauterized the tube. I could smell the tissue burning, nauseating and sweet, putrid, and foul, similar to the smell of leather charred over a flame. Kyle nervously babbled to the doctor, boasting that he had no pain, just an uncomfortable tightness and tugging.

Once the procedure was complete, Kyle slowly sat upright, moaning as I helped him get dressed. Finally, he sat slumped over in a wheelchair while I escorted him to the car, lifted him gently into the passenger seat, and then buckled his seatbelt. As we drove away, I stared through the windshield with my eyes glazed over; unrelenting thoughts circulated through my mind, drowning out the sound of his voice.

I struggled to understand what I had done so wrong. I thought I gave Kyle everything he needed; I was a good mother, we were madly in love, we had an incredible sex life, and I was successful and in the best shape of my life. I blamed myself; this is what I deserved for tearing his family apart, for working too much and being distracted with the kids, the new house, and the wedding planning. The self-destructive thoughts percolated, and I believed I would never be enough for him.

Chapter 17: Rebuilding

As Kyle and I made love for the first time after the infidelity, I lay beneath him, fighting back the tears, yet the moment I closed my eyes, visuals of Kyle and Angela ran like wildfire through my mind. My throat tightened with the intensity of his movements as I held my breath, intentionally trying to focus on the present moment. Kyle felt my energy and paused to adjust his eyes in the darkness as he leaned closer to kiss my cheek. He tasted the saltiness of my tears on his lips, placing my head on his chest as I wept in his arms. I sighed heavily, letting my head drop buried under his arm, yet a sword of deep sorrow pierced my soul, turning a silent cry into deep whimpers and moans, unable to draw a breath with saliva filling my throat. I wept so hard that my words bled together, trembling in my voice.

I asked, "Why? What did I do so wrong?"

Kyle tightened his grip around my quivering body, nudging me closer and with his voice stammering.

He said, "You are more than enough. This is not your fault. It's mine. I was weak, searching for something to fill the void inside me."

Kyle paused for a moment holding me in the silence. The night was dark, with subtle reflections of light from the moon cascading against our bedroom walls; my swollen eyes fixated on the faint shadows as he gently glided his fingers through my hair.

He said, "Serena, you are perfect in every way. This is my burden to carry, and I will do whatever it takes to earn your trust. I'm so sorry that I hurt you."

My heart was vacant, and the pedestal that once held him high above all others shattered. The unspoken and unwarranted power I poured into him through my adoration was too much to bear. I destroyed his ability to be human, imperfect, and make mistakes leaving him isolated and empty. I blamed myself for not seeing his struggle or recognizing the pressure of being everything to everyone.

I surrendered in his arms, clenching onto his skin and pulling him closer.

I whispered, "I forgive you. Can you forgive me?"

He sat upright in confusion, and I turned my gaze toward him, looking deep into my tired eyes.

He said, "Thank you for loving me unconditionally despite the pain I have caused. But I don't deserve your forgiveness. Let alone, why would you need forgiveness? You did nothing to deserve this?"

I interrupted his chatter by placing my finger over his mouth and reminding him of our vows. I shared that I could've created a better experience for him, so he didn't have to hide his emotions. I knew I was distracted by the whirlwind of changes circling us, and I could have been more present. Kyle slowly melted into bed, embracing my head in his hand, then kissed me on the forehead as we fell asleep.

I realized I was constantly distracted balancing three children, navigating co-parenting conflicts with our former partners, sports, my career, and my parents living with us. As a result, we rarely had privacy or time for each other, and the days and weeks blended together.

I never truly felt safe communicating boundaries; the volatile relationships in my past left me feeling disconnected and responsible for every situation. I lived in a false illusion that I could control and fix everything by simply looking within to identify what I did to fuel the problem. Yet, reality set in in the quiet moments when I was alone. I knew that we couldn't overcome this on our own.

I searched online for hours, eager to find a solution or resource that could bring us back to where we were before our lives unraveled. Finally, after reviewing countless websites, one stood out to me. It was a simple statement: A lot of us are emotionally drained and mentally tapped out because we're looking for what we need in others before providing it to ourselves—first.

I felt it in my gut. This program resonated with me more than any other website, article, retreat, or counseling session. The more I read about the program, the more it validated that we needed it. It was an alternative approach to traditional marriage counseling, marriage retreats, marriage seminars, and workshops. Instead, it was a four-day program that included a combination of mental games, drills, intense self-discovery, and experiential exercises to overcome marital challenges. The next session was out of state, and without a second thought, I registered for the program and booked flights for us to attend. Kyle didn't even question my decision. I knew he was struggling with his own demons and was just as eager to put this behind us so we could move forward.

The first-day session started at eight o'clock in the morning, so we arrived early, anxious, and uncertain about what to expect. When we checked into the hotel, the concierge directed us to a large conference room. I could feel the tension rising as we walked through the long hallway. The facilitators locked the doors with over a hundred couples outside the conference room, waiting for the session to begin. I scanned the hotel corridor, curious to observe the other couples; many individuals stood alone, others stood in opposition, and only a few stood beside each other. Again, I could feel the energy in the air like a dark cloud of heartache and hopelessness. I held Kyle closely beside me as I absorbed the emotions in the room.

Finally, the doors opened dramatically with intense music playing as the coordinators firmly directed us to our seats. The primary facilitator had a military demeanor; he seemed stern and authoritative. He stood in the center of the room, surrounded by chairs, and waited quietly, observing each person as we found our seats. He was tall with a cleanly shaven bald head and a thick mustache covering his upper lip. The crowd's murmur silenced as he began to speak, giving him their full attention. He introduced himself as David and started talking with a deep, shrewd tone.

David said, "What you are about to experience will not be easy; this will be the hardest thing you've ever done. I have one rule; you give this program one hundred percent. If you're unwilling to make that commitment, I ask that you stand up and leave now."

The crowd began whispering among themselves as he patiently waited, scanning the room.

He repeated, "This is your last opportunity. So once again, if you are not willing to give one hundred percent, I'm asking that you leave now."

One man stood up and left the room, leaving his wife behind. She turned to reach for him, but the man refused her, and with a defeated expression, she looked to the floor, shaking her head. David knelt before her and instructed her that she could not attend the session without her husband. One of the facilitators escorted her out of the room as the crowd stared in silence. David stood in front of the room and repeated the statement.

He said, "If you are unwilling to do the work, you shouldn't be here."

Holding my breath, gulping quietly with my legs shaking, I gripped Kyle's hand as the unsettling fear of what we were about to experience set in. The first exercise was to separate from your spouse and find a partner. I didn't quite understand how we would work on our marriage problems by being away from each other, yet I followed along and stood beside a woman with long blonde hair and glanced nervously at her, hoping she would pair with me. Instead, she acknowledged my gesture, and we validated our partner selection. Next, they asked us to sit in a dyad, explaining that we face our chairs toward each other and sit upright, allowing our knees to touch. The facilitators then instructed us to choose the letter A or B by tapping one another on the knee. Next, the person who selected A shares with your dyad partner what your spouse says or does that angers you, informing B to listen without a response. Finally, my partner began to speak in a monotone voice.

She said, "My husband doesn't appreciate me. He doesn't acknowledge when I do things for him, and when I ask for validation, he becomes irritated."

The facilitator paused and instructed partner A to explain their "triggers" by not blaming their spouse but instead using "I feel" statements that describe how it makes them feel. My partner sat in speculation and then proceeded to restate her emotions.

She said, "I don't feel appreciated. When I do things for my husband, I feel like he doesn't acknowledge me, and I feel like he becomes irritated when I ask for validation."

The leading facilitator, David, explained, "Shifting the statements from blaming to recognizing your emotions will help give you perspective. Partner B, your turn."

I sat quietly for a few minutes contemplating what to say; I took a deep breath, and with my voice shaking, I hesitantly began to share.

I said, "I feel unlovable, inadequate, and unattractive because my husband was with another woman. I'm terrified that I will never be enough for him, and I feel like it's my fault."

My partner reached for my hands, empathetically staring into my eyes as I struggled to speak. David scanned the room, then added.

David said, "This is not an opportunity to comfort your partner. The rules of the exercise are to listen to their feelings. It's not your job to fix their issues; it's your job to fix your own."

My partner quickly sat up in her chair; her body language seemed annoyed yet reluctantly compliant as she looked toward David rolling her eyes and crossing her arms. David explained the second part of the exercise and asked us to share our past experiences and identify the root of our triggers. A sudden burst of clarity struck me as I realized the reason for the exercise was not to victimize ourselves but to uncover the issues within us that led us to where we are.

Once we understood the past experiences that led to our current actions, we were asked to share bad traits or situations that we observed with our parents; then the following questions were "How have their hurt, bad traits, or situations been passed onto you? How can you break the generations of damage and keep from passing it on to your children?"

The questions were powerful and profoundly enlightening; I felt connected with my dyad partner and could break through the root of my feelings. However, I wasn't prepared for the next exercise. The facilitators guided us to observe the room. They asked that we sit in a group of four with two females and two males, excluding our spouse. I was curious as to why each exercise separated us from working through issues with our spouses, yet I continued to follow along. David instructed each person to choose a group member to represent their mother, father, and mate. Then asked that each person take turns confronting our fears, pain, and past trauma by addressing the member as if they were our actual father, mother, and mate by telling them how they hurt us.

My group selected me to begin; I closed my eyes for a moment to muster up the courage to face one of my deepest fears. I was looking into the eyes of the man sitting to my right, a complete stranger addressing him as my biological father.

I said, "Father, you took my virginity before the age of five; you tormented me and made me believe that I was only worth what I could give you. You stole my innocence and made me believe that I would only receive love by sacrificing my body."

The stranger beside me began to tremble in his seat as his eyes welled up with tears. I spoke with courage and conviction and then turned to the woman on my left.

I said, "Mother, I know you experienced so much pain in your life, and yet you chose to be blinded by a man that violated you and your children, placing us in a dangerous home with an evil man. Which ultimately led to my sister, and I being tossed from one foster home to the next. Why didn't you protect me?"

The woman beside me took a deep breath and locked her gaze in mine. The more I spoke, the more I realized how much I had held inside, and my heart started racing as I looked toward the man across from me. A surge of anger flowed through my body as I glared in his direction. The strange man across from me noticed my body language shift and began to tilt his head, looking toward the floor.

I said, "Kyle, look at me."

The man quickly scrambled in his seat, lifting his gaze toward mine.

I said, "I trusted you. I poured my heart and soul into you, and instead of protecting my heart, you chose to humiliate, betray, and make me feel like I was worthless. You placed your need for attention, admiration, and temporary gratification above everything else without considering my feelings or the consequences. Then, in addition to dealing with the heartbreak of your decision, you threatened to take your own life, sending me on a rollercoaster of emotions."

The words fell from my lips in a torrent as the man across from me sat in disbelief. Once I realized the outpour of emotions I had spewed onto strangers, I immediately felt ashamed and began apologizing. Yet, in the midst of my attempt to backpedal, the small group leaned in to comfort me, validating my feelings and encouraging me to be vulnerable.

I felt an intimate connection with each person as the exercise continued, and they shared their experiences. At the end of this exercise, it taught us how to forgive our parents and spouse for our past hurts, realizing that forgiveness doesn't mean tolerance, yet forgiveness of others allows us to be set free from holding on to the past. Then, each member circled the group once more, verbalizing forgiveness for each behavior that created their self-limiting beliefs.

The intense exercises continued throughout the four-day workshop, with each day starting at eight o'clock in the morning and ending at nine o'clock in the evening. The days were exhausting and emotionally challenging but kept us engaged the entire time working towards self-discovery, forgiving others, self-forgiveness, resolving trauma, improving communication, overcoming triggers, and repairing past pain. As a result, Kyle and I felt more connected and aligned than ever before. It seemed like our marriage was resurrected and gave us hope for the future.

After returning home, we settled back into our daily routine. We were more transparent and open about our feelings and issues, yet the weight of rebuilding trust seemed unbearable. I knew Kyle struggled with a constant need for affirmation and attention, so I circulated ideas about satisfying his needs. *I want him to feel like he can be open and honest with me, but I don't want to be controlling or overbearing. What if I made things more exciting? I want him to feel like he can share his deepest desires without feeling judged or rejected. Maybe if I fulfilled his fantasies, he wouldn't want anyone else.*

It started with little things like lingerie, adult toys, boudoir photos, sexy videos, role-play, sexting, and dabbling in taboo fetishes. Then it quickly escalated to more risky behaviors such as light bondage and exhibitionism. The more we experimented, the more transparent he became about his fantasies. I started feeling intensely connected to him; he poured out new ideas and got excited about even more possibilities.

One evening after a hot steamy sexual experience, we laid in each other's arms, sweating and panting. I looked at Kyle, observing his mischievous smirk, and leaned in to lay on his chest. His heart was beating rapidly, and his body was still shaking; he giggled quietly, and I could sense another wild idea brewing in his mind. I knew the next adventure would need to be even more extreme to satisfy him. I wrestled with my thoughts for a few moments before quickly blurting out.

I asked, "What do you think about joining a swingers club? Of course, I would only want us to be together, but it might be exciting to watch other couples."

Kyle immediately jumped up with excitement, then recognized his overzealous response and composed himself by pausing to analyze my body language. He gently leaned in, placing his hands on my face as he intently examined my expression, piercing my soul with his hazel green eyes.

He asked, "Would you be comfortable in that environment? I know my past actions have caused you deep pain, and I wouldn't want you to go through that again."

Kyle had a rebellious spirit that enticed me. I intentionally responded because I didn't want my insecurities to diminish his vulnerability.

I said, "I want to experience this together. As long as we create clear boundaries and don't participate in sexual behaviors with anyone else, this could be our little secret."

A part of me wanted to give him this experience so he wouldn't be tempted to stray outside of the relationship while keeping our sex life exciting. However, the other side of me knew it was uncharted territory and hoped this would allow us to explore together without creating more damage.

It was a swirling plethora of emotions as Kyle, and I explored a new terrain of possibilities to spice up our sex life and deepen our relationship. We searched numerous websites, narrowing our search to find a swing "lifestyle" event or location that was upscale, exclusive, and highly confidential. We discussed our fears and reservations, openly assessing how to respond in a worst-case scenario, and even established clear boundaries to ensure that we both felt secure and safe in this new environment.

We were curious yet extremely nervous – and our anxiety manifested in the funniest ways possible. I would find myself lost in my thoughts in the middle of the day, thinking about how the event would unfold. Kyle would regularly get that mischievous grin and start acting playful and giddy. The closer we got to the date of our first event, the more excitement ran through our minds. We had numerous conversations questioning what to expect. *What kind of people would be there? What experiences would we be expected to participate in? Could we just watch? What if we see someone we know? What if it's a cult, and they murder us?*

The day finally arrived; I spent the entire afternoon preparing for the evening, from nails, hair, and makeup, and trying on several outfits until I felt comfortable, sexy, and confident. As we arrived at the event location, the club resembled a speakeasy. The only indication we were in the right place was an unadorned, unmarked door in an otherwise nondescript downtown area with no signage. At check-in, we were greeted by a friendly host and asked to provide our photo ID; we were each given a wristband to enter. Once the host realized that we were new to the lifestyle, she was polite, knowledgeable, practiced, and well-versed in describing what to expect and assured us that it was a safe, sexy environment. The host encouraged us to participate in an orientation, including a guided tour of the club's various areas and playrooms. She provided rules, expectations, suggestions, advice on how couples interact, and information about the club's practices to ensure a safe and enjoyable experience for everyone attending. The tour was conducted in good taste and humor, allowing us to learn about the premises without trepidation. The host emphasized safety, cleanliness, and consent several times during the tour, which put our minds at ease.

As we curiously peeked around every corner, the club was oddly inviting. The space plan was open with dimly lit mood lighting. Near the dancefloor, they served 'naked sushi,' featuring two beautiful semi-nude women lying on a table surrounded by floral arrangements acting as a living, breathing human platter with sushi covering their bodies. Yet, their most intimate anatomy was concealed tastefully with flowers and leaves.

Strobe lights sent streams of color in every direction; the speakers vibrated the room as we watched couples entangled in the beat on the dance floor. Pheromones filled the air with a natural yet spellbinding effect that made it impossible not to be captivated by the intense emotions flowing through the dance floor. A maze of playrooms surrounded the nightclub, also known as a backroom or black room. A public playroom is a room, typically at a lounge, sex club, erotic cruise, or swinger hotel takeover event, where couples can discreetly play with one another. The host described the etiquette of a public playroom by using examples of prime directives and communication norms and emphasized that consent is required to proceed with any interaction. For example, single men were prohibited from entering the club as couples and single females were pre-screened and verified before entry was granted. In addition, the host often emphasized discretion as the members who attended these events were typically in high-profile positions, such as lawyers, doctors, business owners, celebrities, and public officials.

Cascading curtains surrounded the play area from the ceiling to the floor, sectioning off small private spaces for those curious but not yet ready to invite others in and large group play areas designed for those who enjoyed being watched and participating. The platform beds ranged from full to king-size mattresses with tightly fitted silk sheets, a mound of pillows, and sheer drapes flowing around each side, creating a semi-private experience.

The host left us to explore on our own. I could hear the faint sounds of moans and panting in the distance, muffled by the bass of the loud music. Kyle swirled his tongue around mine, licking the sweetness from our lips as we savored each other with sweat dripping down our bodies. We locked our gaze while we flowed with the rhythm of the music. Kyle pushed my hair away from my face, kissing my neck and touching my body.

Kyle whispered, "I don't want anyone else; I only want you."

He reached for my hand, guiding me to a private area. We made love for hours, listening to the sounds of erotica filling the club.

In that nightclub, we got what we craved: total permission to feel euphoria and an untouchable bond. It was intoxicating and fed our primal curiosity for this forbidden underground world. After experiencing the passion of that night, it sparked a fire within us that only made us crave one another even more, taking our sex life to an unreachable level.

Discretion is paramount in the swinging culture, mostly because people fear exposure. This taboo lifestyle has a stigma that could hurt relationships, damage careers, and destroy reputations. Little did I know I was about to gain a deeper understanding of how this secret world would impact my own life.

Chapter 18: Exposed

In the following weeks, I was submerged in work preparing to present a comprehensive marketing strategy to the Presidents and several high-level executives at my work. I felt unsettled when I arrived at the office on the morning of the presentation. The executive office was desolate, with only the typing sounds from one administrative assistant. I approached her, questioning where the management team was, and she informed me that the meeting location had changed and provided me with the new address. I gathered my laptop and handouts and rushed to the meeting. I arrived shortly after the first speaker began, quietly finding a seat around the conference table. I was slightly nervous as I was unprepared for a change of location, but I was still in high spirits because I was excited to share the results of the campaigns with my team. The session broke for lunch rather quickly, and the President asked that I stay behind. Assuming it was to discuss my presentation, I eagerly waited for all the associates to leave the room. I noticed two members of senior management stayed behind, so I patiently waited for them to exit. Instead, they sat on each side of the President at the large conference table and asked me to find a seat across from them. Curious and anxious to share my recent work, I began to open my laptop. The President motioned me to stop.

He said, "You won't be needing that right now."

One of the executives stood up, closed the conference room door, and found his seat beside the President. The three men seemed unusually withdrawn and oddly uncomfortable; I tried to lighten the conversation with a playful joke, yet no one laughed. Instead, the President to whom I reported began to speak while the two senior managers beside him sat with their eyes fixated on the marble table.

He said, "Do you have something that you want to share with us?"

Uncertain as to what he was referring to, I jumped right into my thoughts about the presentation. The President, seemingly uninterested, abruptly stopped me by clearing his throat.

He said, "I received some personal information about you this morning that was printed and left anonymously on my desk. Do you have anything you would like to share?

Wrinkling my brow, I examined their expressions as I tried to decipher the question. The President was a three-time New York Times and Wall Street Journal Bestselling Author, known as an expert in Organizational Culture, and highly regarded in the Mormon church. Although I didn't share his beliefs, I admired his accomplishments and aspired to earn his approval. He typically had a calm demeanor unless he was angry, which was sometimes unpredictable and harsh. He was always clean-shaven, his freshly trimmed hair with white and silver highlights gracefully framing his face. The prominent fine lines around his eyes and lips formed a stern expression, and his perfectly pressed suit seamlessly fit snugly around his shoulders as he tapped his finger on a manila folder placed before him. I felt the tension rising in the room with every tap as I contemplated how to respond to such an ambiguous question.

He solemnly opened the folder, pushing a document toward me across the conference table. I feverishly began reviewing the document and quickly realized it was a copy of a personal email I sent Kyle reminiscing about our erotic experience. My body temperature rose, and my heart started racing with each line I read. My eyes began to twitch as disturbing thoughts ran through my mind. *How could they see my personal email? Who would've had access to my credentials?*

I scanned the top of the email to confirm the address was my personal account, yet my stomach twisted in knots with the explicit details outlined in the message to my husband. I couldn't find the strength to lift my head to look the President in the eye as my lips quivered and tears started rolling down my cheeks.

He said, "We have already terminated the person who anonymously printed the document. However, you accessed your personal email from company property, and per the handbook, this violates our company policy. We are a public-facing company, and the information in your message could damage our reputation."

Not only was I the only female Vice President in the organization, but I also used my work computer to write a sexually explicit email to my husband. Of course, this would be forbidden in any company, let alone a highly religious one, so I understand their apprehension. Yet, I pleaded for another opportunity to prove my value.

I said, "I take full accountability for my actions. I am humiliated and ashamed. Is there any way I can earn your trust?"

The President halted my stammering statements; I looked up with my lips trembling while the two executives sitting beside the President couldn't even look me in the eye as they shook their heads in disapproval and disgust. I quickly tucked my chin into my chest and tried to clench my hands from shaking in my lap. My boss sternly placed a second document in front of me.

He said, "This document is a legal agreement stating you voluntarily resign from your position. If you sign this statement, you will receive a severance package, and we ask that you leave immediately. If you do not wish to sign this document, I advise you to consider other options."

The heavy weight of this letter sent a stream of muscle strain throughout my body; I could barely lift my neck to acknowledge his voice. I sat silently scanning the document, with my hands tightly pressed between my thighs, shaking uncontrollably; my throat tightened while I reached for a pen to sign the agreement. He handed me an envelope and asked one of the executives to escort me to my vehicle. Frozen in fear with my knees locked, I slowly gathered my belongings and left the room in utter humiliation.

The devastation crept in as I drove away, shifting from shock and disbelief. What I hoped would save my marriage destroyed my career. Anxiety and fear surfaced in places I never expected. I didn't simply lose my job and financial security; I lost my identity.

The tears poured out and flooded my face making it impossible to see the road. Finally, I pulled over to compose myself. Still, the pain was insurmountable, as though I had lost my livelihood; I was humiliated and defeated, shrouded in the misery of my own making.

I had lost the one thing I had spent my entire adult life trying to achieve as it fell through my fingertips. I spent years climbing the corporate ladder, and now at thirty-three years old, I single-handedly destroyed everything. The emotional impact extended far beyond the financial stress. The relationships I formed throughout my career were shattered instantly by my careless act, prompting a veil of shame, anger, and sorrow.

I lost a part of myself when I learned about the infidelity, yet the piercing pain of being publicly exposed seemed even more humiliating. As I arrived home, I knew I had to face the consequences of my actions and tell Kyle what had happened, but I reluctantly sat in the driveway, sinking into my seat, trying to collect my thoughts before entering the house. Then, with my head against the steering wheel, I heard a tap on the window, and as I looked through the window, Kyle slowly opened the door.

He said, "Love, what are you doing at home so early? How did the presentation go?"

The words spewed out of my mouth in a panic as I hunched over in my seat, rocking back and forth, breathing rapidly, gasping for air. Kyle gently slid his arms around me, trying to calm my nerves as he guided me into the house, but my knees buckled, and I fell to the floor, crying uncontrollably.

He said, "I can't understand what you're saying. Slow down and take a deep breath."

Kyle held me against his chest, slowly breathing in and out while encouraging me to inhale. Finally, I began to catch my breath while struggling to explain what had happened.

I said, "I logged into my personal email account online during my lunch hour when I sent you those emails, and someone logged into my computer and printed our private messages, then left them on my boss's desk. So, they asked me to resign."

Kyle was enraged and appalled, demanding that I get a lawyer and ranting about how unfair it was, but my guilt drowned out the sound of his voice as I knew it was my fault; I deserved this. He saw the defeat in my expression, with my eyes glazed over. He paused, placing his hands against my cheeks as he looked into my swollen eyes.

He said, "Love, I know how much this job meant to you, but you are capable of much more."

His thoughtful words fell on deaf ears as I used my last ounce of strength to pull myself up and climb into bed. I woke up the following day with a delusive feeling: the whole world around me was on its way to work as I submerged myself under the covers in a pool of guilt. I felt my life slowly rolling into an abyss of inadequacy, losing my sense of purpose and meaning. I refused to pull myself out of bed for several days while Kyle patiently consoled me.

Once I finally found the strength to get up, Kyle lovingly encouraged me to search for another position to regain my confidence. I was disheartened, but I knew I had to pull myself out of the pit of despair, so I began to update my resume while searching for positions online. Every job submission seemed daunting as I rehearsed what I would say about why I was unemployed during an interview. Finally, after several hours of searching, I closed my browser and went downstairs to clear my head. My mom was sitting at the dining room table. She knew what had happened because I had poured my heart out to her days before. My mother glanced at me with a soft smile, then asked me to sit beside her, and with my head down, I leaned in as she kissed my forehead.

I said, "I don't know where to go from here."

She replied, "We've all been in a place where we felt hopeless. But you are not like everyone else. You're better."

I looked to the floor and laughed as she continued to speak.

She said, "You pour your heart and soul into everything you do, and if you invested even a quarter of yourself into your own business, there is no way you wouldn't be successful."

I scoffed and gently nudged her shoulder, motioning her to stop making jokes. However, I noticed that she wasn't laughing.

She said, "I'm serious. You should start your own business."

I replied, "Mom, you're just saying that because you love me. Plus, I'd like a paycheck."

She said, "Well, if you're not going to do it for yourself, then do it for me."

I rolled my eyes, laughing at her convincing argument in a sarcastic tone.

I replied, "You're so manipulative. You know I wouldn't do it for myself, but I would wholeheartedly do it for you."

She laughed and said, "I know. I'll even name the company."

As crazy as her idea sounded, my mom knew I would be determined to prove everyone who doubted me wrong if I did it for her. Plus, she wouldn't let me sit around feeling sorry for myself.

I replied, "Fine. I'll do it for you."

As much as I hated the idea of starting my own business, I wanted to prove to my mom that I could beat all the odds against me, so I stood up and marched back to the computer to begin researching the next steps. I wrestled with starting my own business because I never graduated college. Although I had over fifteen years of experience in marketing and advertising, I had yet to learn how to run a business, let alone start one. I led corporate marketing initiatives for multimillion-dollar companies. Yet, I felt unqualified, as if I was an imposter trying to fake my way through the process; however, the reality of having no income and starting a business with no knowledge of the treacherous journey ahead was just the beginning. Yet I desperately needed to provide for our family and knew Kyle's income alone wouldn't sustain us for long.

The following day I jumped out of bed with a newfound purpose. I had a healthy breakfast, dropped the kids off at school, then planted myself in an oversized chair near my desk, wearing my pajamas and fluffy slippers, ready to conquer the day. As I began typing, I heard my parents whispering while tiptoeing out the door. I giggled to myself, curious about what they were up to but continued to focus on the task at hand. A few hours passed, and I heard them laughing mischievously as they walked through the entryway.

Ken yelled, "Bumpkin! Bumpkin!"

A silly nickname that he came up with when I was twelve years old. My mom was giggling with excitement as they urged me to come downstairs. I skeptically walked down each step as they hid in the kitchen.

I said, "What are you two doing?"

They both laughed and giggled, standing before a box on the dining room table. Then, in unison, they stepped aside and shouted, "Surprise!" Confused and curious, I peeked my head around the corner to see what all the commotion was about, and just as I was about to turn the corner, my heart melted. The white box sitting on the table was a brand-new laptop and with joyful tears in their eyes, they handed it to me.

I said, "Oh my gosh! You didn't have to do this."

My dad responded, "I know we didn't have to. We wanted to because we love you."

My mom piped in, "Plus if you're going to start a business, you need the best of the best."

My parents reached around to pull me in for a group hug as I stood in awe of their incredible gift. Then, with tears of joy in my eyes, they embraced me, reminding me they believed in me while squeezing me tightly.

I said, "Thank you so much; this means the world to me."

My mom replied, "Now you have no excuses!"

I laughed nervously, thanking them repeatedly as I opened the box and started to set up my new laptop. I knew my parents didn't have the money for something this expensive, so it only fueled my determination.

Within a few months, I reduced our monthly expenses, created a business plan, set up the legal structure, registered with the state, opened a business bank account, designed a logo, and developed a basic website. I set up an office in a small loft above our staircase to create a semi-private area to work. Our savings account quickly dwindled with three kids, my parents, Kyle, and myself. So, while Kyle worked in the fitness industry, he would meet local business owners and set up meetings for me to offer marketing consulting services.

One afternoon as I intently focused on a small project for a local fish store, I heard the door open. I peeked above my laptop to see Kyle standing at the bottom of the staircase with his chin held high, shoulders back, chest thrust out, and legs spread wide in a proud stance with a gleam in his eye. I raised my brows curiously and hesitantly stood up.

I said, "Love, what are you doing home so early?"

In an animated posture, with a mischievous grin conveying surprise, he lifted his heels and raised his arms to emphasize his words.

He said, "I quit my job!!!"

If I hadn't stood up at that moment, I would have fallen out of my chair. But instead, I froze momentarily as my eyes widened, then began blinking rapidly as I tried to comprehend what Kyle said. Then, in a tone of disbelief.

I said, "Um, what?!"

He repeated, "I quit my job! If I'm going to sell anything, I'm going to sell something I believe in, and I believe in you!"

Anxiety and panic set in as I leaned against my desk for support, nervously smiling, pressing my fingers firmly behind my neck, slowly massaging the tension in my shoulders, needing a moment to process the information as I struggled to find the right words.

I said, "Oh, Love, I don't remember discussing this. But, um, how are we going to pay the bills?"

He ran up the stairs in high spirits and wrapped his arms around my waist with a giddy expression.

He said, "We'll figure it out! We can do anything together. We will be a power couple."

I tried to manage my expression as I could see his face light up with every word. My heart was pounding out of my chest, so I bit my lip and closed my eyes while Kyle hugged me tightly, practically jumping up and down. As terrified as I was to start a business with only one income, the idea of having no income and a family of seven gave me a mixture of conflicting emotions. Yet, I knew he was an incredible salesperson, and I couldn't let him see my doubt, so I clenched my arms around him and prayed for a miracle.

After a year of working fourteen-hour days, depleting our bank accounts, maxing out our credit cards, and reducing every expense down to the penny, we had forty dollars left in our bank account after paying the three employees we hired to support with design and projects. I was feeling deflated and exhausted, yet Kyle always seemed to dream big, never allowing himself to feel discouraged. Finally, Kyle and I scheduled a trip to attend a trade show in Las Vegas in our desperate attempt to pursue potential clients.

Before leaving the area, we met with a national home builder to present a marketing proposal. Although the meeting went well, I was deeply concerned that we wouldn't make payroll next week if we didn't close a new proposal within the next few days. In addition, I struggled with the idea that I was in a cozy office just a year prior with a six-figure income, and now I couldn't even afford to buy a cup of coffee.

As we pulled into the motel parking lot, an eerie feeling came over me, sending a stream of goosebumps down my body and raising the hair on my arms. The motel was in a questionable area, so I curiously searched the FBI Crime Report and realized that the crime rate in downtown Las Vegas was 93% higher than the national average. I skeptically looked at Kyle with my eyes wide open, silently questioning if we should check into the run-down motel, and with a carefree grin, he laughed.

He said, "It'll be a memory!"

Kyle had a way of making every experience a memorable one, so his smile always seemed to put my mind at ease. As we walked toward the entrance, the parking lot was full of old beat-up cars, and wrought iron covered all the motel windows. Kyle took my hand, kneading his fingers between mine, slowing his pace to match my uneven steps, and led me into the lobby. The foul smell of cigarette smoke pierced my nostrils as Kyle tapped his finger on the rusty service bell to ring the attendant. While he checked in, I stared blankly at the neon welcome sign in the window as I observed unusual characters tailgating in the parking lot.

The door to our room had two bolt locks with separate keys, and as we walked in, there was a false ceiling with paperboard squares supported by strips of metal and dingy yellow walls with rust stains. A heavy, oversized chair lined with a maroon fabric covered the seat. The carpet and blankets were damp, and the queen-sized bed had a thin red floral quilted comforter that smelled musky. An odd piece of plywood was strategically placed behind the door as an additional measure of security to prop against the door handle. The orange curtains covered the windows just enough that it felt like someone could watch you through the crack.

We were exhausted from the long drive and knew the following day would be busy at the trade show, so we snuggled close together on top of the dingy comforter, using towels for blankets as we listened to the guest in the adjoining rooms fighting and yelling.

The following day we walked up and down every aisle on the trade show floor for hours. I observed Kyle's charisma and charm in every interaction; his introduction and elevator pitch was effortless. Kyle was in his element, projecting sophistication and style, wearing a midnight blue three-piece suit, a classic light blue collared shirt, a sleek plaid pattern tie with a matching pocket square, and a subtle pair of leather dress shoes. He initiated small talk with light-hearted jokes, shaking hands, and exchanging business cards with every vendor. Kyle was devastatingly handsome with a magnetic personality that practically captivated any audience. After ten hours of dispensing all our energy, we decided to drive home instead of staying another night in the nightmare motel. On our drive home, I scanned through my emails and noticed that the home builder we met prior to our departure had signed the proposal electronically. Kyle glanced at me with an assured expression and winked.

He said, "I told you I can sell anything I believe in and believe in you."

My heart was overflowing with excitement as I leaned over, gently kissing him on the cheek.

I said, "I thought we were going to lose everything; thank you for believing in me."

Within just a few days, our business account went from forty dollars to twenty thousand dollars. We were officially in business.

Chapter 19: Unraveling

After a few years of running the business, with Kyle managing sales while I oversaw the operations, accounting, projects, training, and development, it felt like our fight to never give up was finally becoming fruitful. Yet, we quickly realized that the challenges never ceased. We fought to keep the business running for our family, team members, and survival. However, we fought even harder to prove ourselves to those who doubted we would make it past the first year in business.

There were moments when I felt like an imposter, unqualified, and that nothing I accomplished would ever be good enough. I made mistakes, failed many times, and hit rock bottom more than once. At times I felt like giving up on everything and everyone. Yet I continued to pour my heart into the people who believed in me, which gave me the strength to pick myself up and push forward.

As an entrepreneur, I felt alone. I lacked the same insight and executive leadership I received in a corporate environment. Although I loved my company and was proud of the team I had in place, I began to feel isolated and alone. I submerged myself into the business, working fourteen-hour days, juggling demands, putting out fires, and struggling with cash flow. As the company grew, my fears grew larger. My fear of failure fueled me to keep going, but my fear of not being good enough or intelligent enough wore me down, and just when I thought I couldn't go any further, I met Marshall Krupp.

I received a call from a woman who ran me through a series of business questions; then, she scheduled an appointment for me to meet with an Executive Advisor. She mentioned that Marshall was recognized for his ability to motivate, inspire, and facilitate the growth and development of entrepreneurs and business leaders. In addition to having a career as an entrepreneur for over thirty-three years, he provides C-level positions with support in crisis management, strategic advisory, and consulting. She also mentioned that Marshall facilitates several peer advisory boards for one of the world's largest CEO peer advisory organizations, coaching small and midsize business leaders who meet monthly to openly discuss issues, challenges, and threats within their companies.

I was only paying myself minimum wage, so I wasn't in a position to invest in a business advisor, but I was growing seemingly desperate for guidance, so I agreed to meet with him.

I met Marshall at a local coffee shop wearing a high-waisted black pencil skirt with a satin button-up blouse and black pumps. As I approached the restaurant, I scanned through the crowd and noticed an older man in his mid-sixties catch my eye. He was tall with broad shoulders, distinct features, a crystal shine to his bald head, and a bristly silver goatee that pleasantly shaped his face. He had a serious demeanor with scythe-shaped eyebrows. Yet, as I curiously looked into his eyes, they had the same startling clarity as a quiet river not touched by the wind. His Roman nose and half-dome cheekbones sat above an oaken jaw. As he smiled, I felt a rare emotion, a sense of external reassurance. Marshall reached out his hand to shake mine, and with my shoulders back and my chin held high, I firmly shook his hand, introduced myself, then sat at the table across from him.

I sat straight with a confident posture, yet Marshall didn't hesitate to assess me with a squint in one eye as he analyzed my body language. I could feel my legs slightly shaking with anxiety as the mood of the conversation quickly changed from a casual introduction to an interrogating interview. Finally, Marshall leaned back with his arms crossed just above his stomach and inquisitively began to ask me questions.

Marshall said, "Why are you here?"

Slightly confused by the question, I repositioned myself in my chair.

I said, "I own a marketing and advertising agency, and it was my understanding that you provided business owners with guidance."

He replied, "I didn't ask what you do. I asked why you are here."

My throat tightened as I realized I had already failed the first question. I leaned back in my seat, pondering the question, overthinking my following answer, but before I could speak.

Marshall said, "Don't overcomplicate it. Why are you here?"

I immediately looked to the floor, uncertain of how to respond, as he sat quietly looking in my direction. I lifted my head, catching a glimpse of his firm lock on my eyes, and at this moment, I decided to be completely vulnerable. My lips began to quiver as I tried to contain my emotions.

I said, "I feel alone."

He replied, "Good. Why do you feel alone?"

I immediately began rambling about how no one understood me, carrying the weight of the world on my shoulders, juggling a million tasks, working long hours, and feeling overwhelmed. Then, finally, Marshall stopped me from continuing down a rabbit trail and asked the question again.

He said, "Why do you feel alone?"

I said, "I feel alone... because I am afraid to fail. I'm afraid that I'm going to let everyone down."

Marshall replied, "Okay, good."

Confused by his response, with a scrunch in my eyebrows, I observed him as he sat quietly formulating his next question.

He said, "What do you need?"

I replied, "I don't know what I need."

Marshall asked, "Well if you did know, what would it be?"

His unusual yet insightful questions spun me into a cycle of confusion. I knew there had to be a reason for his methodology. I stared at the ceiling for a few moments as he sat silently. Then, finally, I began to share my story, giving him the grim details of how my life began and what led me to where I was. His demeanor changed as he listened intently to the explicit stories of my childhood, teenage years, and adult life. He uncrossed his arms, leaning forward with empathy as he felt my vulnerability pour from the depths of my heart. I paused momentarily, realizing the answer to his question was clear in my mind.

I said, "I need help."

When those words fell from my lips, I felt a weight lifted from my chest. My legs stopped shaking as I took a deep inhale.

I said, "I don't believe I have ever asked anyone for help."

Marshall responded, "Good. Thank you for being so vulnerable. I know I can help you, but I don't think you are qualified to join my peer advisory group."

My brief moment of relief immediately transformed into a fierce passion for proving that I was qualified. But before I could craft a response, Marshall began to explain the monthly investment to participate in a private advisory board and his executive coaching fee. I gulped, placing my chin on my chest, defeated that something this valuable would be beyond my reach.

I knew that I could barely afford to make payroll let alone increase my expenses, so I humbly thanked him for his time and left the meeting disappointed. As I drove home, I was determined to find a way, deliberating how to reduce expenses to take advantage of the opportunity, support, resources, and guidance I would gain.

However, Marshall struck a chord deep inside me, and this seemingly simple meeting ignited a newfound purpose.

I rushed into the house to tell Kyle about the meeting, giving him every detail as he watched my face light up excitedly. I knew we didn't have the money to join a business advisory group or hire an executive coach, so I found every opportunity to reduce our business and personal expenses. Once I realized we still couldn't afford it, I decided to forfeit my pay, as little as it was, to join the group.

I was still determining what to expect on my first day at the peer advisory group. Each group member was in a high-profile position, including chief executives, presidents, and other entrepreneurs. The goal is for each individual to dedicate one full day to meet as an advisory board to solve business challenges, discuss strategies, share best practices, and identify critical growth and performance issues. Needless to say, this was quite an intimidating crowd.

I was pleasantly surprised when I realized that each person was just like me. They each shared their experiences, struggles, legal issues, financial challenges, and personal stories of the isolation and exclusion they felt from running a business. I finally had a place where I felt understood and accepted yet challenged and inspired.

Within less than a year of working with Marshall, we grew from a two-person company starting in our loft with no income to leasing our first office space with a team of ten employees and over a million in revenue.

Together, Kyle and I overcame insurmountable obstacles that we couldn't even fathom, working long hours and raising small children. To offset some of the financial challenges, we invited a foreign exchange student from China to live with us who attended private school with Adian so we could cover the cost of tuition.

The sacrifices were endless, and within a few years of starting the business, our lease ended for the house, and we could finally afford a new home. The house was in a brand-new neighborhood in the community of Chaparral at The Ranch. We purchased the lot in the first phase, so the excitement of selecting our location and watching our new home being built from the ground was a fun experience for the kids as we created new memories.

It was a two-story home with almost four thousand square feet of living space, five bedrooms, four full bathrooms, an office, an oversized loft, and a three-car garage, and this time it would be our own. Kyle and I selected the cabinets, flooring, granite, appliances, and paint colors so the natural colors flowed effortlessly throughout the space, creating a warm and inviting environment. The grand entry, formal dining, kitchen, main dining, office, and living room were gloss coated with luxurious epoxy flooring in modern shades of gray, making every step into the house feel like you were walking on a piece of art. The grand entry opened directly to a view of the California room accented by double sliding glass doors highlighting a secondary outdoor living space. The formal dining room was situated to the right of the entry with arched openings to the gourmet kitchen surrounded by dark Kona-stained upgraded cabinets, sea pearl granite countertops, stainless steel appliances, a double oven, an oversized center island, and a walk-in pantry.

The guest suite was perfect for my parents as they could enjoy the privacy of their own bedroom and bathroom conveniently located on the lower floor. The spacious study was just to the left of the grand entrance, surrounded by windows drawing in the natural light as a perfect home office for late-night or early-morning projects. The U-shaped stairs tucked away to the left between the office and guest suite were two parallel flights of straight stairs joined by a landing that created a 180-degree turn in the walk line leading up to the generous loft that we planned to turn into a movie room or game room with a pool table for the kids to gather with friends. The dramatic master suite was strategically located at the top of the stairs across from the loft, with an expansive master retreat to unwind after a long day. Including an oversized walk-in shower, beautifully upgraded with modern light gray tile, and double vanity sinks separated on each side of the master bathroom with a deep inset jacuzzi bathtub surrounded by elegant tile complimented the two-tone white and gray paint colors and chic epoxy coated floors. The upper level also featured three spacious bedrooms, two separated by a jack-and-jill bathroom for eleven-year-old Nevaeh and eight-year-old Ashton, leaving

Adian at the ripe age of sixteen with direct access to his very own private bath.

We visited weekly and took family photos as we watched the builders lay the foundation, frame the structure, and install the windows and doors until the final completion. During the same time, we leased a twelve hundred square foot office space for the business just minutes away so our family and staff could each have their own space. Finally, our company was thriving, and our lives were coming together in perfect harmony.

Kyle frequently traveled for business attending trade shows, networking events, and visiting our clients nationwide. Just a few months after moving into our new home, Kyle and I planned to participate in the next business event in Las Vegas, Nevada. Especially because now, we could afford a decent hotel room and enjoy a date night after the trade show. I surprised Kyle with a romantic dinner the night we arrived. I stepped out of the hotel bathroom wearing a sexy short black cocktail dress, six-inch strappy stilettos with my platinum blonde hair perfectly shaping my face, dramatic makeup with smokey eyes, and plump pink lips.

Kyle gasped, "You look breathtaking."

I smiled and winked gently, reminding him that I still had it. Kyle looked down with a blushing expression, grabbed me aggressively, passionately kissing my lips and unzipping my dress with one hand, then tossed it to the floor to remind me that he still had it.

As busy as our lives were, juggling three kids and running a business, the fire between us always burned with passion. After seven years of marriage, our sexual chemistry never wavered. We were infatuated with each other and could hardly keep our hands to ourselves when the kids were around. So, when we were alone, we wrestled in the sheets until dawn. I'm sure we kept the surrounding hotel guests wondering if we would ever take a break so they could sleep, but our minds fixated on each other.

We walked the trade show floor for several hours the following day and decided to lay by the pool to cool down from the scorching Vegas heat in mid-June. So, we quickly grabbed our swimsuits and headed to the rooftop pool. The pool deck flowed with music that vibrated the floors as you walked through the central area. Servers greeted us, taking our drink orders the moment our towels hit the lounge chairs, while the private cabanas surrounding the main pool had bottle service and beautiful people in every corner. It was a perfect break away from the overcrowded event.

I basked in the sun, lathering my body with tanning oil while Kyle jumped in the pool, and within a few minutes, we had drinks in our hands, enjoying our mini getaway together. As Kyle relaxed in the pool, I heard an odd notification sound on his phone; I stood up from my lounge chair, reached for his device, and leaned towards the pool to hand it to him. Just before I could fully rise from my seat, the unusual notification sounded again, and I glanced at his screen. The preview message on his lock screen popped up, and I caught a glimpse of the message.

> You said you were leaving her?
> You said we were going to be together???

My heart dropped into my stomach, and my body froze in shock; Kyle swam toward me, reaching his arm out to grab his phone. I slowly stepped backward as I read the private messages between him and another woman—his reply to the woman just moments before getting into the pool.

It's not that easy; it's complicated.
Just give me more time.

> I have been patient.
> How much longer should I wait for you?
> You said you loved me."

I am in love with you.
I just need to wait for the right time.
I have to think about the kids and the business.

When I thought everything was falling into place, it quickly began unraveling. The familiarity in the tone of those text messages did not ring true for just a one-night stand. Instead, it immediately brought back every ounce of pain I experienced in the first two weeks of our marriage.

My knees started shaking; saliva began pooling in the back of my mouth; my heart was pounding, ready to explode; my eyes scanned left and right in a panic until Kyle caught a glimpse of my heated glare dripping with fury. Then, in a deep raspy voice.

I said, "Get out! Get out of the pool now."

Kyle seemed confused and began rushing toward me to calm me down, not realizing that I had seen the messages.

I yelled, "Fuck you! I sacrificed everything for you. EVERYTHING! How could you do this to me again?

Kyle quickly realized what I was screaming about and began back peddling.

Kyle pleaded, "It meant nothing; it was a mistake. You were working so much, I was lonely, and you were so focused on everything else."

I yelled, "I was focused on all three kids, trying to balance the business and you. But I did focus on you; I practically worshiped the ground you walked on."

The people around us gawked and pointed, waiting eagerly for the chaos to unfold as my life unraveled before them. The more he tried to deflate the situation, the more elevated I became, until everything went dark. The darkness seemed like an endless nightmare. The darkness seeped in as my eyes adjusted to the sun's brightness. It was as if someone was holding a blindfold over my eyes, and I could only ascertain tiny glimpses of the moments to come. It all happened so fast that once I realized where I was, I thrust my body towards Kyle in the hotel lobby, swaying back and forth with my fists clenched, punching his chest as he tried to diffuse my outrage. Each step towards the elevator took every ounce of my strength as I felt a gut-wrenching pain in my stomach. I could feel a sea of eyes watching me as I let out an agonizing scream.

I yelled, "WHY? Why me?"

Kyle tried to calm me down, but each time he touched me, I flared up with anger pushing him away. We stood in the crowd waiting for the elevator doors to open; as I glared in Kyle's direction, he stood weaving in place with his head down, crouched into his chest as he stared blankly at the casino floor. An outpour of tears covered my face while my body trembled with rage. Just as the elevator doors opened to take us to our hotel room floor, Kyle quickly reached into his pocket, rattling the car keys, then bolted towards the parking lot. I observed as he erratically pushed through the crowd with a numbing sensation running down my body; I couldn't find the energy to stop him and felt utterly indifferent about his attempt to run away. As I stepped into the elevator, I felt a sense of deep heartache as a sharp, piercing pain in my chest intensified. He single-handedly cut out a piece of my heart, leaving me numb and hollow.

I tried to piece together a timeline, replaying our past conversations and the messages between him and Ellie. Finally, I realized that Kyle suggested we invest in a timeshare in Las Vegas just a few months prior because he was traveling so much. When I told him we couldn't afford it, we debated the topic in a heated argument, and now it all made sense. He didn't want the timeshare for us, our family, or the business. He wanted a secret place to live his double life with her in Las Vegas.

The more I kept loving, giving, morphing, accommodating, believing, hoping, and chasing his attention, affection, love, and validation, the more I inflated his ego. I created a monster, and I had nothing left to give.

Once I reached our hotel room, I fell to my knees as the door closed behind me, wailing, and crying out.

"Why? Why am I never enough? What's wrong with me? Why doesn't he love me?"

My voice thickened with every cry, and in my attempt to dilute my screams, I crawled onto the floor near the bed and buried my face in a pillow, violently sobbing. Tears drenched my face as I swayed back and forth, pleading for the pain to stop with bouts of yelling and shrieking. Salvia and mucus saturated my lips as blonde strands of hair stuck to my flushed cheeks. Finally, I managed to make my way to the bathroom with my knees hitching. I placed my palms on the counter, slowly lifting my head toward the mirror to look at my reflection. My swollen, bloodshot eyes blurred my vision, and as they slowly adjusted, I realized that I had burst the blood vessels in my face, triggering me to step back against the wall, slowly sliding down to the cold tile floor. I coiled my body in the fetal position and wept.

After several attempts to regain my composure, I began to breathe deeply in and out to calm my racing heart. I sat on the tile floor with my knees tightly nudged against my chest as I reached for my phone to call Kyle. The phone rang twice and then was forwarded to voicemail, so I tried again; it rang once and then was sent to voicemail. Finally, I texted him, demanding that he return to the hotel room so we could talk. No response.

I tried to keep my composure by telling myself he was probably in a bad area or had no service. Just as I leaned forward, placing my arm against the ledge of the bathtub to lift myself, I received several notifications on my phone. I glanced down at the text messages from Kyle and saw a video and images he sent of himself driving drunk with his legs covered in blood from deep incised wounds on his thighs caused by a sharp object or what seemed like a pocketknife. The text message read.

My life is over. I really fucked up this time. I don't know what I'll do, but I can't face you and the kids. It's over.

When I thought it couldn't get any worse, the room began to spin in circles. I urgently jumped to my feet, panicking, taking short breaths, and feverishly calling Kyle. The phone rang numerous times until he finally answered. All I could hear were belligerent sobs, gasps, heavy breathing, and the sound of an engine revving at high speeds. Desperate, I scrambled to find the right words; I didn't know what to say as I had an influx of emotions and feared driving him deeper off the edge.

I pleaded, "Kyle, please stop! Please come back to the hotel so we can talk. I don't want to lose you. It's not worth it. We have overcome so much. We will overcome this too."

I listened intently for several moments to the same treacherous sounds, along with an occasional shriek of the tires. Again, I felt helpless, knowing Kyle was capable of anything, and I couldn't live with myself if something happened to him. Then, finally, I whispered in a still, small voice.

I said, "Kyle, I'm here. I need you. Please don't leave me. We will get through this. I forgive you; please come back."

I could hear him panting through the phone in a deep, jarring tone.

He said, "I don't forgive myself. It's over."

The phone disconnected, and I stood silently beside myself, helpless and alone. I didn't know where Kyle was, who to call, or what to do, so I solemnly walked toward the large window overlooking the Las Vegas strip, fell to my knees, and prayed.

Chapter 20: Shattered

    I didn't know who to call or what to do; we had been here before, and I knew that calling the police would only lead to more chaos. I wrestled with what I would say without knowing where Kyle was or how to find him. Instead, I knelt beneath the window with my face pressed against the dingy hotel carpet, powerless. I was paralyzed in fear as my mind abandoned my body from the upheaval of emotional exhaustion. I tried to reach Kyle, but every effort ended with the defeating sound of his voicemail. Then, finally, after laying in silence for what seemed like an eternity, I was startled by the sound of the hotel keycard beeping against the door. Kyle stumbled inside; the door closed behind him as he stood before me. His eyes were dull, limpid, and blank, while his lips quivered with a debilitating expression. It was as if he had left his soul behind when he entered the room. Kyle swayed back and forth as he walked into the bathroom and closed the door. I heard the lock latch against the metal plate and the sound of muffled cries echoing against the walls.

    It took every ounce of my being to pull myself off the floor, repress my emotions and walk toward the bathroom door. I stood with my forehead leaning against the frame as my knees buckled.

    I whispered, "Kyle, please let me in."

    I heard the lock unlatch, and I calmly opened the door to find Kyle, his face nudged between the porcelain bathtub and his back against the toilet's base, curled in a ball on the cold tile floor. I laid beside him, wrapped my arms and legs around him, and held his body against mine. I could feel his heart beating with every breath he took as I gently grazed my fingers through his hair. Finally, Kyle turned toward me with bloodshot eyes, a pungent odor of sweat, and a sour tone of alcohol and nestled his head into my chest.

The waves of emotions ran so deep that I could feel his debilitating energy in my veins. As infuriated as I was with Kyle, I couldn't imagine losing him. I wrestled with the idea that he could easily threaten to end his life without a fight. It was as though he found it easier to leave our family behind and the life we built together instead of fighting for us. I had an unrelenting desire to protect him, and I would have sacrificed my life to save his. In essence, I did so by abandoning my emotions to tend to him. I wasn't blind to Kyle's manipulation or my codependent behavior; I was terrified, alone, and exhausted, so all I could do was hold him in my arms.

The four-hour drive home the following day was a fog of uncomfortable silence. I wanted to leave this all behind us, but I knew the remains of this earth-shattering pain would slowly seep back into our lives if we didn't face it head-on. Yet, I was too exhausted to speak. As we arrived home, the kids ran out, greeting us with hugs and kisses. They were sharing stories about their weekend, but all I could hear was a ringing in my ears. I smiled, pretending everything was wonderful while suppressing the agony of the twenty-four hours prior.

That evening after we tucked the kids in bed, I grabbed a bottle of vodka, made a few drinks, and hid in our walk-in closet, crying secretly until I knew Kyle was asleep. Then I tiptoed into the bedroom, sliding gently into my side of the bed, and laid awake reliving the nightmare I had experienced the day prior until the sun rose.

That morning I pretended to be energetic and bubbly as I made breakfast and packed lunches for the kids. I couldn't let them see Mommy's heartache, and I refused to uproot their lives because of my pain. I knew Kyle was an incredible father, and no matter the sacrifice, he would move mountains for them; even though Adian and Nevaeh were not his own, he gave them just as much love as he gave Ashton. I couldn't find it in my heart to shatter their perception of him. I had an unwavering desire to protect his integrity in their eyes, even at my own expense. This was my battle to face, not theirs. Our children, family, and business would be ripped apart if I exposed these secrets, and I wasn't willing to destroy everything because of his inability to be faithful. I refused to be the victim and was determined to heal our broken marriage.

Over the following weeks, I scheduled counseling sessions, joined marriage groups, read books about healing, attended retreats, and searched online for every article, resource, podcast, or tool I could find to expedite my healing process. I was desperate to forgive Kyle and move past the pain, yet any progress I made quickly digressed when triggered by the slightest inclination that something didn't feel right. I began writing my thoughts in a journal to seek relief. In my first entry, I wrote:

July 8th, 2018

A tired soul keeps fighting even when there is no strength left.

When I left my first husband, I thought I had finally found "the one" God purposely designed for me. The reality is that I only found more pain. My choices were simply a gateway to the pain I was about to experience. I chose this path based on my selfishness and pride. I sacrificed my life to fulfill the selfish desires that fueled me. The truth is that I left a broken relationship to begin a newly broken relationship. My heart was so focused on fulfilling its own needs that I didn't consider the consequences that would come.

My heart and flesh may fail, but my God never will.

> *It's devastating that Kyle and I lost the honesty and humility in our relationship. At times I believe it was never really there. Instead, the truth is that our love was founded on lies. I chose this path; I chose him. The imperfections and all, just as he chose me. I honestly believed that I was different, that I was special. I don't fully understand why destiny brought us together; I can only seek to understand, being open and willing to grow from these lessons. The reality is that a relationship founded on deception and infidelity only uncovers more damage. When you decide everything is worth sacrificing for someone else, the truth is...*
>
> *You only sacrifice yourself.*

This journal entry was the beginning of my healing process. These words were written from the pit of my soul, resurrecting my inner child, begging to be loved and accepted, searching for validation in others, and not recognizing how to let go of my five-year-old self. Shortly after I finished writing, I looked in the mirror and saw myself as a child with greasy blonde hair and dirt-stained feet with smudges covering my face. Yet, even as a thirty-eight-year-old woman, I was still that little girl struggling to protect myself and, in the process, continued to revert to hiding in the closet.

Every night for months, I battled with these thoughts; they haunted me and replayed repeatedly. I'm not enough. I'll never be enough. My healing halted, and my depression overpowered my will to move forward. Kyle never seemed the same after that evening in Las Vegas; he appeared cold and apathetic. Indifference replaced his once passionate demeanor. There were moments when I tried to express my feelings, Kyle's response would dismiss my concerns, and he would get angry when I continued to communicate. I felt like I was walking on eggshells, so it seemed easier to suppress my emotions. Kyle followed my lead by masking his emotions during business hours and with our family acting overly happy, energized, and motivated. Yet, when the chaos of the day subsided, he seemed harsh, increasingly angry, and withdrawn.

I clung to the love we once had, but my heart was wounded, and I couldn't find the strength to look at Kyle without anguish and disgust. I began to fall deeper into depression. I was a master at pretending that everything was perfect on the outside, but on the inside, I was deteriorating— body, mind, and spirit. The drinking continued every evening, and my escape to our master bedroom closet was my only sense of comfort.

A few weeks later, it was a typical morning juggling the kids' schedules and getting them ready before dropping them off at three different schools. Adian was in high school, Nevaeh was in junior high, and Ashton was in elementary school, but this particular morning was more hectic than usual. Our three dogs pooped in the upstairs loft, and as I shuffled around, I stepped in their mess. Kyle seemed agitated and continued yelling at Ashton to hurry up as we ran in different directions to prepare for the day. I was running behind for my first meeting, and just as I passed through the kitchen into the garage to rush the kids off to school, I noticed Kyle's travel bag by the door. It was unusual, but I was eager to drop the kids off so I wouldn't be late. As I pulled out of the driveway, I realized I had left without kissing Kyle goodbye, but I reassured myself that I would see him at the office and kiss him twice.

As I arrived at the office, I noticed that Kyle's car wasn't there, but in a scurry, logged into my computer to prepare for my meeting. I scanned through my emails to address any urgent requests and saw an email confirmation that Kyle had registered to attend a trade show in Las Vegas on the same day. I forwarded him the message asking him to stay because I needed him here to support me with the kids and the business, then hurried to my meeting.

During the meeting, I couldn't focus; *Kyle wouldn't attend the trade show without saying a word, would he?* It consumed my mind. I remember him saying he would see me at our office, but he never arrived. After the meeting, I checked my inbox and noticed that Kyle didn't reply to my email. This was unusual because Kyle's phone was practically attached to his face at all times, and he was always quick to respond. A few days prior, he mentioned a trade show, and I shared my concerns about him attending. We discussed it a few times earlier but had too many distractions to come to an agreement. Just then, I received a text message from Kyle and immediately read his text.

I decided to go.

I felt darkness run over me as I began to respond, but before I could process my reply, I immediately felt my stomach turn in knots. I jumped up from my desk and walked to the bathroom inconspicuously so my employees wouldn't see me upset. When I closed the bathroom door, I fell to my knees, wrapped my arms around the toilet bowl, and violently vomited. My face was flush, and my stomach was empty, but I continued to dry-heave until I could burst into tears. My mind spun in circles, *why would he go to Las Vegas alone after all we've been through? I know Ellie lives in Las Vegas, but he promised it was over between them. I'm probably overreacting, and he wouldn't be this obvious.*

This is the first trip he took by himself to Las Vegas since I found out about Ellie, and coincidentally, this was the exact date that we attended Marriage Boot Camp five years prior due to his affair with Angela.

I spiraled into a tailspin of chaos, checking the location of his phone every few minutes, logging into our cell phone records to see if any of the phone numbers he called or texted in the past few weeks were to a Las Vegas zip code. Then I completely lost my mind. I paid for an online record to access all her contact information, address, phone numbers, and relatives. I even found her place of employment through a social media platform and contacted the Law office listed as her office to confirm that she was still a paralegal at their firm. The receptionist confirmed that Ellie was working and had just left for lunch. I logged into our cell phone account again and began combing through every phone number under Kyle's activity.

That's when I confirmed my suspicions; he'd been calling her office weekly, so it would seem like he was making business calls. I knew logically if I didn't want to find something, I shouldn't have been searching, but by this point, I was so deep in my detective skills that I could only assume the worst. I checked his location every hour and even called the hotel he had reserved to ask the host if another person had accompanied Kyle. I pretended one of my female employees was supposed to meet him there, even to the extent of sharing that I was concerned about her arrival. The host confirmed that Kyle checked in alone. That didn't pacify me as I continued my pursuit by reviewing our bank activity, tracking every transaction to follow his trail.

Once I arrived home that evening, the kids asked where he was, so I downplayed his unexpected absence by reassuring them that Kyle was working additional hours to make sales for the company and had a last-minute obligation.

After I tucked them into bed, I reached for a bottle of vodka, made a few drinks, and found myself in recon all over again. I noticed Kyle's location was unavailable, my text messages weren't being delivered, and when I called his phone, it went directly to voicemail. In a panic, I called him several times, but still no answer. My heart was racing as I fell back into my cycle of research. Finally, over an hour later, Kyle returned my call. His tone was animated and in good spirits, utterly oblivious of the rabbit trail I'd been chasing for hours.

Kyle said, "Hi, my love; I got here safely and wanted to let you know."

I replied, "I'm hurt; why did you go without talking to me?"

He replied, "I tried, but you were too busy, and every time we talked, you were distracted with work."

As agitated as I was, I tried to keep my composure, so I took a deep breath before I continued.

I said, "I understand that's how you feel, and I'm sorry I wasn't fully present. Can I ask you a question?"

Kyle responded, "Of course!"

I asked, "Have you spoken to Ellie?"

Kyle's tone quickly changed from spirited to defensive.

He said, "No! I thought we had resolved that issue. How long will it take for you to trust me again?"

I paused, staring blankly at the ceiling as he continued rambling; I inhaled deeply and closed my eyes as I deliberated how to reframe the question.

I replied, "To build trust, I need you to be honest. Let me ask differently. Have you tried to contact Ellie?"

Kyle said, "No."

I said, "Kyle, I checked our phone records and saw that you called Ellie's office yesterday and again today.

Kyle hesitated, stuttering, stammering, then finally admitted to calling her office. My entire body began trembling as he backpedaled.

He said, "I wanted to apologize for all the chaos I created, so I called her office, but she didn't answer. I'm sorry I should have told you."

I had a mixture of feelings between relief and skepticism, yet I was too exhausted to continue the conversation, so I simply thanked him for being honest and ended the call.

I sat on the edge of the bed swaying back and forth; the softness of the sheets pulled me in as I leaned sideways, gently laying my head against the mattress. The room was dark, and the house was still, with only the sound of the murmur from the air seeping through the vents. I could still smell Kyle's scent as I nestled my face closer to his pillow. I closed my eyes, desperately clenching his pillow between my breasts, yearning to be close to him, breathing in the smell of his aftershave as a single tear floated against my cheek. The silence only intensified my racing thoughts, and I began to feel my heart pounding as a sharp pain pierced my chest. I tried to calm my nerves by telling myself, *I know he's not good for me, but I love him. Everything is going to be okay. I can't imagine my life without him. I don't want to leave; I'll be alone and have to start all over again. I need to stop focusing on where he is. I'm going to drive myself crazy.*

Instead, my body felt lethargic and numb while saliva filled my mouth as a stroke of nausea swirled in my stomach, giving me a slight choking sensation. I quickly sat up, leaning my back against the headboard to alleviate the sense of vomiting, taking deep breaths in and out. It felt like my mind was holding my body hostage, so I gave in to my compulsive need to find answers.

I reached for my laptop, setting it between my thighs as I propped myself up with pillows. My eyes squinted from the dimly lit glare of the screen as I frantically reached for my glasses on the nightstand extending the tips of my fingers until I could feel the edge of my black Prada case. I pulled the strands of hair from around my face into a loose bun as I repeatedly scanned my phone to check Kyle's location. I watched intently as the map refreshed and displayed "Location unavailable." I again clicked on the circular arrow in the top right corner, and his location was still unavailable. I could feel the sweat from my palms as I continuously pressed the refresh button, hoping for a different outcome—still nothing.

I began obsessively searching online to see his last transaction through our bank account. The most recent activity was at a Venezuelan wood-fired grill approximately thirty minutes from the hotel he booked. Kyle's hotel room was centrally located in Las Vegas, surrounded by hundreds of restaurants, and with the traffic driving through the busy city, it wouldn't make sense to travel miles away for dinner. In a flurry of paranoia, I scanned Ellie's background report and noticed that her home address was only a few blocks from the restaurant. I felt my neck muscles tensing under my skin as I rolled my head back, rubbing my shoulders and clenching my jaw. My blood began to boil as I repeatedly tried to refresh his location on my phone but still nothing.

The disturbing visuals of him and this woman together made me cringe. Ellie's background check included social media accounts, so I impulsively searched through her profile, photos, work history, and followers. I realized that she was born in Russia, and based on her posts and pictures, she had thin ashy blonde hair and a slender and fragile frame with an intelligent expression but seemingly dull for Kyle's taste. Ellie was in her forties, dressed conservatively and uninteresting, even in pictures with friends. Nothing stood out about her; she was ordinary. Kyle was thirty-one years old, handsome, and captivating with a fashion sense that would turn heads from every walk of life; his repertoire included pale pink suits, sequined dress shoes, expensive watches, and designer briefcases. Although I knew he typically preferred older women, particularly curvy, sexy, and sophisticated, I was slightly confused about what drew him to her. I incessantly glanced at my phone, refreshing his location every few minutes. Finally, after two hours of driving myself down a research rabbit hole, his whereabouts were suddenly restored, and I could see him en route back to his hotel.

I wish this had given me a sense of relief, but instead, I couldn't help but think she followed him back to the hotel, and this was just another game in his bag of tricks. This obsession with observing his every move threatened my identity, and I began to unravel at the seams. I knew I had to get a hold of myself, so I closed the laptop and curled under the covers trying to talk myself off the edge as I fell asleep.

Kyle returned from his trip late the following evening; the house was quiet, and the kids were asleep, so I could hear his footsteps approaching our room. I couldn't bring myself to say a word, so I pretended to sleep as he slid into the bed next to me, turned his back toward me, and without a kiss, went to sleep. I could feel his cold, distant energy but was desperate for his smell, touch, or affection. I snuggled up behind him and silently prayed that he would acknowledge me, but he didn't recognize my attempt to be close to him. I withdrew, curling my knees into my chest, turning my back against his while we slept on opposite sides of the bed.

Over the next few weeks, Kyle became more distant, agitated, and harsh. I made every effort to minimize our problems, dismiss my emotions, and pretend that I was working on myself, but the grave reality was that I was deteriorating. I submerged myself into the business, working early mornings and late into the evening to find reprieve as I fell deeper into despair. Day in and day out, I replayed Kyle's statement: "You were working so much, and I just needed affection, but you were too busy." Focusing on running the business and raising the kids was more manageable than inviting more conflict into our lives. I neglected my needs and emotions. I was ultimately causing my health to decline, drinking every night to numb the pain, and isolating myself further from those who loved me.

Kyle and I met weekly with our marriage counselor as the months passed. I tried to focus on healing my broken spirit, yet I felt a heaviness holding me back, like the resistance of running through deep waters, gasping for air as I immersed further into darkness. Kyle attended every session masking his emotions and carefully crafting his responses.

One evening before our next appointment with our counselor, I tossed and turned all night. I had a deep suspicion that Kyle was still pursuing other women, so I waited patiently for Kyle to fall asleep, carefully slipping my toes against the carpet, quietly lifting my weight off the mattress, then discreetly crept around the edge of our canopy bed frame. I knelt down, crawling beneath Kyle's nightstand, cautiously reaching for his cell phone. Once I felt the phone with my fingertips, I quietly removed it from the charger and crawled toward our walk-in closet.

I nestled between the clothes hanging from the valet rod and immersed myself in the darkness with the dimly lit glow from his cell phone as I began searching through his applications. Kyle was a master at downloading hidden message apps with icons that resembled games or calculators, so I was determined to find his newest addition. I viewed his recent downloads, but every application was password protected.

Although defeated, I was determined and continued scanning through his text messages. I knew Kyle meticulously deleted his history and risky messages, but I noticed a name I didn't recognize and began investigating further.

It seemed that the text correspondence was between Kyle and another male bantering about what they would do to a woman acquaintance, using explicit words describing derogatory acts they would perform on her and how the other didn't have a chance. As I read further, they bet on who would have sex with her first. I knew if I had evidence, Kyle couldn't twist the narrative or tell me that I was crazy, so I began to take screenshots of the messages and send them to my cell phone. Suddenly the closet light turned on, and in a panic, I threw Kyle's phone under the dirty laundry, buried my head in the pile of clothes, and pretended I was sleeping. I could feel Kyle standing over me as I pretended to yawn with my eyes squinted while peeking through my lashes.

Kyle said, "I know you're not sleeping."

I rubbed my eyes as my pupils adjusted to the light, then stretched my arms, but before I could formulate a logical excuse.

He said, "Serena! You left your phone on the nightstand, and the vibration from the screenshots you sent yourself woke me up."

My heart started racing, and with my palms sweating, I leaned against the pile of clothes to prop myself up as the humiliation set in. Kyle's expression of disgust only silenced my need to explain. Instead, I looked up at him with courage, then nervously backpedaled.

I asked, "Why would you want to have sex with some girl when you're married? After all that we have been through."

Kyle calmly leaned down on one knee, crossing his legs as he sat beside me on the closet floor. He looked into my eyes and placed his hand on my knee. Then in a soft, cavalier tone.

He said, "You need to stop doing this to yourself. It was a harmless conversation between guys, and you're driving yourself crazy. I deleted the screenshots on your phone. Now come to bed."

I knew it wasn't harmless in the pit of my stomach, but with my incessant need to diffuse the situation after being completely mortified that he caught me sitting in my shame, I decided to comply and concede. Kyle stood up, reaching for my hand, and I followed him back to bed with my tail between my legs.

Before meeting with our counselor, Kyle was distant and cold. I dreaded our upcoming therapy session because Kyle responded in a harsh, short tone whenever I tried to communicate my feelings. Our marriage and family therapist, David, has been counseling Kyle and me for several years. We originally began our sessions with David after the first infidelity. We were introduced to him through our church and immediately connected. David was passionate and personally invested in supporting each of us individually, then our relationship. His philosophy was to foster complete transparency to create a safe environment for Kyle and me to share our struggles and fears without judgment. David recently moved several hours away, so we attended our sessions virtually every week. As David joined the meeting, Kyle immediately changed his demeanor, seemingly upbeat and excited, sharing his weekly accomplishments and explaining how fantastic he was doing.

I immediately withdrew, confused about his sudden transformation from the agitated husband I had encountered minutes before the call. I sat back in my chair, perplexed by Kyle's cavalier attitude, while I observed his behavior. Finally, David noticed my body language and paused.

David asked, "Serena, what's on your mind?"

I knew that was a loaded question, yet I was annoyed by Kyle's patronizing disposition.

I responded, "I guess I'm just confused by how Kyle is acting. Just moments before our call, he seemed completely different."

David replied, "Let's not focus on your perception of Kyle. Instead, share more about how you are feeling."

I sat upright, leaned forward with a sigh of confusion, then tilted my head to observe Kyle's body language. Kyle glanced over at me, shrugging his shoulders as if he was clueless to my frustration.

I responded, "I feel isolated and alone. Unworthy of Kyle's affection. I'm exhausted from trying to rebuild trust when I feel like every time we make progress, it's broken again."

Kyle immediately interrupted, then redirected the conversation by sharing his version of what transpired the night before. Oddly, Kyle softened his expression, drawing his eyebrows together, looking steadily in my direction, then in a sympathetic tone.

Kyle said, "She's been really struggling. It's heartbreaking to see her this way."

David asked, "What comes up for you when you see her struggling, Kyle?"

Kyle moved closer beside me, cupping his arm around my shoulder, and pulling me in, then cautiously chose his words.

He said, "Well, David... She's been drinking every night after the kids fall asleep, and last night I found her hiding in the closet, searching through my phone. Serena was reading some harmless messages between a buddy and me, then when I tried to communicate with her, she withdrew and shut down."

The knots in my stomach twisted into my chest, making me nauseous; I rolled my shoulders back while trying to swallow my breath. Then, I began blinking rapidly, looking side to side, trying to compose myself as Kyle insisted on sharing his feelings.

He said, "I love her so much, and watching her go down this path is painful. I feel hopeless."

I cringed at his attempt to make me seem crazy and quickly repositioned myself leaning away from him. I stared at Kyle with an absent gaze. I could feel my skin crawling with every word that fell from his lips. I didn't trust him blindly; my eyes were wide open. He believed that he was so clever, yet his hidden agenda was in plain sight, but David didn't notice.

I started feeling unhinged and knew that would only make matters worse, so I retracted and refused to participate in Kyle's double game. He was like a magician creating a false reality with smoke in mirrors. I sat through the remainder of the session, allowing Kyle to lead the conversation, nodding my head with a fake smile until it was over. When our meeting ended, Kyle casually stood up, kissed me on the cheek, and walked away with a smug grin.

After eight years together, I felt like I was living with a stranger. Kyle's unpredictable behavior made me feel like I was losing my mind. One moment, he was playful, caring, and the life of the party; the next, he was agitated, apathetic, and rigid. I couldn't keep up with his erratic tendencies, so I stopped trying, avoiding any sign of conflict. Instead, I did what I did best; I pretended that everything was fine, masking my emotions with a smile and impersonating the perfect couple everyone thought we were.

Chapter 21: Denial

Several months passed, and my health continued to decline. I was thirty-eight years old, exercising four times a week, yet my body was deteriorating. I worked fourteen-hour days, submerged in the business, finding any distraction to eliminate the gaping hole in my heart. I began to experience digestive issues, decreased appetite, anxiety, and grief. I felt nauseous and became constipated after only eating small portions, leaving me without a bowel movement for up to six days. My stomach distended with abnormal swelling, and when the cramps became unbearable, I vomited several times a day to relieve the pressure in my abdomen. I was unable to eat most foods, my diet consisted of dry toast, vegetables, fruit, and light meals, yet I was rapidly gaining weight, sleep deprived, and exhausted. The pain in my stomach was unbearable.

My body felt weak and inflamed, like needles or an electric shock running through my veins. The buckling pain instigated frequent headaches, difficulty concentrating, lethargy, and faintness. I tried to seek answers from doctors, specialists, and hormone therapists but was left with more questions. I took several blood tests, CT scans, and stress tests and tried homeopathic remedies and procedures. Still no answers.

Despite my unknown health issues, the agency was thriving. Our team was executing marketing and advertising projects for multimillion-dollar businesses, traveling nationwide to create high-end video content filmed by Emmy award-winning cinematographers. Our incredible team produced commercials, managed six-figure advertising budgets, developed websites, and nurtured client relationships. The agency was publicly recognized, winning dozens of awards for our web design, graphics, photography, filming, and video production. Growing at such a speed that our twelve-hundred-square-foot office was bursting at the seams, and we were running out of space.

My only source of reprieve was meeting with Marshall and my executive peer group each month. Every meeting gave me a sense of hope, providing value, insight, and guidance in the moments when I felt alone. Although I hid my marital issues from my peers, they offered wisdom and support that fueled my determination and allowed me to keep my head above water. With the whirlwind of growth in the business, my peer group suggested that we apply for a small business loan to expand our team and lease larger office space.

Within a few months, the business was approved for an SBA loan, and we were on the search for our dream office. We hired several new employees to keep up with the demand. With all the excitement of growing business, it became an even more significant distraction while I further neglected my health.

Kyle was traveling more than ever. With our salesforce growing, we began integrating our team members into the sales process and encouraging our employees to build deeper relationships with our customers by traveling to trade shows and attending onsite meetings and networking events.

One new hire, particularly, tugged at my heartstrings; Jayden was vibrant, optimistic, eager to learn, and self-motivated. Before accepting the position, I realized that Jayden and her husband were attending a music festival in Nevada when an active shooter opened fire on the crowd from his 32nd-floor suite in the Mandalay Bay hotel. The active shooter fired over a thousand bullets, killing sixty people and wounding at least four hundred. As her husband realized the tragedy that was taking place, he directed his wife, Jayden, and a couple of their friends toward a gate near the venue's south end; two bullets struck him in his lower back. Both narrowly missed his spinal cord as he safely shepherded Jayden and his group through an open gate. Although this tragic event happened a year before she joined our company, her story moved me, and I wanted to give her a sense of hope.

    We had an upcoming trade show in Las Vegas and thought it would be an opportunity to replace tragic memories with new ones so she could move past her trauma. When I offered Jayden the chance to attend the trade show, she seemed slightly apprehensive but eager for the new experience. I genuinely wanted to nurture her personal and professional growth, so I encouraged her to talk to her husband before committing to attend. Jayden approached me the following day to confirm her travel plans and was genuinely grateful for the opportunity.

    As the trade show quickly approached, I was knee-deep in projects and juggling the kid's schedules, so Kyle and I decided it would be best if I stayed behind. That afternoon, I pulled Jayden aside to make sure she still felt comfortable traveling, and she expressed her excitement, so I felt confident that she would enjoy the experience. During the trip, I sent Jayden several uplifting and encouraging messages reminding her of her strength, and when they returned from the event, she was glowing, sharing stories and pictures of all the fun they had. Jayden was finding her purpose and growing professionally. However, within the coming weeks, I noticed that Jayden's glow began to fade in the day-to-day operations; she struggled in her official position as a project coordinator and expressed that she wanted more opportunities to develop her sales skills. It would be an excellent incentive for Kyle to coach and guide her in more of a sales role, allowing me to focus on training the new hires and searching for the new office space while supporting Kyle with sales.

After just a few weeks, we finally found the perfect office space for our team. The new location was only a few blocks from our existing office and was over three thousand square feet of open space in a private commercial building perched on a hilltop overlooking rolling hills and a beautiful canyon. The new office was a clean slate with concrete floors, an open concept floor plan, and an exposed ceiling surrounded by oversized floor-to-ceiling windows with breathtaking views of the valley. I knew that with the business growth, it would be the perfect time to create a hybrid position for Jayden where I could take her under my wing, allowing her to support me with managing some administrative tasks, such as the office move, tenant improvements, and planning our re-grand opening event. At the same time, Kyle continued to develop her sales skills. Jayden was eager to earn our approval, yet she struggled to find the balance between both roles at such a fast pace.

I quickly realized that the disconnect between Kyle and me in our marriage was seeping into the business and was becoming harder to mask, which sent me into a tailspin of trying to cover up any signs of conflict between us. The new office space only complicated our pre-existing issues by making it impossible for us to communicate, leaving Jayden in the middle. At the same time, Kyle and I simultaneously ran in different directions.

One afternoon, Kyle, Jayden, and I met at the new office space to discuss the budget, construction, furniture layout, and moving arrangements. Kyle was in a three-piece suit, already measuring the dimensions for the furniture as Jayden and I arrived. When we entered the double doors, Kyle was prepared with a shopping list of furnishings and accessories to decorate the space. I pulled him aside in a concerned tone.

I asked, "Can we review the project timeline and budget before discussing the furniture?"

Kyle's expression quickly changed from gleaming with excitement to a sour sneer, as if I burst his bubble in a sarcastic tone.

He replied, "Whatever you want, I just don't have time to sit here all day."

I felt the tension rising, so I laughed nervously, deflecting his comment in an effort to diffuse the situation.

I said, "Um, why don't you share your thoughts first? Then, Jayden and I can review the budget and timeline later if you don't have time."

Kyle seemed agitated and didn't hesitate to correct me.

He said, "I didn't say I don't have time. I said I don't have time to sit here all day."

I bit my lip and rolled my neck back, trying to appease Kyle and allowing him to lead the discussion. Kyle has always been a visionary with big ideas and an excessive spending habit, so I spent most of my time trying to rein him in, but I took my cue as I realized he wasn't in the mood to discuss our financial parameters. Instead, Kyle motioned Jayden to follow him around the space as he directed her to create a list of items to purchase. I observed as Kyle pointed to every corner of the room, instructing me to write down measurements while Jayden documented things to buy.

I said, "Kyle, we already have a list of furniture and pricing for you to review that fit within our budget."

He ignored my reasoning and continued walking around the office, measuring as if he didn't hear me.

I said, "Kyle, we already have the measurements and the floor plan. We even created a space plan for you to review with the furniture specifications."

Kyle paused with his back towards me, slowly turning his head, and glared at me with disgust. I glanced at Jayden, hoping she couldn't see the irritation in his expression, but she quickly turned away, pretending not to notice. I closed my eyes, took a deep breath, and allowed Kyle to continue. After an hour passed, Kyle gave his final remarks and insisted that he was late for an appointment. I had scheduled this meeting weeks in advance, so I knew he didn't have a meeting, but I was not in the mood to argue, so I told him that Jayden and I would review everything and obtain his feedback before making any purchases. Kyle rushed off while I was left to smooth things over with Jayden.

I said, "I am so sorry, we've had a rough week, and I should have communicated better before the meeting. I'll talk to Kyle tonight to ensure we're on the same page before moving forward."

As time passed, these little disputes became more frequent, causing the tension between us to build up. I concealed my emotions, pretending everything was perfect while physically watching my body and health decline. Finally, after numerous doctor visits and online research, I was convinced that all my health issues were related to the breast implants I had done several years prior. I scheduled an appointment with the surgeon who performed the procedure to have them removed.

Kyle desired to improve his physique and was eager to learn more about procedures to enhance his already perfect body. He was approximately two hundred pounds of pure muscle with a naturally lean and athletic build, yet he was never satisfied, constantly wanting to increase his muscle mass. Although I hesitated to invite him because I didn't want to over-extend our finances, he insisted.

As we arrived at the plastic surgery center, Kyle was like a kid in a candy store, looking through every brochure and debating which procedure he should consider. I sat quietly, observing his behavior, and slightly enjoying the glimpse of the excitement that I hadn't seen in him for quite some time. Finally, the nurse called us into the exam room as I meticulously explained my symptoms; she began to take notes, measured my heart rate, and reviewed the next steps of scheduling the surgery. I wanted to feel normal again, so I urgently requested the next available date. The nurse asked a few more questions and then excused herself to gather additional items for a pregnancy test. I laughed sarcastically.

I said, "You won't have to worry about taking a pregnancy test. My husband had a vasectomy several years ago."

The nurse reassured me that it was a part of the process and asked me to provide a urine sample. I thought this was absurd, but I followed her directions and returned the container. I sat on the edge of the exam table, barely covered by the open-front disposable medical gown, as Kyle and I waited in the consultation room. I wiggled on the uncomfortable leather cushion listening to him try to persuade me while reviewing all the benefits of his wish list of surgical procedures.

The nurse quietly stepped into the room with a conflicted expression.

She said, "Your test came back positive. You're pregnant."

The exam room began to spin in circles as I adjusted my eyes to the test results she held in her hand.

I replied, "There must be a mistake. How could I possibly be pregnant?"

I felt the tension rise in the room as though a cloud of darkness seeped in. I nervously laughed in disbelief as I slowly turned toward Kyle. As my head tilted, I could immediately sense his agitation. I calmly observed his body language; Kyle's lips curled, pulling back in disgust while he clenched his jaw. Steadily yet forcibly, I expelled all my breath as I tried to comprehend what was happening. My lips began to quiver, yet my words refused to take form. I could see in my peripheral vision that Kyle was enraged just as the nurse stepped out.

Kyle demanded, "Who's baby? It's obviously not mine!"

I quickly backed away, increasing my distance from him as I gathered my clothes. As my bare feet pressed against the cold, sterile floor, I began to feel my body go into shock; I rolled my shoulders forward, placing my shaking legs through the opening in my dress, my chest caved in, and my chin plunged between my breast, shrinking my shoulders forward as I pulled my arms through the sleeves. My mind raced with confusion. *How is this possible? I have only been with my husband; this can't be right. We haven't been in the lifestyle since before, Ellie, so there is no way I could be pregnant.*

Kyle's glare grew deeper the longer I stood in silence. He paced back and forth, shaking his head.

He mumbled, "I can't believe you, making me out to be the villain."

His voice began to rise as he sharply approached me.

He said, "Who is he? Who have you been fucking?"

I stood up, pressing my shoulders back, and looked him straight in the eye.

I said, "Kyle, I haven't been with anyone but you. Something is not right; we need a second opinion."

Without another word, he turned his back to me and stormed to the parking lot. I followed closely behind, pleading with him that he was the only one, but he refused to listen. Finally, after thirty minutes of silence, Kyle pulled into the parking lot of Planned Parenthood, abruptly parked the car, and gestured to me to go inside. I still couldn't fathom being pregnant at thirty-nine, let alone his absurd reaction, so I knelt my head down and walked into the lobby. Kyle rushed behind me as if I had something to hide, hoovering closely over my shoulder as I leaned down to speak through the small opening in the plexiglass.

I said, "I don't have an appointment but would like a pregnancy test."

The receptionist was cold and short, pointing at the clipboard beneath me; I wrote my name on the sign-in sheet and found a seat in the waiting room. While Kyle and I waited for my name to be called, we quietly argued about the possibility of the test returning positive again. I repeatedly reassured him that I hadn't been with anyone else, and this must be a mistake.

The nurse called my name; I jumped up, eagerly explaining the situation. The nurse escorted us to an exam room and directed me to take a urine test, and the results returned positive. I pleaded with the nurse that this couldn't be possible and began asking more questions, so she suggested that they conduct a blood test to verify the results.

Unfortunately, the blood test results would take a few days, so she encouraged me to schedule an appointment with an Obstetrician.

Kyle and I left planned parenthood without a word and drove home. I pleaded with Kyle in tears.

I said, "This must be a false positive test result because there is no way that I am pregnant. I haven't been with anyone but you. Did you ever schedule a check-up after the vasectomy?

Kyle rebutted, "Now you are trying to pin this on me? Are you kidding?"

I replied, "This doesn't make sense; it can't be positive. Did you schedule a check-up?"

Kyle said, "It's been six years since the procedure! I'm pretty sure we would have known sooner if it didn't work."

I begged, "Please, Kyle, can you schedule an appointment to see if something happened before you blame me for being unfaithful?

Kyle rolled his eyes, irritated by my persistent nagging, and finally agreed to meet with his doctor. A sigh of relief fell over my shoulders as I slid deeper into the passenger seat. I begged Kyle to keep this between us until we met with an Obstetrician and his urologist to be sure we didn't overreact without fully understanding the circumstances. I was in complete denial, and there was nothing he could say or do to convince me that this was possible.

After several sleepless nights, my appointment finally arrived. But, again, the stress and anxiety of the unknown consumed my thoughts. My nerves were on edge as we approached the doctor's office, and with my chin tucked into my chest, I steadily counted the minutes until the nurse called me into the examination room.

The sonogram nurse slathered my belly with a sticky gel substance, then rubbed a small ultrasound probe with a sterile cover around my stomach for what felt like an eternity. All I could hear was a subtle wave of static vibrating from the monitor beside me. Finally, the nurse excused herself with a concerned look, quickly leaving the exam room. When she returned, she had a distressed expression. She placed her hand on the ultrasound monitor and slowly turned the screen to face me. Her eyes said everything I already knew in my heart. Then she uttered the words that will forever haunt me.

She said, "I'm sorry; there is no heartbeat."

I stared blankly at the screen, observing the stillness of the lifeless human on the monitor. Not a flutter. I felt my heart go completely dark. I was submerged in shame and grief, blaming myself for the loss of this poor baby inside me. The nurse explained that I would need to schedule a minor surgical procedure called a D&C to scrape and remove tissue from the inner lining of the uterus. My lips quivered as I struggled to grasp what she was saying.

I asked, "Tissue? What will happen if I have a miscarriage before I can schedule the D&C?

The nurse gracefully touched my shoulder as I shivered in fear.

She said, "You are between ten and twelve weeks pregnant, so if your body begins to expel the tissue before your procedure, you might find a sac with an embryo inside, about the size of a small bean."

My expression went cold as though a damp cloth covered my face, then a throbbing white noise pierced my ears, silencing her voice. I refocused my sight on her slightly blurred face as she described that I would experience cramping, minor pain, and bleeding during the miscarriage, similar to a period. Then, she continued to explain that the signs of the pregnancy will gradually get lighter within two weeks, and any additional symptoms, such as nausea and tender breasts, will fade in the days after the miscarriage.

As she left the room, I reached for my clothes and caught a glimpse of Kyle glaring at me in disbelief; his expression of accusation was as sharp as a razor blade, with an incriminating look in his eye, deeming me as unfaithful. It was almost as if I could hear his thoughts demanding that I was no different than him, yet he didn't say a word. Instead, he impatiently wrestled the keys into his pocket while he waited for me to gather my things.

The next day I went back to work as though nothing had happened. Yet the reality of what I was experiencing was a depth of confusion and sadness. I felt like a ticking time bomb and a walking tomb all at the same time. In the days following, I researched everything I could find on having a miscarriage. While, at times, the language could be dehumanizing and the words difficult to read, the knowledge became a powerful tool to process and understand what would likely happen in my immediate future.

That afternoon Kyle met with his urologist, and just as I suspected, his original vasectomy failed. Kyle never returned for the post-vasectomy semen analysis after his initial procedure. My heart dropped into my stomach as the stark reality of the miscarriage finally set in. Kyle began speaking rapidly, defending his reasons for not scheduling a follow-up appointment after the initial procedure. I stared at his face blankly, trying to process my emotions but I couldn't form a clear sentence. A heaviness ran over my chest; I struggled to breathe as I stepped back, reaching for something to stabilize myself. It felt like a band tightening around my neck, and my hands started to shake uncontrollably. Kyle became more animated, speaking in medical terms.

He said, "Vasectomy failure is extremely rare and only occurs in one out of every two-thousand patients. It could have been due to technical errors during the procedure or early or late recanalization. Late recanalization can occur up to seven years after a vasectomy. So basically, the tube can regrow."

The pressure around my neck made it hard to swallow as I stood in silence, trying to articulate a response. But before I could fully absorb Kyle's defense, he casually walked away, mumbling.

He said, "Don't worry. I already scheduled an appointment to redo the vasectomy on March 18th, and the doctor will perform the procedure at no cost."

Before he could utter another word, I quickly interjected, stammering.

I said, "Kyle, that's the same day I scheduled the D&C. I need you there to support me. Why would you reschedule the procedure without talking to me first?"

Kyle seemed agitated and oblivious to how this would affect me. He shuffled backward with a confused look, his eyes narrowed, and his mouth dropped as if I had said something completely unreasonable.

He said, "I thought you'd be happy. So why are you overreacting?"

I was in shock, unable to fathom his eagerness to schedule the procedure so impulsively. However, I wasn't mentally prepared to process all the emotions flooding my mind, so I dismissed my feelings and withdrew.

I said, "I didn't mean to overreact, it's just a lot to take in, and I need some time to reflect."

Kyle calmly reached his arms around me, reassuring me that everything would be okay. This was one of the first times he consoled me in months; a part of me wanted to melt in his arms, clinging to every moment just to be close to him.

I had no idea of the physical and prolonged pain I would face as my body took control over ending the pregnancy. Mentally and physically, I felt depleted.

The following day I was abruptly awoken by sharp pains penetrating my stomach. I assumed I was experiencing cramps, so I ignored the discomfort and continued preparing for the day. Finally, the pain became so unbearable that I could barely breathe, so I informed my staff that I would work from my home office and asked Jayden to meet me there to review the final details for the launch party. Once Jayden arrived, she sat across my desk with a notepad reviewing the agenda, but before I could catch my breath from a wave of sharp pain, I suddenly felt a gush of fluid explode between my legs. I knew something didn't feel right, but Jayden tended to overreact and panic in stressful situations, so I didn't want to startle her. Instead, I glanced at my computer screen, slowly turning towards her, patiently waiting until we locked eyes. It took every ounce of my being as I pretended to be calm and collected.

I asked, "Would you mind if we reschedule our meeting for tomorrow? I have an important issue I need to address."

Jayden responded, "Of course! Is everything okay?"

I inhaled a sharp breath, anxiously collecting the scattered papers on my desk, searching for my phone to text Kyle with a nervous smile.

I replied, "Yes, yes. I'll have Kyle wrap up any last-minute details with you."

Jayden seemed confused that our meeting had ended abruptly, but I couldn't bear her finding out I was sitting in a puddle of blood. I could hear Kyle's footsteps approaching my office and quickly diverted her attention to him. As she turned to face Kyle, I silently motioned him to walk her out. When the door shut behind them, I shouted for my mom, who was just steps away from my office.

I yelled, "Mom! Please bring me a towel. I need a towel. Now!"

My mom rushed into my office with a bathroom towel, and as I leaned forward to reach for it, another rush of fluid came flowing through my legs. When I stood up, a massacre of blood poured out of me, dripping down my inner thighs as I hovered over my office chair. Without hesitation, I wrapped the towel under my midsection, folding each side around my legs. I was in complete shock. I shuffled to the guest bathroom and didn't know what was happening.

My mom shrieked, "There is a huge puddle of blood where you were sitting. We need to go to the hospital."

Kyle rushed into the house, following the trail of blood splatter I left in my wake. He stood over me with his mouth wide open without saying a word as I leaned my chest over my knees, rocking back and forth. Smeared shades of red covered the white porcelain toilet seat. Kyle helped me undress while he prepared the shower to rinse my body. I shook uncontrollably as he wrapped his arms around me to guide me under the running water.

I stood naked, shivering under the hot water, staring blankly at the pool of blood streaming down the drain. I heard Kyle leave the bathroom and quickly return, so I leaned forward, pressing my head against the tile and slowly peeking my nose around the shower curtain. I noticed Kyle leaning over the toilet swirling the chunks of blood and tissue with a coat hanger, taking pictures with his phone.

I gasped, "Kyle, what are you doing?"

Kyle didn't respond; instead, he stood up and walked out of the bathroom. I felt emotionless and frozen in time; I couldn't fathom what he was trying to find. My mom quickly rushed in with a clean towel and a change of clothes. Unfortunately, the bleeding wouldn't cease and continued to soak through my clothing. My mom swaddled the towel around my legs and ushered me to the car. I paused once I realized Kyle wasn't in the vehicle. My mom motioned me not to worry as she began driving to the hospital. I was fixated on the passenger side view mirror, hoping to see Kyle closely behind us as our house disappeared in the distance.

Chapter 22: Surrender

The next thing I remember is the subtle beeping of the hospital monitor beside me. My eyelids were heavy, and my vision was slightly blurred as the nurse began to pull the tape from my skin, slowly removing tiny hairs from my arm while she disconnected the IV tubes. The faint but unmistakable scent of blood seeping through a veil of antiseptic filled the air. The lingering smell was bitter, with undertones of an artificial fragrance, some combination of bleach and cleaning products. My mom slowly sat me up in the hospital bed and positioned me on the edge of the mattress, gently guiding me toward a wheelchair near the edge of the bed.

I felt disoriented and nauseous, struggling to stand without shivering. My legs were still numb from the anesthesia, like having wet, heavy sand pulling me down while I attempted to regain my balance. I wobbled back and forth as I slowly stood upright. The tips of my toes pressed against the cold green, tiled hospital floor while my mother removed the hospital gown, still covered in blood from the procedure. I vividly remember a wave of grief and darkness looming over me. Suddenly, what was happening around me felt like an emotionless, mechanical transaction. I had just lost the little life inside me. I felt immensely connected to this little person and was terrified that they had physically removed this precious soul from my body.

The tremendous shame about losing the baby saturated my thoughts, and the worst culprit of this reflexive blaming was myself. *I must have done something wrong. This is my fault. I was still drinking alcohol before I knew I was pregnant. I was under a lot of stress. Or maybe, I didn't deserve this baby.*

After naturally giving birth to two children and raising Ashton as my own, I couldn't come to terms with letting go of this tiny soul without saying goodbye. I sat quietly in my room that evening, thinking of what might have been. As the tears coated my cheeks, I knew the only way to release the pain was to face it. I began writing in my journal but paused as I suddenly realized this baby deserved a name. My heart became heavy as I embraced the silence and submerged myself in the present moment. A still, small voice whispered in the depths of my mind, *Matthias*. I felt a calm sense of reassurance as my pen hit the paper. I wrote:

To my beautiful angel,

My heart feels empty without you here, but I know God found a special place in heaven for you. You slipped away from me before I could feel the flutter of your tiny body swimming in my belly or before I could listen to your heartbeat, and yet, we were together for every moment of your life.

Some would say you were barely there long enough to make an impression on me. But the truth is, even in such a short time, you made your way into my heart. Losing you was the most painful experience of my life. It breaks my heart to know that you were growing inside me when I was too distracted to notice.

I am truly sorry that I doubted your existence. Instead, I should have poured love into you. I never want you to feel like Mommy denied you; rather, I denied myself the opportunity to hold you in my arms.

You are blameless, innocent, and pure. I take full responsibility for not taking care of myself to nurture you. The hollow grief washes over me as I sit in shame, blaming myself for not embracing you. I am stunned by the intensity of its power. You would have experienced so much love, especially from your older brothers and sister, as they would have showered you with kisses and fought over who got to hold you first. I want you to know that no matter how much time passes, I will never forget the impression you made in my life. I will use this tragedy as an opportunity to celebrate the lessons you left behind. Before I say goodbye, I want you to know the name I chose for you. Your name is Matthias, a name of Greek origin, meaning Gift of God. You will always be a special gift in my heart.

I love you forever and always,

Mommy

As the weeks went on, my health issues were still unanswered. Yet, the grief became more bearable and easier to carry with the day-to-day distractions of raising a family, school schedules, the business, tenant improvements, and the new office launch party preparations.

The kids were older, and their ever-changing personalities kept me on my toes. Adian was seventeen, playing high school football, working part-time in the agency, supporting me with accounting, discovering his identity, and falling in love with the most beautiful girl in school, Marley. Nevaeh was thirteen and taking the world by storm; she went from competing in National dance competitions in her younger years to joining an all-boys flag football team, then focused her attention on basketball, then Volleyball. She has always been fiercely determined to show the boys who's boss. Ashton had just turned ten years old. At his core, he had an engineering mindset, effortlessly connecting the dots and solving problems while simultaneously surprising everyone with witty remarks and clever jokes. He loved exploring new adventures and playing outside for hours.

The loss of the baby reminded me to be present and intentional with each child, which was a more extraordinary gift than I could have imagined.

The new office was finally coming together, and the entire team was planning for our exclusive red-carpet event. The kitchen was a focal point, with sleek white lower cabinets accented with black hardware and a modern yet timeless black granite with dramatic gray veining. The urban industrial floating shelves drew your eyes to the open ceilings and added interest and depth to the kitchen, displaying Kyle's sought-after Whiskey collection. The open ceilings were a signature element of the contemporary office design, with striking industrial pendant lights and Edison bulb string lights streaming across the room, creating a chic, relaxed vibe. The polished concrete floors spanned the office, separated by handmade wood desks, flexible huddle areas, open gathering spaces, fluffy oversized rugs, and cozy couches. It was a dream come true to see it all finally come together, creating a collaborative and fun environment for our team.

Before I knew it, the big day arrived; a red carpet led guests, clients, family, and friends on an exclusive tour through the vast open office space. A bartender made custom cocktails for all our guests in mason jars engraved with "Raise Your Glass" to celebrate our new beginning. The smell of a harmonious collection of wildly bold Mexican aromas filled the air as a quintessential Southern California food truck began making gourmet tacos and appetizers just outside the main entrance. Live music filled the air as my incredibly talented cousin played the acoustic guitar while singing cover songs on request. We even had one of our favorite photographers carefully craft a memorable experience by capturing every moment of the big event. It was a night to remember.

Just when I thought everything was coming together, the harsh realities of being an entrepreneur unraveled more unexpected challenges.

Once all the dust settled from the launch party, I quickly recognized that I had lost sight of some significant issues in the business. With all the commotion of planning the event and tenant improvements, we were considerably over budget, leaving the company desperate to increase cash flow. I pulled Jayden aside to get clarity on what happened, and before I could get an answer, she burst into tears. I discreetly guided her outside the office toward a private outdoor bench and sat beside her as she explained.

She said, "I was trying to stay within the budget, but you and Kyle pulled me into a million directions. In addition, I've been having problems in my personal life, so the pressure of pulling all this together felt impossible."

My heart sank into my chest; I knew I should have been more supportive and present in guiding her through this process. I felt personally responsible for not providing more coaching or checking in with her sooner. I leaned closer to her on the bench. I allowed her to regain her composure, reassuring her that I empathized with the amount of responsibility I gave her and took accountability for my part.

I said, "I apologize for not recognizing that you were overwhelmed. You did an incredible job coordinating the event while juggling the unexpected construction delays. The one thing you could've done even better is to ask for help or communicate your concerns about the budget."

Jayden paused, drying her tears, sat upright, and took a deep breath.

She said, "I need some time to collect my thoughts. Do you mind if I take a few days off?"

I reassured her that despite all the chaos within the business, we care more about her well-being and family. I encouraged her to take all the time she needed. Jayden seemed scattered yet relieved, so she waited until the team left for lunch, then gathered her belongings.

As Jayden left, I reminded her once more that I was proud of all her time and investment in the company. She glanced up with a soft grin and thanked me for understanding. I knew in the pit of my stomach that she was on the brink of breaking down, so I gave her a giant bear hug and sent her on her way.

Jayden recently shared that she experienced a head trauma injury a few weeks before joining the company and regretted not informing the leadership team until after accepting the offer. This discovery explained the signs of extreme anxiety, lack of memory retention, and emotional instability. These factors contributed to her poor performance, yet I was determined to support her success.

Following Jayden's leave of absence, I checked in on her frequently, encouraging her to call me if she needed to talk and requesting a status on when she would return to work. Unfortunately, as the days grew longer, Jayden became more distant, not returning my calls until I received the following text message.

> Hi, Serena! I'm sorry, I'm just seeing this. I can't talk right now, but yes, we definitely need to chat soon. I'm still deliberating on the best decision. I still need a little bit more time before we chat. I just have so much going on in my personal life, I'm torn on whether or not I'm a fit for Pulse with my current personal state. I will call you tomorrow.

Once I realized that Jayden had no intention of returning, I knew I needed to accept responsibility for not being the leader I should have been. I was no different from Jayden, yet instead of having the courage to admit that I was struggling, I acted like I could hold it all together. I replied.

> We support your decision either way and want you to make the best decision for you and your family.
> If you choose to resign, please provide a letter, and schedule a time to return the company equipment and to inform the team. I hope you find the answers you are looking for. Please let me know if there is anything I can do to support you during this time.

That evening, I received a call from Jayden confirming her resignation. I felt a sense of closure and relief, having experienced a week of unpredictable circumstances. However, I realized that I had more significant issues coming to the surface. In addition to the depleted cash flow, our sales dropped forty percent, but before I could process a plan, I received notification from one of our largest clients that they had a change in management and no longer needed our services. This one client made up sixty percent of our business, and the loss of a client; this substantial could have a drastic effect on every aspect of the company.

Kyle and I desperately tried to negotiate our contract terms with the new management, but they were unwilling to come to an agreement, leading to a breach of their annual contract. While reconciling expenses, I realized that I approved over sixty thousand dollars in pre-paid media and trade show expenses on behalf of the client. Our relationship with the previous executive was based on three years of loyalty, so I didn't anticipate the new management refusing to reimburse the agency for media expenses, leading to open litigation. Unfortunately, the company was spiraling out of control, and just when I thought we were in a good place, Kyle surprised me with an unforeseen ultimatum.

The following day during a weekly session with our marriage counselor Kyle and I discussed how the issues in the business were affecting my health, our well-being, and, most importantly, any progress we were making in our marriage. Our counselor David guided us on the journey to healing ourselves and provided the tools for Kyle and me to have a healthy relationship for several years. Our trust in him grew stronger as he weathered every storm we faced, providing a safe environment for us to be fully vulnerable.

During the session, as Kyle spoke to David about his concerns, I was depleted from numerous days without sleep; the more I tried to focus on the conversation, the more I struggled to keep my eyes open. Finally, David noticed my inability to hide the exhaustion and asked me to share what was on my mind. I instantly sat upright in my chair and tried to respond without overstepping the established communication rules.

I said, "We made a vow to be there for each other during the good times and the challenges. I feel like I have been supportive, patient, and unwavering even in the darkest moments of our marriage, but to be fully transparent, I feel alone. I understand that Kyle is fully dedicated to sales and can't always be there to support me with business issues. However, he disappears for hours, and when he returns, and I ask him for help, I receive habitual negative responses or feel like he doesn't acknowledge my concerns. I shouldn't be in this alone because I didn't create this mess alone."

Kyle turned toward me with a tightness in his eyes; I noticed a slight twitch under his right eye as I continued to speak.

I said, "I know sometimes I seem emotional or flustered; all I ask is your willingness to understand and offer support. I need simple acts of kindness to feel appreciated, like offering to help when I'm overwhelmed or sitting with me as I work through issues."

I could sense the tension building in the room and noticed that Kyle seemed rigid; he began readjusting his posture while taking a deep breath and releasing a heavy sigh. Finally, Kyle leaned forward, planting his elbows against his knees, and pressing his hands against his forehead as he began shaking his head from side to side. David observed Kyle's body language.

He asked, "What comes up for you, Kyle?"

Kyle's demeanor suddenly changed; he softened his expression, pursing his lips, raising his eyebrows, then looking into the distance in deep reflection before he proceeded.

Kyle replied, "I want to be respected as a man, and I feel as though Serena has taken away my masculinity by not allowing me to lead. I want her to listen to what I'm saying without reading into the emotion or creating her own interpretation. Sometimes she dismisses my ideas before I finish a statement, making me feel like my opinion isn't valued."

I held my breath steady as I listened intently. I genuinely felt Kyle's defeated energy and began empathizing with how he perceived my behavior. Finally, Kyle dropped his shoulders, ducking his chin into his slightly caved chest.

Kyle continued, "When I try to help, she talks too fast, over-explaining the process as though she's communicating with a child—not allowing me to speak or provide ideas. I want to help her and feel valued and respected, but it's emasculating. I hear her saying that she wants help but then continues to carry the weight of the world on her shoulders. She is unwilling to let go. It kills me to watch her deteriorate."

A deafening silence swept through the room, dividing my thoughts as I refrained from responding. Instead, I fixed my gaze on a dimly lit lamp beside Kyle, uncertain how to process my emotions. David gracefully broke the silence.

David shared, "No man is happy when he is not being challenged. When a woman takes away all the challenges from a man, the man will seek unhealthy challenges. Extreme on either end is unhealthy, being extremely independent is unhealthy, and being extremely dependent is unhealthy. You are both on a journey to find the healthy version of yourselves, and there are peaks and valleys on every journey. Let's reframe this conversation and determine what each of you wants."

To avoid speaking over Kyle, I gestured to him to share first. Kyle turned to face me, drawing his eyebrows together, moving closer and leaning in, placing his hand on my knee. His hazel eyes drew inward as they filled with tears.

He said, "I want a healthy, thriving relationship, meaningful conversations, and quality time with you. I want affection, romance, and intimacy. But most of all, I want you to trust me again. I know that this may hurt you, but I also need independence. I see the business impacting your health, your relationship with the kids, and our marriage. So, I want you to step away from the business to focus on you, and so we can work on our marriage."

My lips began to quiver as I felt my body collapsing, tilting my head back and blinking quickly to keep from bursting into tears. The shame of losing myself in the business and neglecting the people I loved more than anything weighed heavily on my heart. I felt submerged under water gasping for air as intense sadness, regret, and guilt ran over me. He was right; I was drowning and, in the process, taking the entire ship down with me.

I lifted my gaze and slowly nodded, acknowledging the truth of the situation. Nausea roiled in the pit of my stomach as I searched for answers within. An outpour of shame consumed me. *I'm failing my family; I'm unable to satisfy his needs or meet his expectations., I feel defeated and disheartened that my progress and healing weren't recognized. I'm embarrassed and humiliated that I've sacrificed so much of myself for everyone else, and now my family is suffering.*

David observed my reservation, gently leading the conversation as he awaited my response.

David shared, "After a mother cares for her children, they leave home to find independence once they grow and can care for themselves. In the same way, a husband will leave when he feels that he has lost independence. A man needs an impossible mission to conquer. Serena, I know you have invested your time, energy, passion, stress, heart, tears, and health for this business. You own it. It is a part of you. What I hear Kyle saying is that he is willing to take on the responsibility of the business so you can find healing. Are you willing to step away from the business? What do you want?"

As I formulated a response, an undulating wave of anger, sadness, and fear swirled within me. I immediately felt cornered by this question, yet I knew in the depth of my soul that I had nothing left to give. I needed a sense of reprieve. I closed my eyes briefly, exhaling a long, low sigh. My chin trembled as I focused my vacant gaze on Kyle and began speaking.

I said, "I'm truly sorry I made you feel emasculated; that was never my intention. I want you to feel respected. I am grateful for your sacrifice in the business and want you to feel valued. I do need time to heal, and I want to trust that you can take on some of my responsibilities so I can find balance. If you are asking me to choose between you or the business. I choose you."

Just as the last words fell from my lips, I felt my body collapsing into Kyle's arms, and a deep sadness ran over me while my heart sank into my chest. Kyle's face lit up with a bright optimism that I hadn't recognized in years. His heart was pounding, brain racing, as though electricity was running through his veins.

Shortly after I made this monumental decision, the session ended. A sudden heaviness expanded in my core. I was frozen, struggling to process my decision; while Kyle couldn't resist his enthusiasm, his face became alive and animated, verbalizing his ideas without hesitation.

Kyle said, "We'll inform the team tomorrow morning! Then, I'll delegate all your projects, and you can debrief each team member before you leave."

I took a hard, pronounced swallow, tensing my shoulders, grinding my jaw, and rolling my neck as it cracked, popped, and snapped.

I said, "Kyle, I manage the finances, accounting, proposals, hiring, training, legal, contracts, and operations and provide final approval on all projects. Our team is already spread thin; they don't have the capacity to take on my responsibilities. We need a plan to roll out these changes over time."

Kyle leaned in closer, grinning from ear to ear with a cavalier tone.

He said, "You won't have to worry about the business anymore. I'll take care of it now."

I observed Kyle's careless behavior and a sudden incapacitating fear rushed through me, torn between the desire to protect my team and the need to protect my marriage. I knew that releasing my grip; would allow him to feel valued and respected. But on the other hand, I was anxious by his recklessness and terrified of how this decision would impact our business.

Kyle immediately called the leadership team to announce the news the following morning. Kyle was energized and verbose while announcing my leave of absence and the new responsibilities of each employee. I could sense the energy in the room, motionless like a pool of stagnant water, as each team member listened skeptically, drawing their attention to my demeanor. I sat with a tall posture, chin up and chest forward, supporting Kyle as he spoke while secretly, my stomach turned in knots as I observed their confusion. Finally, I motioned Kyle for a moment to share my thoughts; he paused to let me speak.

I said, "I know that this may come as a surprise. First, I want you to know how much I value each of you. Second, I want to be completely vulnerable in sharing that this decision is not easy; it weighs heavy on my heart. The moment we admit that we are helpless is the moment we are open to receiving help, and the truth is, I need your help. I know you will adapt to this change and continue to thrive."

The leadership team experienced firsthand our struggles and empathized with the decision, despite their concerns or apprehension.

Yet, in the following days and weeks, I received numerous phone calls, text messages, and emails from each team member, verbalizing their frustration with how Kyle led the organization. He was delegating an overwhelming workload to each person and demanding unreasonable deadlines for projects they needed to be trained to execute. Kyle was changing our processes, disregarding best practices, overpromising, and under-delivering. At first, I tried to encourage each team member to have feedback directly with Kyle, but when I realized that he wasn't listening to their concerns, I knew I needed to get involved.

That afternoon I began reviewing our financials, preparing to run payroll, and I saw that our account balance was deficient. We didn't have enough to make payroll. I needed to find a solution, so I tried to reach Kyle, but every call was forwarded to voicemail. Finally, I sent him a text message asking him to call me, but he quickly responded by telling me he was too busy. The panic set in, and my blood started to boil as I became infuriated. The repressed anger I unconsciously avoided, denied, or pushed down for years finally rose to the surface. Kyle's carelessness in the business and our marriage ignited a rage inside me that I had never acknowledged before. The anger brewed in my mind. *I have accepted, forgave, and justified his behavior for long enough, and now he is throwing everything we built away by running the business into the ground.* Forgiveness does not mean tolerance, and I will no longer tolerate lies, manipulation, gaslighting, and blatant disregard. I have given him every ounce of my being, yet he continues to raise his expectations even higher, then chooses not to acknowledge all the time and energy I've invested.

I will no longer sacrifice my needs or the company for him. It was time to take back my life, and it was time to tell Kyle that I'd had enough.

Chapter 23: Unhinged

That evening, I drove to the office to tell Kyle we didn't have enough money to make payroll. In the past, when we struggled to make payroll, I always sacrificed my pay to ensure he received his paycheck. But in recent months, I had paid myself so little that I was concerned that we wouldn't be able to pay our mortgage. My palms were sweating as I clenched the steering wheel, rehearsing how I would tell Kyle that we didn't have enough money in our personal or business account to cover his pay.

As I approached the office, I sat in my car for a few minutes trying to calm my racing mind. Then, I noticed that he was sitting at my desk, intently focused on the glaring screen of his laptop. I took a deep breath and began walking toward him. He momentarily acknowledged my presence, then motioned me to stop with an agitated expression gesturing that he was too busy to talk.

The office was quiet as most of our employees had already left for the day, so I sat beside Kyle, patiently waiting for a moment of his time. A sheen of sweat glistened on my cheeks, chin, and forehead while I frantically bounced my right knee. My gaze was fixated on the polished concrete floors as I formulated my thoughts. Just as I lifted my head to interrupt his focus, I glanced at his laptop screen and noticed he was searching online for hunting gear. I cleared my throat, hoping to capture his attention casually, but he ignored my signal. I reached toward his leg to gently nudge him when he suddenly snapped back.

Kyle said, "Can't you see that I'm busy? I need to order this gear before my next Elk hunting trip!"

I had forgotten that the hunting trip was only a few weeks away and didn't realize Kyle still planned on going when we couldn't afford to pay our mortgage, let alone save for an expense this large. I knew it meant the world to him, but this only fueled my anxiety. The mounting frustration was building, and I became unduly irritable, yet he avoided eye contact. As the minutes passed, I became even more intolerant until I finally insisted on commanding his attention.

I said, "Kyle, we need to talk."

Kyle slowly turned toward me; I could sense the tiny hairs stiffening on the nape of his neck as his eyes widened. He moved slowly and deliberately, pushing his chair away from the desk and then leaning back as he reluctantly gave me his full attention. I could feel the tension rising, so I stood up and asked him to follow me outside.

I said, "We don't have enough money in our business account to make payroll. I can process payroll for our employees, but you and I won't get paid. We also don't have the money in our account to pay our mortgage. So, I need your help."

Kyle scoffed, tilting his head down, shaking it side to side. He lifted his gaze, locking his eyes in mine with a slight squint, then snapped his head back, expelling an audible yet cut-off breath.

He said, "Is this what you wanted... to see me fail? So, you could say I told you so."

I replied, "No! I wanted you to feel a sense of purpose. I'm concerned that you do not recognize the impact of this decision, and we need to figure this out before it's too late."

Kyle inhaled deeply, turning away from me, pausing for a moment as he looked out over the canyon behind our office. As the day ended, the sun slowly set in the west, peeking through the clouds while a soft breeze grazed against the trees. We seemed frozen in time as I waited for Kyle to respond. Instead, he stood in silence with defeated energy, embracing the heat of the dimly lit sun on his cheeks; he calmly turned with a vacant expression and monotone voice.

He replied, "I'm going on this hunting trip. You are not going to take that away from me. You can have the business, and when I return, I will start my own. I'm sure you'll figure out how to pay the mortgage. You always do."

I stood motionless, with a throbbing, pulsing sensation in my throat. The heaviness of Kyle's despondent response made my heart sink as he gathered his belongings from the desk and walked away.

An uncomfortable silence lingered through the evening and into the following days. Kyle tediously prepared for his upcoming travels as hunting packs flooded our loft with piles of tactical gear, gadgets, flashlights, headlamps, camouflage apparel, waterproof sleeping bags, firearms, scopes, accessories, and emergency supplies. I tried to initiate a conversation to apologize for how our last discussion unfolded, but Kyle seemed to shrug it off while he focused on the excitement leading up to his trip.

Finally, the evening before his departure, we enjoyed a night alone while the kids were away. As Kyle began to prepare dinner, I leaned over the oversized kitchen island, reaching around to touch his hand as he hustled through the dining room. He paused and caught my gaze.

I said, "Kyle, I love you more than anyone in the world, and I am truly sorry for the experience I created by making you feel unvalued. That was never my intention."

A genuine smile framed his face as he gently kissed my cheek. A feeling of relief washed over me.

He said, "I was just trying to help, and I'm happy about our decision."

Slightly stunned by his response, I couldn't hide the confusion in my expression. He laughed and began chopping fresh vegetables while I stared blankly at his mysterious grin. His face lit up with enthusiasm as he attempted to hold back his excitement. I curiously asked what was on his mind, and without hesitation, he began sharing his new business idea. I felt a sense of reprieve that his anger toward me had faded; even amid my confusion, I was grateful to listen intently while he boasted about every detail over dinner. His eyes sparkled with joy when he finally revealed his plans to start an executive coaching company. Kyle's passion fueled the conversation as he popped the cork on an expensive bottle of wine we had saved for a special occasion. We lifted our glasses, cheering for his newfound purpose. It felt like an eternity since the last time I saw him glowing. He continued by sharing that he would use his personal experience to guide and inspire business professionals to achieve new levels of success.

He said, "It's going to be challenging and uncomfortable, but I'm ready to start something of my own."

I said, "You deserve this! I'm so proud of you."

I knew Kyle always felt like he was living in my shadow, and this monumental shift gave me hope that he found his own identity. After dinner, Kyle finished packing the gear into his car while preparing the last-minute details to leave early the following day. Our sex life had been rigid the past few months because his needs never ceased. I thought that the more I fed his desires, the less likely he would seek them elsewhere. Yet this night was special. Watching his eyes light up ignited a fire within me, and I wanted to give him a night he wouldn't forget. So, I quietly tiptoed upstairs, placing candles throughout our bedroom and carefully tossing rose petals up the stairs leading to a romantic bubble bath. I slipped into some sexy lingerie, refreshed my makeup, then subtly called out to him, asking when he was coming to bed.

    I heard his footsteps coming up the stairs, so I quickly jumped on the bed, giggling as I impatiently waited for him to notice my seductive surprise. But instead, he peeked around the entryway with a mischievous smirk, breathing in the sweet smell of the vanilla cream candles with a hint of bourbon as the flickering flame framed his masculine jawline. Then, he lunged aggressively toward me, fumbling his hands through the waistband of my panties, forcing his fingers into the tight space under the close-fitting lace as he closed his palm around my thigh and thrust me against his body. We rolled around a mountain of pillows beside our canopy bed. The sweat from our bodies melted into each other, panting, and moaning in passion until our energy depleted. I felt the breeze from a nearby open window while I nestled my head against Kyle's warm chest as he gently brushed each strand of hair away from my cheeks. I felt a soothing sense of comfort as I listened to his heartbeat; indulging in these special moments together made me feel safe in his arms.

    A few days after Kyle left for his trip, I thought it might be fun to dress up and text him some sexy photos to remind him that I was thinking of him. He mentioned that he wouldn't have cellular service before leaving, but I still hoped for a response. Yet his messages seemed sporadic and indifferent. Finally, I asked him if everything was okay, and he reassured me that he was enjoying the trip but had a lot on his mind. I knew that although he was with his uncle and cousin, Kyle spent several hours alone in the forest, waiting silently for a target to approach. I didn't want to disrupt his solitude, so instead, I decided to keep myself occupied by setting up his laptop with all his new business information. I searched the office and the house turning our closet upside down, trying to find his computer, but I couldn't find it anywhere. Finally, I realized; He had probably left it in his car at his aunt and uncle's house. So, I decided to drive by to see if it was there.

It was a chilly day in October; the leaves were molten-red, falling graciously from the trees, dancing against my windshield with every breeze. I was soaking in the orange and red tones while admiring the suburban neighborhood near their home. Once I arrived, I quickly jumped into his car and turned on the ignition to warm up while I shuffled around to find his briefcase.

Kyle recently bought a new car, so when I noticed the dashboard displayed a name I didn't recognize, it caught my attention, but it was so cold I continued to search under the seats until I discovered his briefcase was in the trunk. I locked the vehicle, dropped the keys inside his aunt and uncle's house, and drove home. I felt uneasy about the woman's name on his dashboard monitor, but instead, I tried to talk myself off the ledge. I began practicing mindfulness, listening to music, and reframing my thoughts. But it just kept eating away at me. *After all that we've been through, he wouldn't cheat again. But that would explain why he has been so distant on this trip. Okay, now I'm just going crazy. This is crazy; I need to stop. It's probably the name of the previous owner.*

As soon as I arrived home, I ran upstairs, set the briefcase on Kyle's bedside table, turned on the running water for a bath, and began writing in my journal. As I prepared the bath, I sat on the edge of the tub, waiting for the water to cool down. We enjoyed such an incredible night together before he left. I couldn't piece together why his demeanor shifted so quickly. I felt like I was on an emotional rollercoaster; the highs were exhilarating, and the lows equally debilitating, often in rapid succession.

I couldn't take it anymore; I impulsively texted him, asking if he was still in love with me. I anxiously stared at the lock screen, studying my reflection. I knew Kyle was in the middle of the woods without service, but it seemed like an unimaginable amount of time to wait for a simple response. So instead of desperately dwelling on the minutes that passed, I dipped my toes in the steaming water, submerged my legs and torso, then tilted my head back beneath the surface. The bubbles gently drifted around my face drowning out the sound of my racing mind. Finally, I closed my eyes and began to float. The strands of my wet blonde hair streamed through the ripples in the bath, tickling my cheeks as the water coated my body. I held my breath to drown my thoughts until water surged into my lungs; I choked, sank, and came up, gasping for air. I sat up, breathing heavily, sliding my fingers through my wet hair and over my eyes as the tears flooded in.

I needed to pull myself together, so I slipped into a towel and began drying my hair. Just then, I received a notification from Kyle.

What are you talking about?

> You said you had a lot on your mind.
> Are you having second thoughts about us?
> Is this what you want?

Are you asking me to make a decision about us?

> That's not what I said.
> I'm simply asking what you want?

My body shivered in the damp towel as my bare feet slid against the cold floor. A heavy weight pressed against my chest as I struggled to swallow. Minutes passed, and still nothing. Finally, I curled my body into the fetal position lying naked, swaddled in the damp towel on the carpet of our walk-in closet, concentrating on the glow of my cell phone while I awaited Kyle's response. My eyes felt heavy, and just as they began to close, I was startled by the vibration of my phone.

I wasn't planning on making a decision when I came home, I was just having a dialogue with you.

> I think we've had enough dialogue. It's time for you to decide what you really want.

I understand.

His tepid response left me dejected and defeated in a state of confusion. That evening I scheduled a private virtual session with our marriage counselor, David. I was aware that I allowed my irrational thoughts to consume me, isolating myself from the people I loved, hiding and masking emotions. I understood that my method of coping was unhealthy and acknowledged its negative effect on my healing process; at the same time, my intuition was gnawing at me. Something didn't feel right, and I needed clarity. David was the only person who undoubtedly saw me, even when I tried to hide. He had a particular way of providing insight and bringing my fears to light.

I joined the session early, biting my nails as I rehearsed how to approach the conversation. I wavered back and forth, questioning myself as I didn't quite know how to explain my feelings. However, my mind went utterly blank once David arrived, with only one question lingering. Curiously David smiled, tilting his head with an inquisitive expression.

David asked, "How can I support you today?"

I took a deep breath, stretched my arms, and rolled my shoulders back as I gradually lifted my chin from my chest.

I said, "I think it's time. I have a deep feeling in the pit of my stomach that I need to make a decision... To leave Kyle."

My eyes widened as I sat in shock for a seemingly endless pause. I couldn't believe the words actually fell from my mouth. David leaned forward, intently listening. I felt my body temperature rise as though I was sitting in a sauna, pressing my sweating palms together while I continued to speak.

I said, "I see glimpses of him, then he fades away. I believe Kyle wants to change with all my heart, but his actions show me that I live in a false reality. I'm terrified."

David responded, "What are you afraid of?"

I began fumbling my words as I rambled an endless list of fears.

I said, "I'm afraid of losing our home, tearing apart our family, hurting the children, losing the business. If I leave, what if he takes Ashton away? Where will my parents live? But most of all, I am afraid Kyle might hurt himself."

David reclined in his chair as I anxiously peeled the cuticles around my fingernails, awaiting his response.

David asked, "Do you think you have that much control over someone's actions?"

I hadn't prepared for his question; I collected my thoughts as the emotions flooded in. David compassionately observed my restlessness.

He said, "You have endured more in your life than most people could survive in an entire lifetime, and I admire your strength. You are responsible for keeping yourself and your children safe. However, it is not your responsibility to protect Kyle. You may be able to influence his feelings, BUT only he is in control of his actions."

His statement struck me like a jolt of electricity. I sat in shock, searching for the courage to release myself from the responsibility of protecting Kyle. It felt as though David had ripped off a blindfold that I had been refusing to remove for the past ten years.

David asked, "What comes up for you?"

I replied, "I am strong, ambitious, and resilient. I'm a loving mother, provider, and nurturer. I have given Kyle grace, mercy, and forgiveness. I'm an incredible wife, plus I am amazing in bed! But no matter how hard I try; I will never be enough for him."

David responded, "You may have all those qualities, but Serena, there is no need to prove your worth or convince others to love you. True love is not earned. It must be freely given, without expectations."

I experienced a breakthrough, an extreme sense of clarity, and the chaos in my mind suddenly stopped. This entire time, I was running in circles on a hamster wheel, trying to earn Kyle's love, affection, and approval. Instead, I had been fueling Kyle's idealization while simultaneously sacrificing myself in an effort to save him.

David had a profound way of speaking directly to my heart. In a simple statement, I gained a deeper understanding of my role in this cycle, and the answer to my questions became inevitability clear.

The following day I woke up as the morning sun radiated through the blinds, curling my head under the covers, wanting nothing more than to bury myself within the soft down comforter, pleading with God to let me sleep my problems away. The conversation with David weighed heavily on my mind. I wanted nothing more than to believe that there could still be a chance that our marriage could overcome all these nightmares. But I knew I needed to pull myself together, if for nothing more than to ensure that my parents and the kids didn't see me this way. So, I showered, threw on a dress, applied a slight extra blush to brighten my face, and mastered a fake smile in the mirror before rushing out the door to drop the kids off at school.

I managed to fake it through the day, and on my way home, the persistent sadness began to seep in. I genuinely believed that we could overcome anything after all Kyle and I had endured in our marriage, but something still didn't feel right. I decided to keep myself distracted without allowing the unwanted intrusive thoughts to play their own narratives recklessly through my mind. As I arrived home, my mom was finishing the laundry while my dad played games on his computer, Nevaeh was entertaining a friend, and Adian had just returned home from football practice. I rushed up the stairs before anyone could catch a glimpse of me and planted myself stomach-first on our canopy bed. I buried my head beneath the pillows while I attempted to relax.

Just then, I remembered Kyle's briefcase. I sat upright, placing the pillows behind me as I propped his computer on my lap. I began organizing his new business files on the desktop, setting up his email, and removing folders he no longer needed. Kyle normally disabled his text messages from appearing on his laptop, but before he left, he canceled his cellular service from our shared plan and started a new account for the business. Within a few minutes, the messages from his phone automatically synced with his laptop, and a multitude of text notifications poured in. Instantly, Kyle's iMessage popped up with an alert from a contact named Nick. Just as I minimized the chat window, I saw a stream of photos loading, so I curiously reopened the message and noticed that Kyle had sent Nick a screenshot of our private text messages from the day before.

A tunnel of darkness encompassed my concentration as I began frantically scrolling through every text between Kyle and Nick. Then, a flash of reality slapped me in the face when I discovered that Nick wasn't a male friend of Kyle; in fact, it was a woman, and her real name was actually Rachael Nicole. I suddenly remembered that Rachael was the name displayed on the screen in Kyle's car, and Nick was an alias he had created for Nicole.

Kyle claimed he didn't have service, yet and sent messages to her the entire time. He sent a photo of their initials he carved in a tree, wrote her name in the snow surrounded by a heart, and told Rachael that when he returned from his trip, he was finally leaving me so they could be together. She replied to his messages with photos of herself and proclaiming her love for him.

Appalled, I threw his laptop against the wall screaming and crying in a manic fury. My mom rushed into the bedroom, with the kids closely behind. Hoovering in the doorway in complete confusion about my outburst, they each tried to comfort me. Again, I wailed violently, accompanied by bouts of yelling and shrieking, covering my face between my knees as I backed into a corner, rocking back and forth.

I cried, "NO, NO, NO! This is not happening again. Why God? Why?"

Saliva, mucus, and tears saturated my face as cries glued my lips in a static open position, whaling from the pit of my stomach. Finally, my mother and the kids knelt on the carpet, coddling my hollow body in their arms.

The various stages of anger unleashed a rage within that I had repressed for years, from internal turmoil to explicit anger. This emotion spread throughout my heart, triggering past trauma in my mind, body, and nervous system, and reopening old wounds.

My chest felt like it was caving in. I began to relax my shoulders, intentionally slowing down the pace of my breath in a deliberate effort to inhale through my nose, then released a loud sigh with each exhale. Once I caught my breath, with my lips quivering, I muttered in a raspy voice.

I said, "Pack all your things. We're leaving."

I refused to reach out to Kyle to inform him of my findings because I knew he would deny the affair. Kyle was scheduled to arrive home in three days, giving us limited time to pack our things before he returned. Ashton was staying with his mother while Kyle was traveling, so I was grateful that my baby boy wouldn't witness the eruption of chaos.

I jumped up, ushering Adian and Nevaeh to their rooms, following closely behind with oversized suitcases for each of them. As I approached Nevaeh's room, she turned and paused abruptly, pushing the suitcase away from her bedroom door with a determined glare in her clear blue eyes.

She said, "I'm not leaving! He should leave. This is our home."

Unprepared to be challenged by my twelve-year-old daughter amid my hysteria, I recognized my loss of control but could not rein it in. Instead, I insisted that she pack her things immediately, then rushed down the hallway to drop off the next suitcase in Adian's room. Adian was flustered, running in circles from his bathroom to his bedroom, scooping up piles of clothes from the floor. Finally, he paused to acknowledge my presence and with a compassionate tone.

He said, "Don't worry, mama, we are going to be okay."

His voice stopped me in my tracks, giving me a momentary sense of peace. He seemed very familiar with my anxious, apologetic smile.

I whispered, "I love you, son."

The house was in complete chaos as we rushed up and down the stairs until my mom touched my arm gently to capture my attention. Her expression drew inward as though she could physically feel my pain. She tried to speak, then paused to reflect.

She said, "Where should your dad and I go?"

In my flustered attempt to find a solution, I scrambled for the right words but couldn't compose an answer. Finally, my mother acknowledged my disbanded thoughts, motioning me to continue.

She said, "Don't worry about us. We will figure it out. You have enough on your mind."

In the reflection of her eyes, I saw myself as a failure. When we bought this house, we included a guest suite, so my parents could be close to us, and due to my efforts to flee without warning, I left them without a home. I knew they were scared in this moment of uncertainty, yet they continued to set aside their fears to comfort me. I was ashamed and disappointed in myself for letting them down.

My parents have given so much of themselves. They have been a pillar of strength in our lives, serving unselfishly, loving unconditionally, embracing our flaws with acceptance and grace, and never asking for anything in return. I dreamed of greatness, wanting nothing more than to make them proud, but instead, my life was in pieces, and I was falling apart before their eyes.

Accepting that my choices led me here weighed heavy on my mind. I am responsible for allowing this to go on without telling anyone, and now their whole world is being turned upside down. It was debilitating, but I knew I couldn't allow my insistent desire to protect everyone else, stop me from protecting myself.

I wandered aimlessly through every room, packing, cleaning, and sealing boxes filled with the memories we shared. Yet even the most positive memories between us have been eclipsed by a shadow of betrayal. Suddenly the stark reality of losing Ashton set in, and I couldn't imagine what he would think when he returned home. *What would Kyle tell him? Would he think I abandoned him? What if my baby boy would never be in my life again?* Once I gathered my thoughts, I searched for a marker in his room and wrote a note on the mirror in his bathroom.

Ashton,

You will always be my baby boy, and I will always be your mommy (#2). Our last name or DNA does not define my love for you; it's defined by the commitment I made to love you unconditionally for all of eternity. It means choosing to love even when it's hard and never giving up on each other. I want you to know that I will never give up on you and always be here for you. I love you more than all the stars in the galaxy.

Love, Mommy

I gently closed his bedroom door, hoping that Kyle wouldn't find and erase the message I had written. I prayed that Ashton would know how much I loved him as I continued packing my belongings.

I had suppressed my feelings for so long that they were explosive when I finally allowed them to surface. Anger, resentment, and disgust came alive and pulsed through my body. These emotions raged within, provoking thoughts of revenge. I was unhinged. Finally, in a moment of weakness, I decided to expose the truth.

I rushed through the hallway, up the stairs to our bedroom, grabbed Kyle's laptop, sat with my ankles crossed on the carpet, pressed my back against the corner of the wall, propped his computer between my legs, and began to log in to his personal social media account. Then, without hesitation, I impulsively composed a public post impersonating Kyle bringing his deception to light. The post read:

> It is with great sadness that I'm posting tonight. I have been unfaithful in my marriage several times, and my recent relationship with @RachaelNicole devastated my children and my wife. I have a journey of healing ahead of me, and I am asking for your prayers.

I tagged Rachael in the post; then, with my fingers shaking, I published the message. Amid my irrational behavior, I hastily closed the laptop and continued collecting my things. I justified my uninhibited actions of publicly exposing my marriage by convincing myself it was warranted. *He deserves this! His selfish actions have destroyed our marriage too many times. He has humiliated me long enough. I will no longer protect his integrity. I'm tired of pretending.*

The guilt set in within a few minutes, and my thoughts dangled from a limb. I was mentally berating myself over my reckless decision. *What have I done? I can't believe I posted that message. I'm such an idiot. What* is wrong with me? I'm so humiliated. I need to delete it immediately before anyone else views it. I rushed back to his computer, lifted the top panel as my eyes adjusted to the glow of the display, and within minutes the dreaded social media post received over twenty comments. I was mortified as I scanned the responses.

> "You need to keep this to yourself. Get on your knees and pray for forgiveness. I pray that Serena and your kids can get through the damage and pain you have caused."
>
> "This has got to be a joke."
>
> "I respect you for being open. Hope your kids will recover."
>
> "I can't believe you just respected an adulterer. Think about that, and just let that sink in. Fuck you and your prayers! Your God will not help you crawl out of this one. You are on your own."
>
> "Dude... what's going on?"
>
> "Praying, bro, you'll be okay."
>
> "Kyle is on a hunting trip without cell service. He didn't post this; it must be an attempt to ruin his reputation. Take this down!"

Before I could read another comment, I took a screenshot of the stream of comments with the message I posted, then immediately deleted it. I quickly closed the laptop and slid it under the bed in a poor attempt to hide my shame. My stomach turned in knots; sweat dripped from my brow as I pinched the skin between my eyes. The deep-seated realization that someone would notify Kyle of the social media post hovered over my head like a dark cloud as I scrambled to reverse the madness I had unleashed.

I lost myself in a flash of anger, provoking more pain. I sat alone in the dark room with my head in my hands as I summoned my strength. I had failed myself, and I needed to own my mistake. I pulled the laptop from under the bed, opened the display, and sent the screenshot to Kyle with a short message.

> You will have everything you want when you return.

Chapter 24: Enough

I tossed and turned all night, dozing off in short periods, with my head suddenly snapping back, waking up to the reality of what I had done. My eyes blinked rapidly, cocking my head from side to side, trying to cleanse the berating thoughts that haunted me through the night. The emotional hurricane drained every ounce of my energy, yet my body was restless as I stared blankly at my phone screen, nervously awaiting his reply. Then, finally, the digital clock on my phone flickered; it was five in the morning, and my eyelids began to close just as the sun started to rise. Suddenly a notification appeared, sending chills down my spine. Kyle finally responded in confusion.

What?! I don't even know what this is?!
I didn't post that.

I sat up, placing pillows behind me, leaning against the headboard, and drawing the courage deep within. I paused for a moment, focusing on my breath, reminding myself to transform the pain into power and honor my commitment to be resilient.

I posted it.
I also listed the house for sale, opened a new bank account, hired a divorce attorney, informed my parents and the children, rented a condo, and packed all my things.
We will be gone before you get home.

I don't think you need a divorce attorney.
I don't want anything.
I'm so sorry that you are going through this right now.
I do love you and don't want you to hurt.
I know you haven't been happy, and my past decisions ruined what we had.

Kyle's deflecting response repulsed me, but I felt an odd sense of relief, knowing the man I once loved was a stranger. He is so tangled in the web of lies that he is unrecognizable. Instead of allowing myself to be twisted in his double game, I held firm in my decision.

> I asked your uncle to confiscate any weapons you have in your possession and informed him that you may be a suicide risk. In addition, I have removed every item from the house that you could use to hurt yourself. I am sorry you chose this path, and I will no longer allow you to hurt me or my children.
>
> Goodbye, Kyle.

Once I received confirmation that the text message was delivered, I blocked Kyle's phone number so I would no longer receive notifications and curled up in a ball with a pillow pressed against my face to drown out the sounds of my aching heart.

For far too long, I didn't know who to talk to or where to turn, so I held my silence, minimized my pain, isolated myself from those who loved me, keeping my secrets locked inside. As humbling and humiliating as it may be, I knew the last item on my list was informing my employees of our divorce. So, I reached deep within my soul to find the courage to face my team.

As I drove to the office, I watched the fall leaves dancing in the blistering wind on a cold October afternoon. I could see Adian and Marley following closely behind through the slightly fogged rear window. Our team was like our family, and I felt the need to protect them from the devastation. Yet, I knew that I could no longer pretend. It was time to honor my truth, allowing myself to be fully vulnerable. Nothing worth holding on to requires a tight grip.

I swallowed my fears and stepped into my power as I entered the double doors with conviction. I gathered everyone closer to share that I had an announcement. The tension in the room was heavy. I sat knee-deep in silence, with my eyes fixated on the floor, collecting my emotions.

The bathroom faucet dripped into the sink, echoing across the office and reverberating around the room like a cymbal, yet no one blinked or moved, waiting steadily for me to speak. I leaned in closer, with a pressing weight against my chest.

I said, "I promised to always be fully transparent with you, yet in my effort to protect each of you, I have withheld the truth. So it is with a broken heart that I share with you that Kyle and I will be getting a divorce. It has been a rough journey, and I had to make some hard decisions for my well-being, my children, and the business. I've never been more devastated for our children and the loss of the man I once knew. Nevertheless, I forgive Kyle and will always love him, although I will no longer allow his decisions to influence our lives."

I paused to take a sip of water, allowing the silence to settle while each person visibly expressed their emotions with sighs, scoffs, and disparaging looks.

I continued, "I am feeling empowered and weightless as I've been carrying this on my shoulders for almost ten years; the kids are resilient, so I know God has a bigger plan. I have always been the agency's sole owner and dismissed Kyle as an employee before uncovering the most recent situation. Despite the challenges, I am confident the agency will continue to thrive. I believe in each and every one of you and know that nothing will hold us back!"

A flurry of activity and questions broke loose as I guided the conversation to the focal point of moving forward, pressing on, and letting go of the past. I strived to reassure the team that we would overcome and prevail, fielding every question with reassurance and certainty. Finally, with my last ounce of strength, I confidently stood up and walked toward the kitchen, scanning the open shelves for an expensive bottle of bourbon. Then I turned to the team with a reassuring smile, raising my arm high with a glass in my hand.

I said, "Let's open a bottle, and cheers to new beginnings!"

We gathered around the open office kitchen, raising our glasses, celebrating our strength, and encouraging each other. Once the excitement began settling and the team dispersed, I overheard them bantering back and forth about Kyle and Jayden. I couldn't hear their words, but I did not want negativity to stiffen the mood. I interjected with a compassionate tone.

I said, "I know this is a lot to process, but we have a no-tolerance policy for gossip."

My son caught my attention like a thief in the night with a stark expression on his face.

Adian said, "Mom. They're not gossiping."

His face was pale with a pained expression; his clouded eyes drew inward, taking a deep, troubled breath as his voice weakened.

He continued, "It is true. Kyle was with Jayden."

I felt a blow to the chest like a bomb dropped at my feet and exploded, piercing my ears with a sharp ring, drowning the barrier of sound. I could only see Adian's face as the entire room faded to black. The space around me transformed into darkness as I tried to focus on Adian's tender blue eyes, with my chin quivering.

I muttered, "What do you mean?"

Adian calmly approached me, reaching his arms around me, holding me tightly while my shoulders caved into his chest, whispering, "I'm so sorry, Mama."

How could Kyle let my son carry the weight of his burden? Adian witnessed the only father he had ever known create a spiral of lies while Kyle openly pursued other women. I couldn't fathom why Kyle would be so careless in front of my son. I stepped back, stammering as I turned in slow motion observing every expression in the room. They all knew? I felt stranded on an island surrounded by an ocean of lies, exposed and naked.

My employees circled me, talking over one another, "We're so sorry; we thought you knew." "We thought that was why Jayden resigned." "It was obvious that Kyle seemed indifferent; he made it seem like you let him do whatever he wanted."

I leaned back, stepping away, noticing two of my managers frozen in shock. Simultaneously they said, "We had no idea, Serena. We would have told you if we knew."

The last flicker of my soul was burnt to the core. Yet, it ignited a fire within that burned brighter than my fears. I was angry that I mentored and supported Jayden while she was secretly sneaking around with my husband, but I couldn't let those emotions dictate my response. So instead, I stood up swiftly, holding my chest out, raising my glass again, and with determination in my eyes.

I said, "We will not fail. On the contrary, we will rise and be stronger than ever."

My employees cheered and surrounded me with a group hug. These are my people, and I refuse to let them down.

Kyle's lies were the bars of an invisible cage that held me captive under my own account. I continued to believe it was a cage I created, but all along, it was an illusion he fabricated to keep me in the dark. As each day passed, it brought new light and clarity, uncovering hidden truths and allowing me to let go, setting myself free.

I found more healing in the ugly truth than in the prettiest of lies.

In the following weeks, amid the chaos of selling the house, I discreetly informed clients of the recent changes, co-signed for a recreational vehicle for my parents, unpacked our new condo, and strived to create a sense of normalcy for Adian and Nevaeh.

Despite my efforts, the inevitable began to unfold. Vicious arguments erupted between Kyle and me as the truth continued to surface old wounds. Kyle refused to let me be a part of Ashtons life, allowing only Adian to visit them at his new lakeside home. Kyle contacted several agency clients, informing them that we were going bankrupt, which resulted in a fury of confusion that my staff and I had to unravel. I contacted each customer, offering a ten-percent reduction to their ongoing retainer fees to illustrate our commitment to restoring the relationship. To minimize the damage of Kyle's persistent threats to defame the business and his ruthless demands for a financial settlement, I agreed to provide him with a settlement package in exchange for a confidentiality agreement, including dismissal terms and withdrawal of claims to prevent him from spreading false information to our remaining clients.

Submerged in an endless storm of financial challenges, I took every measure to stabilize the business and rebuild a fresh start for my children. I applied for state assistance, hardship programs, mortgage relief, deferred payments, and reduced expenses. I was desperate to minimize the destruction yet submerged in one crisis after another.

I committed to my team to model our cultural beliefs, and by doing so, I knew that it was my duty to be fully transparent about the company's instability. In despair, I scheduled a mandatory meeting with all my employees. As the meeting began, I could barely hold back the tears as I shared my fears and concerns. Without hesitation, the entire team offered to reduce their hours in an effort to save the company. I was awestruck by their willingness to sacrifice and inspired by their unwavering loyalty. This was a pivotal moment for me; my world was caving in, and they were there to hold me up.

In the following weeks, I received calls, emails, and messages from peers, clients, family, friends, and even former employees reaching out, reminding me of my strength. Unfortunately, I was equally inundated with untold stories from our mutual friends that began to surface, with an inevitable trail of gossip. Kyle fully embraced the bachelor lifestyle, juggling relationships with multiple women, abusing substances, destroying friendships, and spinning a web of lies to cover it all up.

Shortly after our separation, Kyle met Vanessa. I felt relief, hoping this newfound love would distract his incessant need to taunt me, but it only ignited his vengeance. Vanessa was stunning, roughly mid-forties, but ageless, athletic, and perfectly tanned with full synthetic lips, voluminous blonde hair, and radiant blue eyes with a sense of high voltage about her. Yet, behind her beauty and designer clothing was a veil of broken pieces from her past.

Kyle found every opportunity to flaunt their relationship, reminding me I could never fulfill his needs as she could. Amidst their newfound love were unhealed wounds, a trail of lies, and an undeniable passion. Their heated passion was fueled by infatuation and the desire to fill a void within themselves, only creating an outpour of unrealistic expectations. They unleashed inner demons that could not be contained, leading to a deeply tumultuous relationship that bled into every aspect of their lives.

I wrestled with the false hope that Kyle would realize what he had lost and try to reconcile the damage. Yet, I knew Kyle on a profound level and understood his tactics for preserving his status. I intentionally surrounded myself with counselors, peers, and mentors to seek guidance as I focused on my healing.

One morning, I received an unknown call. I suspiciously answered the phone only to realize it was Vanessa. Slightly curious yet guarded, I asked why she was contacting me, and within minutes she unloaded a slew of questions and unsolicited information. I leaned against the edge of my bed, sliding to the floor, catching a glimpse of my reflection in the grainy, sliding mirror closet doors as I quietly listened. I was lost in thought, only partially retaining her words, then she shared that Kyle took her on a trip to Napa, describing all the wineries and restaurants they toured. I slowly curled my knees closer to my chest, pressing the phone firmly against my ear as the knots in my stomach twisted. It struck a chord that he would have the nerve to take her where we signified our love with our families. She continued by sharing that Kyle wanted to marry her. My throat tightened, making it hard to swallow as I pushed out the words.

I said, "Vanessa, what made you contact me?"

She faltered her words as she recognized the concern in my voice. I sat in confusion, wondering why she felt the need to divulge their personal information with me. Finally, she sighed and began unloading all their problems in my lap. I laid my neck against the curve of the mattress while I stared at the ceiling fan circling above. Vanessa rambled about Kyle sneaking around with other women, uncovering lies and volatile fights between them. But then, her voice drew inward.

She said, "Kyle threatened to hurt himself if I left him. Do you think he's trying to manipulate me, or do you believe he's serious?"

I could sense the defeat in her tone. I inhaled, rolled my neck forward, and sat upright on the floor, searching for the right words.

I said, "To be fully transparent, I wouldn't doubt that he is trying to manipulate you. However, Kyle is very emotional, and if he said he would hurt himself, I wouldn't take that lightly. I encourage you to seek help, but honestly, I am not the person you should seek it from."

A moment of counsel was all I could give; I couldn't allow myself to get wrapped up in their stories when I was barely unfolding my own; this was the first time in my life I finally felt free. I wished Vanessa the best and gracefully ended the conversation. As I hung up the phone, a multi-layered twist of complicated and conflicting thoughts surfaced painful emotions. I wondered if she had an underlying motive for calling me; my prior lack of skepticism typically left me unguarded, so I sent Kyle a message casually informing him of our conversation. Within seconds Kyle responded.

He said, "Vanessa and I broke up; she's being over dramatic and trying to probe you for information. Just ignore her calls. She's crazy!"

I was curious about his response but wanted to avoid immersing myself in his love triangle. They each hold similar characteristics fighting a battle of manipulation and mind games. So, I quickly ended the conversation by agreeing not to answer future calls from her.

In the following weeks, as I picked up the pieces of my life, the world was in the midst of a global pandemic. The media swept the nation with frightening updates on the spread of a fatal disease. The outbreak struck in January; a crisis so severe that states began to implement shutdowns to prevent the risk of contracting the lethal virus. By March 2020, the U.S. shut down its economy, shuttering businesses, mandating school lockdowns, and requiring all nonessential workers to stay home to slow the spread. As Americans stock-piled essentials preparing to stay indoors, the scenes of anxious customers tearing through grocery aisles, loading toilet paper and canned goods created mania declaring a National Emergency. An unnerving sense of ambiguity sent a current of fear through every home as we prepared for the unknown.

It was late one evening while the kids and I huddled together around the television, anxiously watching the State premiers fronted by the media revealing how many people had tested positive for COVID and the number of heart-wrenching families that lost loved ones. Then, my phone began to ring; interestingly, Kyle called, so I ran up the stairs to my bedroom for privacy and skeptically answered.

I said, "Um, hello?"

Kyle replied, "Hey, I'm worried about you and the kids. Why don't you and the kids come to stay with me?"

I was dumbfounded by his carefree tone and oddly upbeat demeanor. How could he possibly have the nerve to act like he didn't just spend the past few months sleeping with multiple women, binging on drugs and alcohol, trying to sabotage the business, and causing an uproar of rumors? He practically proposed to Vanessa in Napa within weeks of our separation, and now he's calling me as if nothing happened between us. It was like he had just returned from a mid-life crisis and was ready to invite us back into his life. Let alone stay at his bachelor pad.

Kyle continued, "I have plenty of food and supplies, so you won't have to worry about anything! You'll be safe here."

Kyle sounded genuinely concerned, but I refused to trust his intentions after he completely dismantled our lives, the betrayal, lies, manipulation, deceit, and all the pain he caused. *Has he forgotten that I was madly in love with him, and he literally tore my heart out of my chest?* I stood leaning against the doorway, lost in a fog of confusion, staring blankly at the white walls in my bedroom.

He asked, "Are you there?"

I responded, "Um, yes. I appreciate the offer but don't think it's a good idea. I wish I could, but I need to guard my heart. It's just not healthy for either of us."

He replied, "Cuddling up with you on a cold night just sounded nice. But you are probably right."

As I ended the call, I felt conflicted. After all, I had just spent the last ten years of my life with this man. What if he was honestly concerned about our well-being, or if he finally recognized the damage he caused and is trying to reconcile? Nonetheless, Kyle hadn't accepted responsibility for his actions or their impact on all of us. Let alone apologized, so I held true to my intuition and stayed home with the kids.

A state of emergency was declared on March 4, 2020, issuing a mandatory statewide stay-at-home order on March 19, 2020. The streets, grocery stores, parks, and schools were desolate. In the isolated moments when we saw other people, they thoroughly covered their faces while making obvious attempts to avoid contact with others, walking six feet around the other at all times with disgruntled looks and scowls if you happened to step too close. It felt like we were all living in an apocalypse movie, complete with eerie music and heightened voices on the news. The virus was a sneaky monster, microscopically growing at historical numbers, lurking everywhere. We waited in anticipation for life to return to normal as the modern world suddenly stopped.

Late one evening, the house was still while Adian and Nevaeh were sound asleep. I tossed and turned, wrestling to get comfortable lying awake in bed, watching the street light flicker through the blinds. My body was tired, yet my mind wouldn't settle. Restlessly, I stumbled through the dimly lit hall towards the bathroom to run a warm bath. Just before I dipped my toe in the steaming water, I heard a notification on my phone. I thought, "Who would be sending me a message this late? Unless it was an emergency." I quickly wrapped a towel around my body to reach for the phone on my bedside table. I sprawled across the bed on my stomach, curiously reading the message. It was from Kyle.

I'm so sorry for all the pain I caused you, and I am grateful for all the memories we shared.

It was three o'clock in the morning, and I wondered why he was up so late. But the curiosity immediately faded as I realized that he had finally apologized! A warm feeling of joy ran through my body as I crafted my response. I wanted to tell him how much he means to me, how much I love him, and maybe this is the start of his healing process so we could be together again. I paused for a moment and deleted my message before pressing send. Talking myself off the peripheral ledge, I knew I couldn't blindly open my heart to someone who didn't protect it. So instead, I decided to compose a simple message.

> Thank you, Kyle, that means the world to me.
> I appreciate you thinking of me.

After several minutes fixated on the glowing screen and waiting for Kyle to reply, I decided to soak in the bath—still nothing. I then curled up under the covers and finally fell asleep. The following day, the sun peeked through the blinds; I rubbed my eyes and stretched my arms, yawning as I reached for my phone to see if Kyle had responded. Instead, I noticed several missed calls and a voicemail from Vanessa. I rolled my eyes and sighed, they must have had another fight, and if she saw his text message to me, I'm sure she had something to say. I tried to listen to the voice message from Vanessa, but she was hysterical, and I couldn't understand a word she was saying. I immediately sat upright on the edge of my bed, clicked on the missed call, and waited anxiously as the phone began to ring. Vanessa was screaming, desperately begging me to go to the hospital. I could hardly piece together the words through her muffled voice.

She said, "Kyle is in the hospital. You're the next of kin, so they won't tell me anything, but I need to know he is okay!"

A man took the phone from Vanessa, and in a calm tone, he gave me the name of the hospital. A whirlwind of panic swept through my mind as my body began to shake uncontrollably. I reassured them I would go immediately as my trembling fingers typed the hospital into my map to pull up the directions. It was the hospital across the street from my condo. I could see the blaring sign from my bedroom window as I shuffled around the room, jumping on one foot and pulling my maxi skirt over my thighs. I stumbled down the stairs yelling for Adian. Nevaeh opened her bedroom door as I ran frantically from the third floor to the main living area.

She said, "Mom! What's wrong?"

I couldn't articulate my words without stuttering and didn't want to worry my twelve-year-old daughter if this was a false alarm.

I quickly responded, "I'm not sure, baby girl. Adian and I need to go to the hospital. It's only across the street. Stay here; we'll be right back."

I yelled Adian's name again as I tripped on the edge of my maxi shirt, stumbling down the second level of stairs to the first floor and sliding into Adian's bedroom door. I opened the door frantically as Adian sat up in bed with a confused expression.

I said, "Sugar, Kyle is in the hospital. I don't know what happened, but I'm worried, and we need to go now."

It was discovered that Kyle posted something on social media last night that said, "ENOUGH!" Then others confirmed that they received a message from him around three o'clock in the morning.

I struggled to swallow as I pieced together the timeline of events. Then, finally, I slipped on my shoes, one foot barely holding on to the edge of the sandal, as I raced to the car. Adian immediately jumped in after me while I called Kyle's sister to let her know that something had happened to Kyle and asked that she inform the family while I checked in to the hospital to get more information.

As Adian and I entered the desolate hospital, there was a cold silence. The faint but unmistakable scent of antiseptic filled the empty halls, a little bitter, with undertones of the artificial fragrance contained in soaps and cleaners. My gaze swiveled over the waiting room; the seats stood empty as many hospitals enforced strict no-visitation rules to democratize hospital visitation policies during COVID-19. I desperately asked the attendant to provide Kyle's room number, sliding my identification card on the counter. As he dialed the nurse, the attendant directed Adian and me to the waiting room. I could hear a low, muffled conversation but couldn't make out the words with the beeping sounds of medical devices and the coded emergency announcements blaring over the intercom. Adian noticed my anxious expression.

He said, "Don't worry, mama, everything is going to be okay."

I took a deep breath, glancing at his clear blue eyes and placing my hand on his.

I said, "You're probably right, son; I just feel uneasy."

The nurse called my name as she guided us to a small, dark, private room with bland walls, flickering fluorescent lights, and a table full of worn magazines. Adian glanced around, taking in the deserted, blue, and white color schemed waiting room sitting on the edge of a hard wooden chair as I paced back and forth, fidgeting, intently watching the clock on the wall as it ticked past nine o'clock. The endless ticking echoed in my mind while we waited for the nurse to return. Finally, we heard a light knock as the door opened. A physician's assistant stood in the doorway as she introduced Deputy Soria, a middle-aged woman with long brown hair wearing a muted black business suit. As the room started spinning, I reached behind my back to stabilize myself on the chair. The physician gently closed the door with a somber expression.

She said, "I'm Jessica, the Physician Assistant. Are you Serena Mastin?"

I stumbled back slowly, sliding into the chair as I confirmed my name. The dark room seemed to be closing in on me as I eagerly waited for her to continue. Finally, Jessica knelt to meet me at eye level and began to speak.

She said, "I'm so sorry, Mrs. Mastin, your husband, Kyle Mastin, was pronounced dead at eight o'clock this morning. The cause of death is a gunshot wound that penetrated the right temple area of his head. Deputy Soria will ask you a few questions and provide additional details about the incident."

My body was engulfed in pain, and knots twisted in my stomach as my eyes glazed over while I stared at the ceiling, illuminated with the flickering fluorescent light. I felt outside my body, removed from reality, and couldn't fully comprehend what was happening. I quickly stood up and demanded to see Kyle.

Deputy Soria responded, "I am sorry for your loss. I know this is a lot to take in. However, I don't recommend seeing the body at this time."

I was lost in confusion; this wasn't just a body; this was my husband. He was the love of my life, my best friend, and at times my worst enemy, but nonetheless, he was the man I spent the last ten years of my life with. The visualization of crawling into his hospital bed and wrapping my arms around him was at the forefront of my mind, and I couldn't fathom why they wouldn't let me see him, hold him, or at the very least kiss him. The deputy calmly explained that Kyle's head trauma was severe and gracefully declined my request. I paused, locked eyes with Adian, and suddenly realized Kyle was gone. It was as though I had lost a piece of my soul as my beautiful son sat beside me. Adian tightly clutched my hands. I felt like my body was in complete paralysis as the deputy described the incident. It took every ounce of my strength not to buckle to my knees on the dingy hospital floor. As he struggled to draw breath, Adian began to speak in a thickly deep voice, coarse and strained.

Adian said, "I don't understand. Kyle seemed happy when I was just at his house the other day. He mentioned that the toxic relationship with Vanessa had ended. What was she doing there?"

I stared up at him, silent. The muscles in my jaw tensed as I slowly crouched down in front of him, nearly falling over, firmly clenching his hand to hold my balance.

The deputy explained, "There was a 911 call from Vanessa at approximately five thirty this morning regarding a suicide attempt. When the officers arrived, Vanessa was in the residence's backyard and advised the officers to locate Mr. Mastin in the living room. The officers saw Mr. Mastin sitting on the couch facing the deputies as they entered. He had a semi-automatic handgun in his right hand, resting on his lap. The officer yelled at Mr. Mastin to put the gun down, but instead, he pulled the slide back, lifted the gun towards his head, and shot himself in front of the officers. They noticed what seemed to be self-inflicted lacerations to his left forearm in the shape of a "V" and left a note that read, "I was never going to be ENOUGH for you."

A moment of silence followed as Adian, and I processed the devastation. After all the years I spent trying to protect Kyle, I couldn't save him from himself. Kyle lit up my world and then burned it down. I loved him so much that I stopped loving myself and lost my identity in the process. I would've given my life to save his.

I couldn't imagine the thoughts that ran through Kyle's mind moments before he took his life. Although, I did know his heart. I believe he felt defeated, hopeless, and exposed. Kyle had an unrestrained desire to be admired, flourish, and make an impact on the world. But when faced with losing everything, he struggled to numb the pain by filling an inner void with drugs, alcohol, money, sex, and attention. Unfortunately, those desires were only a temporary reprieve, leaving him empty and without the clarity to see past the present moment. Kyle had a depth of emotion, feeling every experience through his veins, but he lost his way, and once he traveled down that dark path, he could no longer see the light.

Certain people will come into your life that will change your life forever, and when they're gone, it won't matter what they did or said to hurt you because the truth is that every experience is a memory, and you get to choose the ones you hold on to and the ones you leave behind. The moment we accept that nothing happens without a purpose, not even broken hearts. Not loss or pain. These moments are lessons and signs that allow us to step back and reflect on our journey.

Grief is like the ocean, the waves of emotions flow in and out. One moment you may feel at peace, the next, you're broken in tears. Yet, even amid our deepest pain, the brave human heart knows love is worth it. We may never move on from the loss of someone we loved, yet we slowly move forward.

Healing isn't linear; it's an ongoing process of self-love, forgiveness, and acceptance. You may not be able to change the experiences you have faced, yet you hold the power to change your perspective.

In the wake of the tragedies I faced, my world continued to crumble as the pandemic swept the nation. Due to the state of the world, the ramifications on my business added an element of uncertainty. The aftermath of loss unraveled more pain as I was left to pick up the pieces. Struggling to provide for my children as the business suffered, the financial devastation of unexpected medical bills, and the terrifying reality of navigating through life alone.

There were many moments when self-doubt crept in, isolation felt like safety, and my unwavering fight to never give up slowly dissipated. I leaned on my determination and resilience through all the devastations I faced. Yet, in truth, this was the moment I questioned my very existence.

And yet, life continues even when we cannot see past our tears.

The path forward for me began with the realization that if I didn't seek to understand my unhealthy patterns, triggers, and behaviors, I would continue fighting an endless battle seeking love in unhealthy places. But first, I had to find the courage to admit that I could not do it alone; I needed to surround myself with a community that would encourage and support me. Then, I reluctantly let go of any pride I still grasped between my fingers.

In my reflection, I saw an empty vessel. For far too long, I denied myself the love I so deeply craved, seeking fulfillment, meaning, approval, acceptance, and belonging in others. Only to recognize that I needed to embrace my flaws to forgive and accept myself wholeheartedly.

I struggled to release the guilt and shame of being unable to protect my children from such painful memories. Yet, the most loving thing I could do for my children when I had nothing left to give was honor the healing process and demonstrate what it truly means to embody self-love.

I immersed myself in the depths of self-reflection, and emotional awareness, seeking resources, knowledge, and counsel from the experience and wisdom of others. Journaling, yoga, exercise, intentional breathing, and practicing meditation were invaluable.

A supportive catalyst for my growth and one of the healing practices I found the most fulfilling was finding a sense of belonging by fearlessly sharing my truth with those who did not pass judgment and accepted me unconditionally. Leaning into the discomfort and allowing others to rise up around me and lift me off the ground when I could no longer stand on my own. My children, family, and friends surrounded me with love, and my team held the agency together as I began to rebuild my spirit.

The more I let go of who I thought I was supposed to be, the more I uncovered who I was. Shifting my focus from sacrificing my needs to investing in myself allowed my healing process to unfold, ultimately bringing more clarity and unveiling my purpose through my pain.

In the words of post-traumatic wisdom, all the obstacles leading to this very moment were necessary to give me strength, compassion, and resilience, guiding me so that I may give you a glimpse of hope. Even in the darkest moments when we feel hopeless, there is always a greater purpose. Wisdom is not something we inherently possess. It is given and received. We never stop gaining wisdom; it narrows our focus and helps teach us what not to do.

Underneath the masks, behind closed doors, we are all routed by the same desires. Those desires can be raw, dark, and deeply shameful.

It takes true strength to be vulnerable. It takes real power to open up about what makes you uncomfortable. It takes real courage to expose the truth. Hiding your problems and pretending they don't exist is the real weakness. Hiding our stories in the darkness does nothing but allow them to rot and decay. When we bring them to light, we create healing for ourselves and empower others to do the same. As long as these wounds remain hidden, they will continue to sabotage us in the shadows. We can find freedom and shift from helplessness to empowerment only when we bravely expose our truth and heal the damaged emotions.

So, get up, dust yourself off, and focus on the lessons you're learning and how to use them to fuel your resilience. Not one drop of your self-worth depends on another person; own your story and use it to empower others.

Challenges and heartbreak are a part of life, we all face hardships, and at times life shows us a different version of ourselves. Everything that is hurting you is also healing you. Everything that is weighing on you is also teaching you. When all is said and done, and you finally pause to reflect, you might not even recognize the person you've become. Instead, you'll begin to see the person you were meant to be with even more courage, strength, and resilience. And that might be the greatest gift you ever receive.

Three fundamental steps have guided me through this process:

First, you must find the courage to uncover your inner wounds by facing your truth and practicing self-awareness. Next, you must acknowledge the pain. Then, release yourself from captivity by letting go of past experiences you cannot change, openly embracing self-forgiveness, and forgiving others. And finally, practice unconditional self-love and acceptance by honoring your story and acknowledging your progress so you can gently move forward. Although my story has been woven by hands that are not my own, they have held me through this journey allowing transformation and healing.

My children are healthy and thriving, I find the utmost joy in watching them pursue their dreams, and after three years of financial hardships, the agency has stabilized, but not without my team's insurmountable sacrifice and support. I am honored and grateful for the outpour of kindness, encouragement, and love from all those that believed in me.

This is my story, but it doesn't have to be yours. No matter how your story began, you hold the power to change the path and write a new ending. You will never know how strong you are until being strong is your only choice. At any given moment, we have the power to say: This is not how my story will end. In fact, this is just the beginning.

www.ingramcontent.com/pod-product-compliance
Lightning Source LLC
Chambersburg PA
CBHW070247010526
44107CB00056B/2370